Legs up & laughing

For Christopher
who was with me
from the start
and for Tristan
who met us at the end.
And for Dalisay,
who forgave me for
all the times
I made her cry.

Legs up & laughing

VANESSA BATES

First published in 2007 by Pier 9, an imprint of Murdoch Books Pty Limited

Murdoch Books Australia
Pier 8/9, 23 Hickson Road, Millers Point NSW 2000
Phone: +61 (0) 2 8220 2000 Fax: +61 (0) 2 8220 2558
www.murdochbooks.com.au

Murdoch Books UK Limited
Erico House, 6th Floor, 93–99 Upper Richmond Road,
Putney, London SW15 2TG
Phone: +44 (0) 20 8785 5995 Fax: +44 (0) 20 8785 5985
www.murdochbooks.co.uk

Chief Executive: Juliet Rogers
Publishing Director: Kay Scarlett

Commissioning Editor: Hazel Flynn
Project Manager: Rhiain Hull
Editor: Karen Gee
Cover design: Alex Frampton
Design concept and design: Heather Menzies
Production: Kita George

Text copyright © Vanessa Bates 2007
Design copyright © Murdoch Books Pty Limited 2007

All rights reserved. No part of this publication may be reproduced, stored in a retrieval system or transmitted in any form or by any means, electronic, mechanical, photocopying, recording or otherwise, without the prior written permission of the publisher.

National Library of Australia Cataloguing-in-Publication Data

Bates, Vanessa. Legs up and laughing. ISBN 9781921208935 (pbk.). 1. Bates, Vanessa - Anecdotes. 2. Infertility. 3. Infertility - Alternative treatment. 4. Fertilization invitro, Human. 5. Medicine, Chinese. 6. Mothers and daughters. I. Title. 618.178

Printed by 1010 Printing International Limited in 2007. Printed in CHINA.

Author photograph on front cover flap courtesy of Susan Gordon-Brown

Every effort has been made to contact the owners of copyright material used in this book. Where this has not occurred, the owners of copyright material are invited to contact the publisher. The publisher will be happy to acknowledge appropriate copyright owners in future editions.

The first year

WATERBABIES

1972, Penang, Malaysia. On this day my family rides in a taxi, with the radio blaring, down to the Chinese Swimming Pool.

> Last night I heard my mama singing a song
> Ooh eee chirpy chirpy cheep cheep
> Woke up this morning and my mama was gone.
> Ooh eee chirpy chirpy cheep cheep
> Chirpy chirpy cheep cheep chirp

La! We're so excited, me (aged four) and my little sisters, Amanda (aged three) and Toni (just one), and we all sing the ooh eee chirpy chirpy cheep cheep bit till Dad shouts at us to Get Out We're Here.

Smell of salt and chlorine, lunch in plastic bags, Hiawatha rubber ring and red red cossie with the matching rubber thongs. Smell of humid sticky limbs with never-quite-dry pits and cracks of bum and that bit between the shoulder blades where the towel doesn't quite reach. Smell of the fountain, all gushing water, white noise, salty smell and white tiled ledge, driving you mad with the incessant whoosh and rush and enticing you closer with the bubbling surging face-wetting ...

Mum sees us, spies us, faces down, mouths open and calls out: Don't drink the water!

Smell of the baby pool, thigh high, wee warm for little girls with tiny little bladders.

Don't drink the water!

And the big pool, grown-ups' pool, mysterious green and bottomless, with the scooped out, hand-holding, phlegm-spitting gutter going round the inside and ... yes Mum, I know!

Don't drink the water!

We frolic in the baby pool, Dad chasing us with a bucket of water and a sharkface grin.

We run and splash and scream with high-pitched joy our little shouts of glee ...

... and wet my red red cossies with little spurts of wee.

Don't drink the water!

In the grown-ups' pool Mum and I play a great game with my Hiawatha rubber ring, she holds it out and I jump and it catches me.

Like a cushion, like a crash mat, like a pair of strong arms for my wild wet leaps.

We stop for lunch. I bolt down my sandwich and have a quick slurp of ice-cold orange cordial from the drink bottle with the little towel wrapped round the outside and the laccy band over the top to keep it secure.

And I run run run to the edge of the pool, the big green grown-ups' pool, and I throw my Hiawatha rubber ring into the air and it lands like a perfect Hiawatha doughnut on the water and I jump.

But I've forgotten something.

Someone.

And without her, holding everything in place, Hiawatha skips nimbly to one side and I simply slip past the ring and plummet down into the green depths. My eyes are huge and open against the salt-tang sting of the water. I see the white tiles and the sharp vents of Underwater World and the legs and torsos of swimmers, miles away, worlds away.

It's so quiet. Silence almost, except for the distant gush of the fountain in the baby pool, and the whirr of the filter motor, and somewhere up there, a family still finishing their lunch. I watch as the golden green shafts play through the slightly murky waters, slipping past, streams of far away, filtered sunlight.

I look down and see myself. My arms. My legs. My red red swimming costume.

> Last night I heard my mama singing a song.
>
> Ooh ee chirpy chirpy cheep cheep.

How long am I waiting, hanging there? Frozen?

A second, a moment, thirty-four years later ... I look up and see ... a man in batik shorts, squatting at the edge, about to dive in. My hand reaches up and he leans down to grasp me and pull me out of the warm soup, the green womb, the wet grave. He holds me by one arm aloft above the surface and through the fuzz in my eyes and the thump in my head I see my mother run towards me.

And I breathe.

June

The Great Big Fertility Ride starts the day I casually tell my GP that my partner Christopher and I can't seem to get pregnant.

Doctor GP seems fairly calm about this; Christopher and I haven't been trying consistently, he goes away a fair bit, blah blah blah ... But then I mention that we've been together for nearly ten years. And that our chief form of contraception in all that time has been ... ahem ... the withdrawal method.

And that I'm thirty-five ...

Doctor GP's face clouds over, great big red lights start flashing around the room, an alarm goes off and a large neon clock descends from the ceiling and begins to monster me with its incessant tick.

'Ah,' says Doctor GP. 'In that case you *must* see Professor Specialist and have some tests.' I feel a bit put out by the forceful nature of his suggestion. I didn't say I was *desperate* did I? Christopher and I have been talking about having babies for a few years, on and off. We just haven't had one yet, that's all. I mean, let's not push the panic button here. Thirty-five's young isn't it? It is for a writer. Last year when I mentioned the baby thing, Doctor GP told me that thirty-four was actually the median age for first- time mothers in this suburb and I shouldn't feel at all worried or concerned. But apparently last year I neglected to mention the 'several years without official contraception' side of things.

'Sure, I'll have some tests,' I say.

It takes several months, but eventually we get an appointment to see Professor Specialist at the Unnamed Sydney Hospital. By the time we are shown into his office I have to admit I'm a little more anxious. Now that we've started this whole investigative malarky I can't help noticing there are *loads* of articles and helpful *Today Tonight* type shows about the general drop in male and female fertility, and particularly about Evil Career Women Who Have Left it Far Too Late to Bear Children, Ha Ha Serves Them Right For Being SO SELFISH.

Having read our referral letter and verified the shocking details for himself, Professor Specialist gazes thoughtfully out the window, tents his fingers à la *The Simpsons'* Mr Burns, and fires off some information about the tests we will undergo. Christopher will have to sprog into a jar and give some blood while I get to experience a whole range of invasive and probably painful procedures.

Oh *goody*.

'Let's start with *this*,' says Professor Specialist cheerfully. He scribbles something down on a bit of paper. He seems so enthused, it could be his mother's recipe for shepherd's pie or the name of that fabulous new wine bar that reminds him so much of Paris.

It is neither of these things. It is something nasty, involving tubes and things poked up my lala.

At home, I ring a nursing friend and ask about proper pronunciation because I know from experience that if you display any uncertainty in a medical situation you get messed around, right from the get-go. *Hysterosalpingogram* I say over and over about fifty times before I ring the receptionist at the Unnamed Sydney Hospital and book myself in.

Okay, so it probably made doodlysquat difference, but it *does* make me feel all 'I know what I'm doing, don't blow me off and book me in in six months, bitch'. And she doesn't, she books me in in *three* which will be, just by the way, several weeks after my thirty-sixth birthday.

It's also two weeks after our wedding.

This is Round Two for both Christopher and myself and, being naturally wary of skipping down the aisle (or in this case down the crumbly stone steps at Darling Point), we have made absolutely sure it's the real deal by living in sin for the past decade.

'And anyway,' I say, 'what better way to celebrate our newly blessed nuptials than by having dye pumped up my fallopian tubes to check for blockages? Also, note that honeymoon and hysterosalpingogram both start with "h".'

I begin this new and exciting experience (HSG not honeymoon) by having my 'genitals swabbed' by a dour nurse with a lump of wet gauze clutched in her plastic tweezers. As she dabs away it occurs to me that it's almost pleasurable. Yes, almost. It must be a bit like those weird guys who pretend to be babies and get their bottoms powdered and big nappies wrapped round them.

Oddly, as soon as this thought enters my brain it's as if a warning light has gone off in hers because in one lightning fast move she drops the gauze, picks up the brillo pad and gives all my girly bits a good hard scrub. And that's not pleasurable at all.

Next, legs up and freshly lathered, I am introduced to the doctor. His surname is perfectly reasonable but the nurses press me to refer to him by his casual nickname: 'Dicky'.

I'm sorry. That's not going to do. Bad enough Doctor Nickname is going to introduce all manner of appliances to my cervix, I'm not *also* going to call him Dicky like he's got some right to be rooting around in there. I make a point of only referring to him by his professional name.

Doctor Nickname calmly explains the procedure to me. It will take only a few minutes (good), some women experience excruciating pain (bad), others experience only 'period-like cramping' (sort of good). Afterwards I may experience cramping for a week (bad) and bleeding for a week (bad) and if the pain becomes unbearable or if the blood loss is excessive I should go straight to my GP (very very bad).

As Doctor Nickname gets the speculum ready he delivers the kicker: if at any time the pain is so bad I need to stop the procedure I should just call out. They'll stop immediately and then I can simply reschedule for another time WITH SEDATION.

What the?

Dear God, I think to myself. What kind of scary-ass procedure is this that I may have to *beg* Doctor Nickname to let me come back and be knocked out?

I try to weigh up my options. On the one hand, where pain is concerned, I am a complete and total wuss. It's not something I'm ashamed about because I feel I have various other skills. For instance, I'm quite good at writing nice things in people's birthday cards. On the other hand, I really want to find out just what the hell is going on in the downstairs department. Why haven't I ever been pregnant? *Ever?*

It's true we never thought we were earning enough money to be parents. And life has been full of scrimping for trips overseas, and strange temporary jobs and writing plays and a lot of just sort of mucking about and having fun and doing all sorts of things where 'having a baby' would make things complicated, but even so it's been ten years of dodgy not-quite contraception.

Ten years. Not one single oops.

No one can be that lucky can they?

I reflect on the length of time required to even get this appointment today and I decide that, short of having my uterus torn out, I will grit my teeth and take it because I don't want to come back here again. *Ever.*

In goes the speculum and I take a sudden interest in the water stains on the ceiling. Next, a thin tube is fed through my cervix. I start to take long, controlled deep breaths. To these I add some loud woooo hooooo noises. It's my own brand of meditative breathing, specially developed to dull any pain and drown out horrid squelchy sounds as the dye begins to wend its way through. Doctor Nickname very kindly gives me frequent updates. He tells me he is 'introducing the dye with a tiny catheter' but this is just medical mumbo jumbo for 'grab your ankles girly I'm pumping in the juice.'

I huff and puff and wooo and hooo. It's not pain as such, but I can *sense* pain, hovering in the wings, waiting for its big moment. I think at this point Doctor Nickname is worrying a little about my breathing. He probably feels that I am going to hyperventilate and pass out, so he asks if I am okay.

Yes, I think to myself, I'm just concentrating on my breathing, but because I don't want to interrupt the flow it comes out as a barked 'yup'.

Doctor Nickname cranks up the X-ray machine and it starts taking photos of my repro bits chock full of dye. Even in my state of near hyperventilated unconsciousness I note that the head of the X-ray machine is protected from my foul female discharges by what appears to be a shower cap. Tee hee.

Doctor Nickname, sounding concerned, calls out again. 'Are you in pain?'

No, I think, not really, but I certainly *am* feeling those famous 'period-like cramps' I was warned about so I'd *really* like him to make it snappy. Again, I don't want to interrupt the breathing and I also don't want any more pfaffing around so I simply grunt 'yep'.

Perhaps it's my alarming breathing or monosyllabic grunts, perhaps it's the natural speed and efficiency of Doctor Nickname, but soon it all stops and I am allowed to relax my legs which, interestingly, have begun to wobble like silicon implants on a plate. I feel like crying and vomiting all at once. I put on my underwear complete with large wad of cotton padding to soak up leaking dye and to have a few more happy snaps taken for the family album and then it's done. I'm free to go and I'll get my results back in about ... ooh ... three months. The results would in actual fact be available *this afternoon* but *of course* I can't get in to see Professor Specialist until then.

Apparently the best-case scenario will be that my plumbing is blocked and a further procedure required to drill out my tubes.

That's right, *drill*.

Any child I might possibly bear had better be an absolute angel. I'm talking breathtaking physical beauty and slavish obedience.

A few weeks later I get called up by an old uni friend who is also having fertility issues. He starts to tell me about the horrors of having his sperm tested. I can't get a word in edgewise, let alone 'hysterosalpingogram'. Instead I listen to him bang on about the humiliation of being put in a room (a *private* room let me add) and told to ejaculate into a jar and then have to ... get this ... *hand the jar to a nurse* 'who knows full well that you've just had a wank'.

I. Am. Speechless.

I mean, call the United Nations because some kind of human rights violation has obviously taken place here. Boo hoo Old Uni Friend, you had to jerk off into a jar, with a room full of pornography and comfy seats, WITH NO ONE ELSE AROUND. I feel like punching him very hard in the face. Even when I try to point out that his wife would have to go through a lot worse, he can only partly agree because the 'humiliation' of his experience was so intense.

In the end I give up trying.

Wanker.

And, he was drunk and ringing me from a wedding reception at midnight.

So, loser also.

October

Many moons later we revisit Unnamed Sydney Hospital to determine why we're failing the human race. It's almost like early Christmas—we've got a slurry of blood, a bit of sperm and of course the infamous HSG results to look forward to. Professor Specialist himself has a slight touch of the Santa Clauses to him, what with his white beard and twinkly eyes.

Sadly, the festive mood dies a little as we wait.

And wait.

And wait.

As the minutes (and for all I know the use-by dates on each one of my eggs) tick past, I watch as Christopher peers over his book at a small Chinese boy who is making engine noises and grinning happily up at him. The little guy's clutching a tiny yellow truck in one chubby hand and threatening to run it into Christopher's boots. It seems they're blocking the Invisible Tiny Truck Super Highway which appears to start under the public noticeboard, wind around the toy box, career under Christopher's chair and end at a discarded orange juice bottle which may or may not be the Invisible Tiny Truck Police checking drivers for overloading and amphetamine abuse.

Christopher obligingly lifts his feet and also makes some extra *vroom vroom* sounds and a few loud truck honks, which earns him some sharp looks from the adults sitting nearby and a gleeful giggle from somewhere beneath his chair.

Yet again I tell myself that Christopher would make a great father. Babies and small children are often attracted to him. He has a good range of silly faces and voices that seem to please. But then again, he also gets on well with old ladies and cats.

I'm starting to feel a little melancholy, so to take my mind off things I look around the room at the rest of the patients. It's not a good move. The place is teeming with small children and babies and heavily pregnant women.

There is another couple sitting a few seats down and they're not reading books or playing with strange children or even looking around at other people, they're just sitting quietly with their eyes on the receptionist, waiting to be called.

And I wonder if, just maybe, they're like us.

An hour and a half later Christopher and I finally enter Professor Specialist's office. There's an almost Academy Award hush as he opens our results.

Blood? Good!

No coeliacs, in case we were worried. (Ah ... no, actually.)

Sperm? Pretty good.

Motility? Good. Count? Good. Morphology? A little spakka, but nothing to worry about there. All basically good!

And the award goes to ... ?

Professor Specialist checks his watch. 'We're running very behind time now so let's just go straight to saying you need IVF.'

My jaw drops. IVF?

Yes that's right, IVF, in-vitro fertilization—that procedure for losers who can't manage to impregnate themselves. Here's a brochure, read all about it.

I stare at him. I'm obviously fifty sorts of stupid because it never occurred to me that this might be his diagnosis. Surely it's some sort of last-resort strategy? For people who are desperate. Or old. That's not us, is it?

I flick through my mental *Cliff Notes* on IVF. Pain. Needles. Cash.

'Hang on,' I hear myself say in a slightly wobbly voice, 'what about my HSG? What were the results there?'

Professor Specialist is slightly taken aback. He rifles through the notes again. 'No HSG results here—when did you have it?'

'A long long time ago,' I say, very quietly. A large stone seems to be pressing down on my lungs, affecting my volume.

'Oh,' he says, 'I'll get Jen my receptionist to bring them in. But even so, I still say IVF.'

Christopher has a go. 'Would the test results change that, once you've seen them?'

'No. Come back and see me in the New Year and we'll talk more.'

I stare at the wall and don't say anything. I want to scream: 'Then why did you send me to have that godawful test if the results mean nothing to you?' but I'm afraid if I even open my mouth, I'll lose control and start crying.

Instead, I look across at Professor Specialist. Did I really think he was like Santa Claus? Maybe not the regular Santa Claus, maybe what I actually meant was Bad Mean Tactless Time-Poor Santa Claus. Professor Specialist has sunk so low in my eyes he seems to have devolved. His forehead protrudes, his greying hair starts filling with fleas and tiny dags of oil-clogged dandruff fall about his hunched shoulders. Crisp shirt and dapper tie give way to crudely formed coverings of animal hide.

Professor Caveman.

At this point his receptionist comes flying in, like that scene in *Broadcast News*. 'Left fallopian tube blocked,' she announces breathlessly.

Professor Caveman grunts. 'It doesn't matter, I'll give them the results when they come back to see me in the New Year. Oh,' he turns to me and shows his teeth, 'I may as well send you for an ultrasound too.'

He hands over a scrap of yellow paper.

'In fact, on your way out you can pop your head in at Radiology and make an appointment.' He says this as if it's a tip for our convenience.

Finally I ask: 'If my left tube is blocked does that mean I only ever had a chance to conceive every *second* cycle?'

He doesn't even bother to look up.

'Yes,' he says.

We leave and make another appointment to see Professor Caveman in the New Year. I struggle to hold back the tears. He's an arsehole, and not only that he's an arsehole I can only get in to see every three months.

Christopher is furious. We get back in the car and now I sob like a hysterical barren woman with dried up ovaries and an only half-functioning uterus. Christopher is as pissed off as only a man with good motility and count but reasonably poor morphology can be.

When we get home I hit the phone and begin calling friends who have had IVF. I Google IVF and start clicking through screen after screen of information. Meanwhile Christopher scrabbles in his desk drawers and brings out a small tattered scrap of paper. I recognise it as the phone number of a Chinese medicine fertility expert someone told us about ages ago. We'd always said we'd call her but we never did. Christopher rings the number and gets us an appointment the following week.

November

Friends who have had IVF or ART (Assisted Reproductive Technology) give me advice over the phone. They are cheerful, supportive, outraged on my behalf, and optimistic.

'It's a snap,' one veteran tells me.

'But the needles …' I begin to blubber.

'The needles are a snap,' she says firmly. 'You can do it. You'll be fine.'

I plan to never return to the hospital unless it is to demand all my test results or bomb the fertility clinic. Not with a bad terrorist sort of bomb, just a sort of pissed-off bomb that doesn't really damage anything or even make very much noise. I don't want to disturb people after all. Maybe all it does is shoot out a long, stretchy elastic hand that reaches around the rooms and finds Professor Caveman and punches him on the nose really hard. Yeah. That sort of bomb.

On Friday we go to see our newest fertility expert. Her office is in a little terrace house and when we walk in the doorway it's like a quick step to Chinatown. Downstairs is a dispensary with walls of Chinese herbs and medicines and cunning little scales on the counter. The wall by the door is papered in baby photos and letters of thanks and baby announcement cards so we know we've come to the right place.

A tall, good-looking youngish Chinese woman sizes us up and scoots us upstairs. This is the Chinese medicine guru? I think I expected an ancient, wizened, white-haired hermit type. Instead she's more of a funky Chinese fertility goddess. Never mind. I also expected to get decent service and compassionate care from the hospital.

Upstairs the Chinese Fertility Goddess peers at us both through her fashionably rimless glasses. We tell her we have been together for ten years. We tell her we have only ever used the withdrawal method.

We tell her our specialist has said we need IVF.

She rolls her eyes at the suggestion. I say that according to the unseen HSG test my left fallopian tube is blocked. She snorts in disgust.

'Why he say IVF because of this?'

We shake our heads, we have no idea. Her eyes glint fiercely.

'Okay, so maybe left fallopian tube is blocked, doesn't matter, I can unblock this, but what is *this* over here?'

She jabs suddenly at the side of my waist and I jump a little. 'Hello? Other side? *Right fallopian tube!* He no say that right fallopian tube is blocked? No! Just left. Okay. And he probably say that left right left right, you only fall pregnant every second month?'

I shrug a little.

'No one knows! No one know this! Yes, it *can* go left right left right but sometimes, it go right, right *right*!'

The CFG presses her lips together. 'Who says all this to you?'

We say, in hushed tones as if we're on a witness protection program, 'Professor Caveman.' She nods. 'Yes. I know him. *Very* conservative. I get you pregnant in one month!'

She waves a thin finger at our goggling faces.

'*Some* women, I say: don't get pregnant now, wait, I have to nourish them, but you, *no*! We start treatment today!'

I am suspiciously close to tears, again.

After checking our pulses and tongues she whisks us into the acupuncture rooms, sticks us with pins and leaves us to dream a little.

She loads us up with bags of herbs—the leaf, twig and chunks of what look like chopped up surfboards sort in paper bags for *me* ('You boil these and see the process!') and the ready-made plastic bag variety for Christopher ('I don't give *you* two lots to cook, too chaotic!'). We also get boxes of Chinese pills and a bag of red Chinese dates. This will replace the sugar in our diets. From now on if we want a sweetie we can eat some of these. They will also purify our blood. As well as cutting sugar we will eat more seafood, vegetables and fruit. We will eat less carbohydrates at night, we will cut out fats and dairy. We will stop drinking coffee and wine.

Christopher asks, forlornly if he can drink decaf. The CFG rolls her eyes.

'Ahh! No decaf. You want cup of coffee? Okay, you have coffee. You want glass of wine? Okay you have wine. Just one, it's okay. Be happy! That's most important. Be happy!'

She looks at me.

'You not happy, you very stressed. You like this for a long time. Not good.'

I nod. Not good.

Thus begins the new regime.

Be healthy. Drink tea. Be happy.

The tea is truly vile and I take a perverted delight in the fact that Christopher has to drink his own brand of Horrid Tea too. We boil them up together and sip them companionably morning and night, grimacing at the sludgy bitter taste. They look like coffee. They don't taste like coffee.

The thing is, seeing the CFG has calmed me down a little.

I don't feel so desperate about the IVF; as if maybe we'll have to look at it later on and that's okay. But for now, I feel like we've got some control back, and we're not hanging on the words of some specialist we can only see every three months. Things look better.

I just wish they tasted more like coffee.

December

As Christmas waves its flabby fist, I ponder the great array of foods we aren't allowed to eat. Anything containing fat, sugar or chilli. Luckily a family decision is made to embrace a 'seafood Christmas'.

But the sweeties! The chocolate truffles and the cashew nuts and the icing on the Christmas cake and the ice-creams and all manner of divine custardy desserts!

God knows the Chinese dates won't hold up to much. They are a great disappointment. Christopher has eaten one, I have eaten two and we have managed to trick visitors into eating about five. The thing is, they are sweet at first but then leave a bitter taste in your mouth. They dissuade your palate from craving sugar by seemingly giving it what it wants and then slapping it in the face. Á la *A Clockwork Orange*, we are brutally weaned from the evil sugar.

We are not perfect. We slip, we slide, we buy a tin of wasabi-flavoured broad beans (!) which we discover have no saturated fat, and hoe into these with delight, tears streaming down our faces, until I discover finally (i.e. half the tin gone) that they are also 50 per cent sugar. The wasabi broad beans now sit sadly beside the Chinese dates.

The Chinese Fertility Goddess is taking off three weeks for Christmas holidays with her family (the cheek!) and so both Christopher and I have been loaded up with multiple sachets of

Horrid Tea. We are given charts to explain when to drink what combination. I am told strictly to relax more.

Christmas comes and goes at a little house down the South Coast and a drive back to Newcastle on Christmas Day. The festivities wash over us in a great wave of prawns and salad and grilled fish, with occasionally crab sushi and the odd nip of plum pudding vodka.

Be happy!

Lots of sun and swimming and three naughty nephews running around for inspiration.

But no pregnancy.

And as the New Year rolls past, babies make their way into the world through the vaginas or slit abdomens of various friends and friends of friends and others are pregnant with their second or third ...

THE BRIDGE

1983. School holidays. My mother said yes.

She knew his mother of course, and he seemed a nice boy. And he was in Year 9 and half Filipino like me, so we should have had plenty to talk about.

My parents were on a holiday on the Gold Coast and my younger sisters and I were staying with our grandparents in Sydney. I had seen him, not long ago, at some sort of Filipino 'friendly day'. We sat next to each other, bored, scoffing at the folk dancing and curling our lips at the traditional food.

On my second day in Sydney he phoned and asked if I could go out with him. I had never been allowed out with a boy before and my grandparents made me ring my mother first.

'A movie? Are you sure? Does his mother know?'

'Of course she does,' I said. 'Just a movie and lunch, that's all, pleeease ... '

'How will you get there?'

'We'll catch a bus into town from his house, come on Mum.'

'Grandad could drive you to his house.'

'Yes.'

'And you'll come straight back after the movie.'

'Yes!'

'Well then ... I suppose you're old enough. Yes.'

Yes!

I punched the air with glee and my sisters stared jealously at my victorious face.

My victorious, old enough face.

Grandad drove the car through endless boring suburbs and we had no idea where we were when he stopped. Everything looked the same—the houses, the apartment blocks, the roads.

Sometimes, driving through the city Grandad would say: 'First one to see the Harbour Bridge gets an ice-cream!' Our heads would crane this way and that, eyes on stalks, and we were always surprised when someone finally glimpsed it, distantly hanging between houses or buildings or perched alongside the Opera House or simply shimmering.

In midair.

Once, he played a joke on us, calling: 'First one to see the Harbour Bridge gets an ice-cream!'

Where?

He laughed at our twisting heads and pointing fingers ... there's the Opera House, it must be here somewhere ... surely ... where is it Grandma? ... it's not fair ...

And suddenly, as the sharp web of steel and sky began flashing overhead, we realized. We were on it. The two old people chortled and chuckled. They were city people, Sydney people, had been for years.

They always knew.

As our car pulled up, his mother came out to meet us at the kerb. He himself appeared at the front door smiling quietly and blushing a little and I found myself, suddenly shy, smiling and blushing back. He was neatly dressed in beige and light corduroy. He would like The Cure a bit later on and wear red and black and a lot of eyeliner, but this year, just now, he was like me.

All whites and pastels and creams. No true colours.

I could see his older brother and little sister, laughing and whispering in the doorway behind him and hear behind me the rustling chirrup of my own sisters, laughing and whispering in unison.

The adults droned on beside us, polite talk, weather and pick-up times and how are their parents and he's been looking forward to today and so has she and so on.

I kicked at the grass slightly, prickling at the awkwardness, the embarrassment of it all and then stopped when I saw it exposed my brown hairy leg to the white sunlight. My mother wouldn't let me shave my legs. I was the only girl in my year who didn't.

I looked back at my sisters waiting in the car (no you can't get out we're just dropping off your sister then we'll take you for a lovely picnic at La Perouse) and rolled my eyes and they rolled their eyes back in sympathy but when I turned away I could hear them laugh and whisper again.

He said something and I turned to look at him. Something about school. I noticed there were little red bumps around his jaw where he had shaved the top off his pimples.

'Yeah, okay,' I said. 'School Certificate, you know.'

'Yeah, and your school's really small eh?'

'What do you mean?'

'Do you have many teachers?'

'What?' I stared at him and he blushed again.

'Sorry I thought that's what it was like with schools in the country—you don't come from Sydney ...'

'It's not a big school,' I said after a minute, 'and a lot of kids who live in the country do go there ...'

... but it's not backwards, I wanted to say, it's not a daggy backwater if that's what you think.

But now it was time to go and the grandparents were waving and pointing at their watches.

'See you at four-thirty,' they said.

'Enjoy La Perouse,' I said, and they were gone.

'So ... we may as well just go too,' he said.

As he spoke I glimpsed the curtain at the front window being twitched aside. We were alone on the street, and yet ...

I felt like all the curtains in the street were being twitched aside.

He saw my hesitation.

'Unless you want to ... you know ... use the bathroom.'

'God! No!' I giggled, embarrassed at the suggestion. 'No, I'm fine.'

I wasn't, I was busting.

'How far is the cinema?'

'Not far. We catch a bus just down here.'

He reached out and took my hand in his. I flinched.

'It's all right,' he said, 'we've gone past the house.'

The last time we spoke it had been about funny things our dogs had done and how many kids in our respective schools liked Boy George. There had been nothing to suggest anything more than perhaps a shared chorus of 'Karma Chameleon' and yet here we were, palms sweating together as we waited for the bus to pull up at the stop. I was grateful for the chance to dry my hands as I felt for my money.

I noticed him looking at my blue surf wallet. There was a rainbow printed on the front and a thick strip of blue velcro on the inside. For a panicked moment I thought he was going to ask me where I got it. I could hardly say 'in my Santa sack', I would have to make up something.

Instead he took me to the back seat of the near-empty bus. I never sat up the back of the bus at home, that was for tough kids, and I enjoyed the sensation. He tried to take my hand again but I held onto my wallet and he dropped it awkwardly. My palm was still clammy from the walk down the hill. He must have been keeping a close eye on me though, because when I slipped the wallet back into my canvas army bag his hand was suddenly there, beside mine. Waiting.

'Oh look!' I called out, awkwardly. 'It's the Sydney Harbour Bridge!'

And it was, not far away, a mesh of blue and grey.

He laughed and his Adam's apple bounced and bobbed in his skinny throat.

'God you're such a bumpkin,' he said.

'No I'm not, it's just that ...' I stopped. There was no way of explaining.

'I'm sorry, that was really mean of me.' His voice was sincere. I looked at him, he seemed genuinely concerned, maybe he did understand. He leaned closer and I could smell his aftershave. His nose was covered in tiny blackheads, little dark pinpricks all over the tip I notice, and then suddenly he was all mouth and tongue. It was so shocking I jumped and our front teeth clacked together painfully. I tried to smile at him, make light of it.

'Oops,' I said.

He went back in for a second go and this time I braced myself so our mouths properly joined at the edges but it was like a wet cavern, a warm gelatinous vacuum between us and I was horribly aware of the driver's upward turning eye and the woman with the headscarf sitting in front of us and the little boy beside her twisting back to stare, and the bright white Sydney sunlight.

I broke away feeling sick at the thought of what we must look like. Two randy Eurasian kids fumbling on the back seat away from their mamas. God!

'No one's watching!' he hissed irritably. A spitty bubble enveloped his front teeth.

'Maybe later,' I muttered. The bus rolled and lurched.

'We're here,' he announced and we wobbled our way to the front of the bus.

'Where are we?' I could see cinemas, one after another, and cars and people and signs ...

'George Street.' He sounded impatient. 'Haven't you ever been to George Street before? The movies?'

I wanted to say no but I've been to the movies loads of times, like going to the movies, that's why I'm here in the first place, not for you, but because I'm desperate to get away from my grandparents and do something else, something fun for a change, something grown-up, not a boring family thing ...

He took my hand again and this time I was happy to be led, threaded through the crowds of people.

He shouted something incomprehensible over his shoulder. He seemed to be waiting for an answer so I shouted 'okay' back at him.

'Whereabouts?' he shouted again and I realized he was asking about a place to eat. We were surrounded by restaurants and fast-food places, too many to pick from. I shrugged weakly and he pulled me through a doorway. I just had time to see the sign. Pancake Parlour.

Pancakes? I had been to one of those places before, it was a chain, a family restaurant chain, and I went with my parents and little sisters, it was a place for kids not for ...

Abruptly he turned and walked past me and I had to scuttle to catch up.

'Is it full?'

'It's too expensive.'

We bolted across the road to McDonald's. He was more relaxed in here, so was I, we knew this place and places like it. They were built for us. For people like us.

Not kids, no. Then what?

We joked as we waited in line and I could feel the tension start to leave my stomach. But when he turned to order I thought about the Pancake Parlour again and felt a flash of confusion. Why had he said it was too expensive? He meant for him didn't he, not both of us. Had he meant to pay for me? Because I didn't want that. He hadn't paid for the bus but maybe that was why he had looked at my wallet like that, maybe he was going to, but I took it out too fast. Maybe his mother had told him that he had to pay, had given him extra money even, probably told him that that's the sort of thing you do in the Philippines. Should I say something?

He was ahead of me in the line and as I reached out to tap his shoulder he turned suddenly and I saw his tray piled high with two burgers, two trays of chips and worst of all a huge thickshake with two straws. The scene from Grease, *where Danny and Sandy smile coyly at each other over the rim of their shared milkshake, flashed horribly into my head.*

Oh God, hadn't enough shared fluid passed between our lips? I had to speak now, had to say something, anything.

I opened my mouth and as I did someone pushed me from behind and I fell into his tray.

Fries flew.

Burgers tumbled into a thick, meaty heap.

The thickshake dropped like a stone onto the polished floor and exploded over my feet and ankles.

A roar went up from the watching crowd and I wished I could faint on demand.

'Oh God, I am so sorry, someone pushed me and I just fell ...'

'Don't worry about it.' He threw the tray on top of the bin.

'Please, let me buy you something else, what do you want?'

Someone whistled.

'It doesn't matter,' he mumbled, 'let's go.'

He pushed his way outside and looked down at my feet, repulsed.

'Have you got a tissue or something? It looks like you've thrown up on yourself.'

'Yes, um, somewhere here.'

I didn't.

In the toilets of the cinema I pretended to be fixing my hair, so I could put my feet in the sink without anyone seeing. I wiped them quickly with paper towelling and ran out, still squelching.

'Everyone's gone in,' he said as he led me to the doorway.

'Wait,' I said, 'I haven't got my ticket.'

He ignored me, handing two tickets over to the doorman.

Oh God, he had paid for both tickets.

'What movie is this?' I whispered as he sat me down in the back row.

'Doesn't matter does it?' He grinned in the semi-darkness.

God! What movie did I think I was going to see?

The screen quickly filled with teenagers. Teenagers dancing, teenagers driving, teenage girls squealing as they unbutton their tight little blouses, teenage boys gaping at the sight of pert bouncing breasts. The camera dived into some girl's cleavage and the audience cheered.

More squealing teenagers, more fast music, they were at a party now. Some boys who were meant to be punks appeared, crashing the party. I caught myself scoffing, yeah right sure that guy's meant to be a punk.

'What did you say?' He whispered in my ear. I turned, my eyes still on the screen.

'I said ...'

His wet mouth suddenly locked over mine.

He missed my lips, misjudged their width apart completely (perhaps he thought I was going to say something like 'aha') instead managing to completely enclose my mouth with his. His nose was resting on top of mine. I began to laugh, I couldn't help it, it was so grotesque and so ... so ... God so embarrassing!

I cut off the laugh so that it came out like a grunt. He rolled his tongue over mine.

It occurred to me to vomit.

I glanced at my watch in one of the few moments he allowed me to breathe my own air. One-thirty. A whole three hours until my grandparents would come back to pick me up. I pretended to be deeply fascinated by the movie. He leaned back in his seat, victorious, one arm clamping me to him.

I thought about what I would tell my friends. What he would tell his friends.

The hairs on my legs were drying in stiff little points, the pads of my feet, still wet, clung greasily to the synthetic inners of my sandals.

One thirty-one.

Later that night I would whisper the whole horrible story to my sisters, and they would be sympathetic first and then all of us together would cackle and fall on the bed and laugh till the tears came and we had to wipe our eyes on our cotton nighties.

And they would tell their horrible story too, boring La Perouse and grumpy Grandad and the too-long drive home. At least I got to see a movie.

I would clench my teeth and open my lips in a parody of that first, on-the-bus kiss, and we would all laugh and cry again. And later that night my sister would reveal the real victory, lifting her nightie to show off her secretly shaved legs, smooth and brown.

But what if Grandma sees? What about when Mum and Dad find out? I would whisper, horrified, but deeply, deeply impressed.

And she would shrug and say: 'I'm not a kid anymore.'

But that was all hours away and now the time was one thirty-two.

I sat perfectly still and tried hard not to think about the long bus ride back.

The second year

10 January

We are at the house of the Naughty Nephews, packing up picnic things and trying to shove even *more* cricket bats and balls and scooters and tricycles in the back of the car when I get a phone call from the Hospital.

Professor Caveman has decided to close his clinic. I will not be able to see him in February as my appointment dictates. Do I want to see Professor Caveman at his private practice?

'No,' I calmly tell the receptionist as I buckle up sandals and dig under the couch for hats. 'I am unhappy with Professor Caveman. I did not appreciate my last experience with him. I will not be having IVF with your Unnamed Sydney Hospital. I am seeing a new practitioner and if I *do* decide to have IVF I shall go private or transfer to a different Unnamed Sydney Hospital.'

The receptionist is dumbfounded. 'Oh dear,' she says.

I am very very glad that we have started seeing the Chinese Fertility Goddess. If indeed I'd had the ultrasound that Professor Caveman so nonchalantly suggested and was awaiting the results of that *and* the HSG, I would have been devastated by this phone call.

Instead, I can concern myself with more important issues like Does Naughty Nephew the 1st Have Sunscreen On?

Be happy!

19 January

As a special treat the Chinese Fertility Goddess prescribes something new. It comes in a rectangular pastel pink box. The instructions are to take 'a ball' a day. This intriguing description becomes clear when I open the packaging to discover what appear to be several wax ping pong balls printed in gold characters. These have to be split apart to reveal another ball, made of plastic, containing fifty small round pills. These must be swallowed. All of them.

I crack one open and begin taking three at a time. After an hour I manage to finish one ball. They are described as having a 'honey taste'. Balls. As per the tea, they taste revolting.

After a couple of sessions I am also given a box of what appear to be chocolates but disappointingly turn out to be slices of deer antler. I am to boil these with the Chinese dates and create a 'tea'. This will be put in the fridge and allowed to cool. One tablespoon of the precious gold liquid is to be ladled into the morning and evening cups of my Horrid Tea. This will cause us to go at it like rabbits, apparently.

Christopher is given his own special capsules to take. These are bright red and go by the name of 'Golden Gun'. They come in a natty little gold box. He is quite pleased with these. They are ordinary-capsule sized and he only has to take two twice a day.

He is not so pleased when he reads the English explanation on the side of the box:

Indications—underdeveloped sexual organs, impotence, infirm erection [sic] and over-exhaustion etc.

I fall on the ground laughing.

We are also given a discreet schedule of sexual intercourse. When the Chinese Fertility Goddess writes it down and explains it to me I laugh behind my hands like a schoolgirl.

'That's good,' she says, as I snicker away, embarrassed. 'You laugh, that's good! More laughing for you.'

And whether it's the Golden Gun or the deer antlers, *something* goes ballistic in the bedroom.

And are we happy? Oh yes!

2 February

Another day, another acupuncture session with the Chinese Fertility Goddess.

Legs up & laughing

I get in early and miraculously there is no other patient lurking about so the CFG and I end up having a good chat. I lie back and think of baby as she cracks open her needles and prepares to get prickly with me.

She asks me if I have a job and I say no, not officially, but when I write things that get performed on stage or radio I get paid royalties and stuff. And sometimes, I say with enthusiasm, if I write something for television I might get paid a Proper Wage. Like with, you know, super.

Her eyes open wide in amazement and I wince and smile bravely, not because of the needles but because having treatments with the Goddess is like paying for a second mortgage. We can't afford a *first* mortgage so it's more like paying rent on a second flat in a much nicer suburb *and* keeping the Doberman who lives there in fresh meat and squeaky toys.

I tell her that having a baby has now become a priority (over, say, food) so don't spare the pins and do prescribe me another box of that delicious fifty-dollar antler velvet ...

The Chinese Fertility Goddess pokes in the last of the ultra-fine needles and twiddles them a little for good measure. She pats my arm and leaves me to relax and think positive babymaking thoughts. Instead I add up in my head the potential savings we make now that we've given up chocolate, coffee, cheese, butter, ice-cream, wine, sugar, steaks, sausages, lamb, actually all meat except fish ...

Against that I have to balance the items we *really* go to town on ... brown rice, tofu, fruit, vegetables, oily fish, chickpeas, rice crackers, dried fruits, nuts, seaweed ...

Woo hoo. Party at our house!

Despite all this mental grocery shopping I eventually fall under the spell of the Chinese Fertility Goddess and her Thin Pointy Servants and once again I slip into a sort of deep trance. Only this time I start having strangely dirty dreams and at one stage I am even aware of my hips moving in a suggestive fashion

... yeah, needles and all ...
And *that's* a little bit weird.

8 February

Early each morning, in that dreamy half-awake half-asleep state, nightie askew and hair fashionably mussed, I reach out for ... no not my husband's penis ... but something that sees infinitely more action—my thermometer. I shove it in my mouth, turn on the bedside lamp, squint crustily at the mercury, memorize the temperature so I can plot it on my little chart and sink back into oblivion.

The theory is that you can tell when you are ovulating (or indeed pregnant, ho ho ho) by charting your temperature on awakening. The rise in luteinizing hormone just prior to ovulation causes a temperature rise and then the presence of progesterone in the body after ovulation keeps it high. If you're pregnant, the temperature stays above normal as new and exciting doses of hormones whizz madly round your body like a bunch of kids on red cordial. If not, it drops just before your period arrives.

Day 28 begins with the surprise discovery that my temperature is up from the day before.

When I go to see the Chinese Fertility Goddess she takes my pulse and hums a bit.

I describe various pains and bodily discharges and finally, a little shyly, I mention the business with the temperature going up.

She goes into hyperdrive.

'Why you not tell me earlier? Some women bring their chart to me and say ... look look my temperature ... !' I begin to giggle dementedly.

'You could be lucky,' she says to me as she begins to stick me with needles. 'You could be lucky.'

When I tell Christopher, he is delighted. But, we say, we're not going to get our hopes up.

In the evening we go to see a movie and I duck into the loo just before it starts. When I come out Christopher looks pale.

'I thought you were in there a bit long,' he says. 'I thought something must have started.'

Apart from the fact that it shows how men completely misjudge the time it takes a woman to wee *and* wash her hands, I thought it was very sweet that he was getting caught up in the whole is she or isn't she, because *this is me every twenty-eight days.*

This is me, and this is all women like me, because this is the time, around the end of a cycle, when you think to yourself: *I could be* ... But of course it's too early to tell your partner, it's almost too early to tell yourself ...

For a few hopeful hours you start to read signs like crazy and they're not always coming from your body ...

A bud on the lemon tree, about to come into flower ...

Two identical fish caught in a tidal pool swimming round and round, like twins ...

We watch the movie and then walk alongside the beach and hold hands and dream our separate dreams.

And then this morning, I take my temperature and see that it's dropped. Christopher is still asleep as I write this.

A little more time for him to hope.

9 February

Despite the ghastly Horrid Tea, even with essence of sliced deer antler mixed through, early this morning, in came the painters.

I was meant to be doing some productive writing but instead I did lots of unproductive lying on our couch, staring at the ceiling and sighing.

Even the news that I've been shortlisted for a play-writing

award didn't cheer me. Instead, I felt slightly panic-stricken because (contrary to the rules of the award) I had sent the play out to another company who now want to produce it in October. I did this because life's too short to hang round waiting when I might not get shortlisted anyway. If I had waited till *after* the shortlist was announced to send the play out it wouldn't have got into this year's theatre season. It may not have got into next year's either, because it's topical and relates to events that occurred two years ago.

You spend ages writing these things. For nothing, mostly. And then you send them to theatre companies and it takes ages for them to get back to you. And of course if they don't want the play, they usually never bother to get back in touch.

I've got three plays in my desk drawer that are not being produced.

One of them was shortlisted for exactly this award a year ago.

Sometimes this industry seems like a complete lottery. Like babymaking I suppose. Some people just get better numbers.

17 February

I believe that Arthur Miller said: 'A man of genius makes no mistakes. His errors are volitional and are the portals of discovery.'

Or maybe it was James Joyce.

Whatever.

Yesterday I talked to my agent about the shortlist problem. I went over all my gripes and concerns and they were many and legion and she listened to them all patiently and finally she said: 'Would you be worrying about all this if you were a guy?'

And I realized, of course I wouldn't. I wouldn't care at all because ... well because the play's *great* and the more theatre companies that get to see it, the better. Share the love.

Sometimes I think if I were a guy I would be a lot less nervous and anxious and worried about what people think of me. Obviously a generalization, but I have this image of Super Cool Writer Guy Who Takes Risks and Laughs in The Face of Failure.

I think I might even be a lot less stressed about trying to have a baby. (Leaving aside the 'if I had a penis' type thing, I'm talking attitude, not gonads.)

Maybe I wouldn't see myself as such a failure or even give my infertility such a huge role. I have to admit it's starting to take over my identity a little, as if all I am is a uterus on legs. Give me a long frilly dress and a charming French accent and you can call me Madame Ovary.

A couple of weeks ago when we were doing our tax (and mine is always a total mess because I keep my receipts in stupid places like shoeboxes and old envelopes and discarded socks) I had to actually think … look … *other people have tax hassles. Playwrights* have tax hassles. Maybe even great ones like Caryl Churchill and David Mamet and Christopher Durang (but not Arthur Miller) but they don't define themselves that way.

It's not like: 'I am a taxation nightmare and in my spare time I wrote *Top Girls*.'

So I tell myself: just chill.

I am a writer.

With a small tax hassle.

And a small fertility hassle.

And a teeny *tiny* shortlist problem.

22 February

During a recent visit to the Chinese Fertility Goddess I told her I was feeling depressed and slightly weepy. Could she put some 'happy herbs' in this week's mix? She said yes.

I was *thrilled*. I had no idea Traditional Chinese Medicine had 'happy herbs'—I just made that up. At first I thought it was some kind of mountain-grown Chinese marijuana, maybe hybridized with a little ginseng, but then before I left she told me she'd put some 'happy bark' in my tea. Cut to me, pouring contents of paper bag into clay pot that night, prodding through the contents to find said 'happy bark'. I find at least four different kinds of bark in the brew so I get a spoon and squash them right down into the water to make sure I extract every goddamned *molecule* of happiness.

28 February

The last of my friends from uni is pregnant.

Four of us from the same first-year drama class have kept in touch and more or less catch up regularly, even though two live in London and two live in Sydney. Lucy had her first child at twenty-four and her second just last year, Michelle had her first baby at Christmas and that left me and Helen.

Helen actually said, the last time she was in the country, that we should both wait till we were thirty-nine to have a baby. Yeah right, I said without any conviction, because at that stage Christopher and I were already lining up for tickets for the Great Big Fertility Ride. What must it be like to be so confident that you can nominate the age of conception?

Back in London she was doing all the hard drinking, hard partying and yummy eating that Christopher and I *hadn't* been doing and lo ... she emails to say she is up the duff. It seems like it happened about two minutes after she and her husband were married. That makes me feel a bit glum, what with all the Horrid Teas and acupuncture and Professor Caveman types we've had to deal with and still nothing to show for it. I would kill for a few squares of dark chocolate or even a measly Kit Kat finger right now, but I make do with three red Chinese dates and a nasty aftertaste which I think we call 'jealousy'.

I feel like that time in primary school when we had to do folk dancing for sport and the boys had to ask the girls to dance. And one by one, all my friends were chosen and got up and took their place for the Convulsing Weasel or whatever the name of the stupid dance was, and I just sat there, smiling uneasily and picking invisible threads off my skirt. I'm sure I wasn't the last girl asked to dance, my memory isn't painful enough for that, but the fear was there.

And then when I add to this the various rejections from theatre companies or awards or grants or indeed the whole being shortlisted and missing out on the main event (yup, all that worrying was for naught) and then the general play-writing malaise ... it seems so very easy to link these two things: fertility and creativity.

I have writers' block and it's probably in my left fallopian tube.

I am heading off for another blood test tomorrow. This time the Chinese Fertility Goddess wants word from the science community on my progesterone levels.

The delightful boiled-dog smell of brewing deer antler is wafting over me as I type.

But in good news, two green frogs have taken up residence on our verandah.

ONCE UPON A TIME

Naughty Nephew the 2nd, aged five, is crazy for Harry Potter.

Or at least he's crazy for the Harry Potter he knows from schoolyard conversations, the video game and the cover of the books his big brother is voraciously reading. He's too young to read and they're too advanced to be read to him. The next best thing is to be told a 'Harry Potter Story'.

In the beginning I started off faithfully, retelling the usual snippets ... the flying car bit, the dementors attack Dudley bit ... but it all got a bit dull and inevitably I would find that Naughty Nephew the 3rd, aged three, was listening too and no one wants to tell a three-year-old about sucking someone's soul out through their lips. ('What's a soul?' 'Why is he sucking it?' 'What's a soul?')

That's when I started telling the Harry Potter Variations.

Usually Harry would be doing whatever it was the Nephews were doing at the time of the story ...

'One day Harry Potter was taking a bath ...'

His pals Ron and Hermione would join him, bringing appropriate props, usually food related.

'Hermione waved her magic rubber ducky and chanted the special words that made a whole box of chocolates fall into the bath water.'

There would be some form of impending danger, nearly always in the form of GREEN LIGHTNING which would warn us, the listeners, that the magic rubber ducky (or bath water, or slippery dip, or shop on the corner) was in fact EVIL but would be foolishly ignored by Harry and his friends.

There would also be a bad wizard named Mouldy Pork or He Who Shall Not Be Sniffed.

Mouldy Pork had proved himself almost as bad as Voldemort, but not quite. For instance, he liked to eat mermaids and chips ('Harry Potter and the Magic Turtle') which rates quite high on the baddie scale but not as high as killing off Harry's parents.

Also, he was usually vanquished by Harry and his friends and ended up exploding ('Harry Potter and the Flying Swing Set') or eaten by a giant hippopotamus ('Harry Potter Gets Grumpy While Stuck in Traffic on the Way to the Zoo') or covered in purple slime ('Harry Potter Has Nits').

Naughty Nephew the 2nd gets very involved in the storytelling, introducing wicked plot twists, additional evil wizards all named after spoiled foods, and correcting me on details of spells and proper pronunciation of incantations ('Flipendo!') which of course he knows from countless hours of computer gamery.

Luckily I have gained credibility by being able to introduce the famous and highly magical incantations: 'Ala! Peanut Butter Sandwiches', 'Open Sesame' and 'ShaZAM!' which I insisted were studied carefully by Harry and Pals but not used as much on account of their extreme power and potential danger.

These stories have gone so well that even weeks later the three-year-old will sidle up and ask me to tell yet again the gripping tale of 'Harry Potter and the Magic Turtle'. In fact, not to drum my own cauldron, but even Naughty Nephew the 1st will drop into the story circle at times to hear how 'Harry Potter Cuts Sick and Goes Surfing.'

At the dinner table, at picnics, in the car, at the beach inevitably I will find a small hand creeping into mine and a little voice in my ear saying: 'Will you tell me a story?'

Their mother and father say quickly 'Leave her alone, she is only two spoonfuls through her dinner', but of course I love it. I make special 'Yes, one moment while I swiftly gobble my food so I can give you my undivided attention' faces and ask the owner of small hand and persistent voice to start thinking up the characters and even the situations that Harry finds himself in.

And that's why, at the park on the weekend, I felt my heart do a funny little skip when I realized that his dad was finally reading Harry Potter and the Philosopher's Stone, *the actual real authentic unabridged no magic turtles or Mouldy Pork version, to Naughty Nephew the 2nd.*

Christopher and I were given a quick perfunctory hug each and then he turned to his dad and said 'Can you read me more?'

And we were dismissed.

Soon the familiar words of J.K. Rowling wafted through the air. I consoled myself by sliding down the hill with Naughty Nephew the 3rd on a handy piece of cardboard we found near the bins. As we climbed up the hill to go again, I looked across the grass to where Naughty Nephew the 2nd was comfortably curled up with his dad and listening hard.

It's great, I told myself firmly. Books are like being in a whole new world.

For a moment I felt like telling Naughty Nephew the 3rd that our scrappy piece of cardboard was actually a flying carpet.

But then a big plane flew overhead and a kid bravely rode down the hill on his bike with no brakes, and a truck tooted its horn as it drove past and the moment was gone forever.

2 March

This morning I grabbed the all-knowing, all-essential thermometer, squinted at the mercury, and in my braindead state decided *what this thing needs is a God almighty shake.*

The stupid thing shot out of my hand, flew across Christopher's head, and smashed against the opposite wall.

Is it a sign?

7 March

I am a big believer in the power of positive thinking, creative visualization, all that sort of hooky spooky guff.

For instance, once, years ago, when Christopher and I were on the verge of homelessness, I made us do some very heavy duty visualizing of our ideal home. I imagined a flat, with stairs, a bit of a view and some lovely yellow light. I also wanted him to chant with me the following mantra every night before falling asleep: 'We are living in a beautiful and creative space.'

Frankly, I don't think Christopher took it all that seriously. Each night, I would hear him start to snore and realize that once again he had forgotten to chant. I would have to prod him awake. Then, instead of chanting in a proper soothing monotone over and over, he would start *performing* the mantra, using stupid accents or changing the inflections on different words.

'WE are living in a BEAUTIFUL and CREATIVE spaaaaace.'

'No, don't say it like that,' I would mutter between gritted teeth, 'just chant it, just *say* the words over and over.'

'But it's boooring,' he would whine. 'I have to make it interesting.'

'No you don't, you just have to say the words, it works whether you are bored or not, just SAY THE DAMN WORDS.'

'Why are you shouting?'

In the end, though, it must have worked because we were unexpectedly offered a fantastic one-bedroom flat in a posh part of town that was way out of our league. It had steps and polished floors and an ultra modern bathroom and was painted a sort of lemon colour so that when the afternoon sun hit the windows the place was filled with gorgeous golden light. In fact, several years and flats later, we still have our post office box in this part of town because it forces us to stop and pick up our mail and maybe linger at a lovely outdoor café and sip nostalgically at our ridiculously overpriced coffees. Sorry, I mean antioxidant-rich green teas.

So the thing is, I have decided to actively use my power of positive thinking to sort of boost the Chinese Fertility Goddess's efforts. I will relax but I will also cunningly focus my mind to visualize my clear and freely running fallopian tubes. I'm basically trying to get more bang for my buck. This is why, in the midst of my acupuncture-induced coma, I do not want to hear:

1. mobile phones
2. man in next cubicle emptying his pockets of change as he prepares to drop trousers for Chinese Fertility Goddess.
3. toilet door slamming
4. extremely small child telling Mummy she is hungry/thirsty/bored/needs to go wee wee.

Mummy is obviously attempting similar acupuncture coma to myself but has failed to realize her supply of crayons and colouring book will be woefully insufficient for satisfying small child and keeping her quiet for minimum twenty minutes. Hence, not only is *Mummy* failing to enjoy full effect of expensive treatment, but so is everyone else. Instead, Mummy makes the situation worse by loudly whispering: 'Sshhh darling. Mummy's resting ... where are your lovely crayons? You go wee wee in the room outside, go on, you're a big girl'

See point three above.

Someone told me recently about various sacred Aboriginal waterholes dotted about the landscape that the women used to visit when they wanted to have a baby. I don't know where any of these sacred waterholes might be and also I'm a bit scared of leeches but I imagine the ocean must contain a lot of spiritual power and I *do* like to walk along the beach.

I'm hoping this will count for something.

Especially if my feet get splashed.

I breathe deeply in and out and imagine myself swimming in a cosmic ocean full of tiny waterbabies, swirling and giggling and wheeling around me. Rather like sea-monkeys, but bigger and with only two legs.

11 March

The Chinese Fertility Goddess has decided that Christopher needs his boys checked out again, aka the infamous 'wank in a jar' test.

Last time he did this was under the orders of Professor Caveman and it involved a drive to a large hospital in the western suburbs with a clinical space and white-trash pornography. (Christopher points out that as this is a multicultural society, surely they should include some variety.)

He did sort of average in those tests, getting a 'could do better' and a terse 'insolent pest' comment for Woodwork. Oh no, sorry, that was his Year 8 end-of-year report. Actually, he does least well in morphology but the sperm count and motility are good. This means that his boys are fast and numerous but with bodgy heads.

This time, instead of going to a large hospital in the western suburbs he is going to a small clinic in Chinatown to see a Chinese Sperm Scientist who only works on Saturdays and does the test results himself. I am interested to know if in Chinatown Christopher will finally get the variety he is seeking in the mag department.

We have a special dinner at a neat little Italian seafood restaurant to celebrate the fortieth birthday of Christopher's brother Keith.

Keith and his wife Neâ are very jolly and of course have three gorgeous boys, being the Naughty Nephews, who we see as much as we can. Keith and Christopher's parents made a surprise visit from Perth to join in the festivities. I experience a slightly smug thrill when I hear that Naughty Nephew the 2nd told his grandmother his 'favourite aunt' was coming to *his* birthday party. Tee hee! That's me!

Dinner is progressing well with lots of drunken merriment abounding (except for the infertile members of the family, obviously) until Christopher tells Neâ that the Naughty Nephews will have a cousin to play with soon. Neâ is suddenly very excited. Christopher realizes that he has been a prat. He then has to explain that it is not an announcement, it is merely an 'outburst of optimism'. Neâ bursts into tears. I burst into tears. Everyone suddenly sobers up.

After an awkward pause, things are okay and we all go back to the stuffed calamari, but this incident makes me realize that we have lots of people around us who are quietly very hopeful on our behalf.

12 March

Aaaarggggh!!!

This is what went through my head today when the Chinese Sperm Scientist said to Christopher: 'But where is your sample?'

No, his receptionist had said *nothing* about bringing a sample, she said *nothing* about collecting a little sample cup prior to today's visit and *nothing whatsoever* about filling it with tadpoles less than two hours before the appointment.

'Okay,' says the Chinese Sperm Scientist with a warm smile. 'No problem.' He hands Christopher a cup. 'You can use the men's toilets outside ...'

'Outside' is a large waiting area that services about ten different clinics. There are people with legs in plaster reading magazines. There are elderly men waiting to have their skin cancers cut off. There are children in line to have their impetigo diagnosed. The toilets are the public toilets for *all* the clinics. Christopher could be ... ahem ... *filling his jar* ... in a cubicle next to any one of these unsuspecting folk.

He looks at me, aghast. Have we really sunk so low?

'Or you can use the examination room next door. That way you can both go in.'

And that's how we discover that in this corner of Chinatown, the material of stimulation is not a fistful of magazines featuring hot Asian babes, it's a faded breast self-examination chart ... and me.

Yup. That was me, whispering in my husband's ear, offering a helpful hand, obligingly passing the sample jar, trying to block out the sound of other patients chatting happily on the other side of the thin walls. And laughing. I nearly made myself sick laughing. Which, thinking back, was probably not the most helpful thing I could have done.

Christopher holds up the cup after the most silent orgasm imaginable and purses his lips a little.

'What's wrong?' I whisper.

'Nothing,' he says, peering at the cup. 'It's just ... not very much.'

The Chinese Sperm Scientist has suggested the next step may be a post-coital examination. If Christopher's sperm turn out to be fine, the 'problem' could be me. My vagina may be harbouring 'hostile' mucus.

Nice.

In the lift we discuss this latest player in our quest for a baby and Christopher points out that the Chinese Sperm Scientist has a wise wrinkly face and a kindly manner, which seems to make up for the fact that he takes cash only and doesn't give receipts. In fact, greenish skin not withstanding, he looks and sounds a lot like Yoda, if Yoda ever took to wearing little knitted vests.

And as far as we know, Yoda wasn't into giving receipts either.

15 March

I imagine a time, way off in the future, when I look back and smile, and perhaps even chuckle gently, at the bitterness surrounding my attempted journey from nothingness to babyness.

I won't remember that today, for instance, I lay on the couch blubbering and saying pathetically, 'I don't understand ... why is this happening ... why do we have to have so many things *wrong* with us?'

This morning we got Christopher's results back from Yoda, and although all his levels have risen some, it turns out that he now also has Sperm Antibodies. This means that Christopher's body sees his sperm as foreign and unwanted (very much like this country's attitude towards refugees, for instance) and, instead of setting them free with joyous abandon, it shackles them and causes them to clump miserably and not want to fertilize my waiting eggs.

Or at least my waiting eggs in the *right* ovary, the left one being closed for business.

So. Imagine the scene. We've got clumping, limping sperm, most of which have deformed heads. We've got walled-up left-hand eggs screaming for release.

We've got right-hand eggs only available every second month, perhaps.

It's a total gothic interuterine nightmare. Sort of like *Hunchback of Notre Dame* meets *Where Did I Come From?*.

16 March

One of my old school friends rang me last night, all excited because he's going to be a dad.

He's gay, and a lesbian couple that he's friendly with have asked him to hand over the goods. It's all going to be organized and drawn up in some kind of semi-legal way and he will be the acknowledged father and contribute and be part of all their lives.

He's always been a fairly solitary sort of fella, a bit isolated and often lonely. He loves children and has umpteen nephews and nieces who all love *him*.

He moved back to (our) home town last year and he's sort of happier. But not really. This news, however, sees him leaping about on cloud nine. He's going to be a dad!

As I imagine him bouncing away he suddenly says, 'We're going to inseminate in June—so you're going to be another aunty.'

I smile thinly. Yup, *that's* what I want to be. Another aunty.

'Or maybe you might be pregnant too and we'll have babies at the same time!'

Mmm. Maybe.

I was really happy for my friend but I couldn't help thinking as he told me: there goes another one.

19 March

Christopher and I sit before Yoda, glumly scanning the test results. We are here for our second consultation to work out what comes next.

Things didn't start well. Yoda's receptionist is a gorgeous young überchic slip of a thing with a mouth full of attitude. She asks both our names but when she sticks her head through the door to tell Yoda we're here she immediately forgets Christopher's, referring to him as 'um … the partner'. She tells us to come back in five minutes because … (actually no reason, just because) and when we do return we have to wait in line behind two white-coated Pathology Dudes who are slavering over her deskpad.

Überchic Receptionist cannot even acknowledge our presence because she is regaling the Pathology Dudes with tales of her Big Night Out and her Lesson Learned (only drink good vodka) and how sucky it was to come in to work this morning 'cos there are, like, patients *everywhere*.

I have already decided that this *must* be the receptionist who failed to inform us of the necessary preparation for Christopher's earlier sperm sample test, and this, combined with my natural anxiety and her natural beauty, is inciting pure undiluted hatred.

I must wait until her long and boring tale is complete, with a warm and understanding smile playing across my face, but in my mind I am committing grave acts of violence using only her freebie drug company biro and the foam esky things the Pathology Dudes are gaily waving about.

When we do finally see him, Yoda is congenial almost to the point of jolly and I calm down and refrain from telling him his receptionist is a moron.

Pleasantries aside, Yoda puts on his stern face and for a few minutes all seems dark indeed. Morphology now completely sucks, motility is barely normal and those scumbag antibodies are clinging around the tail tip of 90 per cent of Christopher's sperm like screaming three-year-olds at a day care centre wrapped around their fleeing mothers' ankles.

Having previously spent a good half hour on Google, I ask knowledgeably about 'sperm washing' as a way of isolating the unfettered sperm. Yoda shakes his head. Sperm washing is so five years ago. 'We've done sperm washing already, it doesn't work.'

I take a moment to miserably stare about his room as a way of staving off yet another flood of tears. I notice he's left on that machine that wobbles things about so they don't set and wonder if it's a waste of electricity but *then* Yoda starts to wield his hi-tech space-age gadgetry (i.e. use his calculator) and suddenly things look brighter.

Firstly, sperm antibodies have a tendency to come and go. They rise and fall as evidenced by last year's sperm study (for evil Professor Caveman) which showed only 50 per cent antibodies. Secondly, it seems that allowing for slowness and bodgy heads etc., Christopher actually has *fifteen million* wrigglers to play with. Hoopla!

Yoda proudly shows off statistics of some of his previous cases, which show parents miraculously created from only 4 and 4.5 million of the crazy tadpole guys. Choice!

He now recommends a post-coital test to see if I really do have a toxic vagina. To determine when the coital part of the test should take place he sells us a $50 luteinizing hormone test (scorning the bargain-price Fortels I buy at the supermarket). Similar to a pregnancy test, the LH test shows when ovulation takes place and when pregnancy is most likely to be successful.

He gives us some convoluted instructions to follow and tells us to ring him at 8.30 am sharp if we get the two lines that indicate that ovulation is imminent. Any later and we'll miss him because he will be playing golf. Or at church.

It seems that Yoda is a Christian. Possibly even Catholic, I decide, because of a previous comment he made about Good

Friday. Also, when Christopher marvelled at the wonders of cervical mucus and the way it becomes fertile at just the right time, Yoda looked up towards the ceiling and smiled saying, 'Yes, *He* is.'

I note that Yoda doesn't say 'have sex', 'copulate' or 'fuck like rabbits'. He says 'make love' which makes him sound like someone from *Days of Our Lives*.

So off we go with our fistful of LH tests and a much happier frame of mind.

We still have a blocked left tube and 90 per cent antibodies. But I'm happy because we've also got fifteen million sperm. Woo hoo!

20 March

One of the things that happens when you realize you are infertile, and that all your friends are having babies, is you spend a lot of time in cyber world reading stories of infertility on various blogs and messageboards because you feel so horribly alone in your real world.

You also start to get very sensitive about all the babies that seem to have suddenly popped up in your vicinity.

Suddenly, pregnant bellies loom large from every doorway. Conversations with pregnant or 'with-child' girlfriends are all about baby sleeping or baby eating or baby kicking. Prams and strollers seem unreasonably enormous and designed purely to run over your toes and show off the pusher's natural fertility.

To cope with this all-encompassing world of goo goo gah gah, I begin to take on protective mechanisms. For instance, I avert my eyes generally when babies or bellies are in the region and do a sort of soft focus, stare-out-to-sea type thing. This is often dangerous in crowded shopping centres but frankly I prefer bruised shins to a broken heart.

My other trick is to *externally* engage very brightly and enthusiastically in conversations about Other People's Babies so that I *seem* to be interested and unscathed by barrenness, but *internally* I wilt a bit and vague out and mentally stare at my toes.

Which is really why the following horror situation occurred:

Scene: rather noisy housewarming party.

Me, chatting with someone in the hallway. I duck around the corner and see my husband talking with a couple of people. One is in the middle of an anecdote. Cheerfully, I join the group only to realize that Anecdote Woman is talking about A BABY. Too late to veer off in another direction, I employ abovementioned vague internal but bright external tactic.

ME *(glazing over yet smiling like a dervish):*

Hi there Anecdote Woman, did I just hear you say you've fostered a baby?

General hubbub as Anecdote Woman repeats herself. I can't really hear what she's said and frankly I'm not trying very hard.

ME: You have? You fostered a baby? Two weeks ago? That's great! That's wonderful!

Awful pause.

ANECDOTE WOMAN: I said, I *lost* a baby. Two weeks ago.

ME: Oh my God.

That was a bad moment but I was well punished for it as Anecdote Woman then went into enormous, gory, terrifying detail. We all gaped in horror. She opened up a silver locket she wore around her neck and showed us the teeny tiny baby footprints. I burst into tears.

After I recovered she continued her story, and as she did I noticed her eyes were sidling over my shoulders to where a woman with a baby was sitting on the couch.

Another girlfriend was standing in our group. And she'd also been trying (and failing) to fall pregnant. And I realized I'd had an earlier conversation with the girl whose house we were warming. And she was also trying (and failing).

And for the first time I realized that in my non-cyber *real* world, I actually wasn't so alone after all.

21 March

Dead in the mucus. This was Christopher's brave lads at 11 am this morning during our post-coital test with Yoda.

Following instructions, we had determined ovulation to be imminent and so at 8 am we had sex (sorry, 'made love') and then trotted back into Chinatown.

Not being the weekend, hellish Überchic Receptionist has been replaced by Scowling Frumpy Everyday Receptionist. Confusingly, Yoda nips out when he sees us hovering by the front desk to tell us he is not here, he is actually at his golf game.

Rather than use the clinic we go instead to the 'Outside' general waiting room where we fill in forms together and Yoda raises an eyebrow at the absurdity of my surname remaining my own instead of Christopher's. (Obviously a case of that Make Love, Him Upstairs Does Good Mucus, Christian thing again.)

Using his Jedi mind powers, Yoda somehow manages to get me into a laboratory across the corridor, bypassing everyone waiting in the queue to deliver me, smilingly, to the blood test lady.

Instead of fiery looks and gnashing of teeth, everyone is smiling. Bizarre. Christopher says these are not Jedi mind powers, these are the results of paying cash in hand.

Five minutes later we're back where Yoda isn't. Now he drags in the groovy doctor from the clinic next door, to administer the post-coital test. She looks like she's heading from Hong Kong to New York but has decided to slum it in Sydney awhile. She has suede boots and square tinted glasses. She also smiles a lot. When I thank her for doing this test despite a waiting room full of her own patients she says 'Well you know, when Yoda calls … we obey.' Yoda nods approvingly.

Christopher is banished to the waiting room for some obscure reason and I'm … legs up and laughing again. Doctor Groovy inserts the speculum and casually asks, 'Okay, which tube am I aiming for?'

'No no,' says Yoda, 'post-coital test.'

'Oh,' says Doctor Groovy. 'No insemination?'

'No no,' says Yoda. 'Withdrawal. Not deposit.'

More giggling all round.

After a bit of pippette fun, Yoda cranks up the microscope. 'Hmm,' he says, after a few squinty seconds. 'Not good. Bring in hubby.'

Soon, 'hubby' and I are peering into the strange and frightening world of Yoda's microscope. I am shown the contents of my cervix and also my 'vaginal pool' which, frankly, needs a good going over with the Creepy Crawley. No wonder Christopher's boys had trouble swimming, they were constantly in danger of being run down by all the floating debris.

The whole scene reminds me of the underneath of our bed, or alternatively the opening scene of *Saving Private Ryan*, because apart from floating debris the place is also littered with sperm corpses. Yoda shakes his head, concerned. I tell him that Christopher and I had sex two nights previously, and Yoda practically hits his head with his stick. It seems we should have abstained to build up supplies. I argue that I thought I was ovulating possibly yesterday. And Christopher had a load on, you know, so we thought that he should jettison the old stuff.

No no no. All wrong. Yoda displeased with young disciples.

Doctor Groovy has just tripped in to grab some meds from Yoda's fridge and catches a bit of this head-shaking.

'Don't you worry,' she says reassuringly. 'Remember, it only takes one sperm.'

I fall in love immediately with Doctor Groovy and shake Christopher's arm at her like a six-year-old brandishing their Show And Tell at the teacher.

'This is my husband, Doctor Groovy,' I prattle. She smiles and says hello. Yoda is smiling too. 'Doctor Groovy and I disagree sometimes,' he says. 'She likes to be optimistic. But I am a fact finder.'

'We're optimistic too,' pipes up Christopher.

Doctor Groovy waves bye-byes to the kids.

The upshot is, for the next two cycles, Christopher and I have to abstain from sex leading up to ovulation. And when we do it, Christopher will have to try 'split ejaculation'. This means pulling out after the first spurt. This is because, according to Yoda, the first spurt contains most of the sperm while the rest contains all the fluid. And this fluid holds up the progress of the boys in front.

As we take a moment to absorb this rather distasteful bit of seminal trivia, Yoda shakes his head in a disappointed manner. At first I think it's us but then he glances 'upstairs'.

'I don't know why He did it that way,' he mutters. 'Doesn't seem very logical.'

It's a shame, because God scored a big tick from Yoda a few days earlier for getting the cervical mucus right.

Christopher asks 'And after the two cycles? If it doesn't work?'

'Then,' says Yoda, 'we try IUI. Interuterine insemination.'

'Not IVF?'

'No,' he says firmly. 'I don't believe in IVF.'

I don't believe in IVF?

Well that's *all* the conservative Christian cards on the table then. I realize now I should have said 'Happy Easter' to him as we left, instead of 'Happy Golfing'.

22 March

Back to the Chinese Fertility Goddess to go over the whole Yoda experience.

I tell her that I'd casually mentioned to Yoda that I, shock horror, had a *shower* after sex. 'And,' I chuckle, 'he got quite stern with us.'

Her eyes open wide. 'You *shower* after sex?'

Christopher and I exchange guilty glances. 'Um ... yes.'

'NO!' she shouts. 'Not when trying to conceive! You wash the sperm away! Soapy water kills the sperm ... no!! No shower! You must sleep! Sleep! Legs up and sleep!'

Lordy. Yet another thing we're doing wrong. If this is all some kind of competence test for child-worthiness, we're failing badly.

We've put 'showers after sex' on the 'NO' list along with chilli, fat, caffeine, alcohol and processed sugars.

26 March

Christopher and I are in the Blue Mountains for Easter. It's incredibly peaceful. The autumn weather is beautifully crisp; the air is cold and so clean I feel like I'm inhaling pure water.

Yesterday was sunny but today the clouds seem to have closed in. As I write I can see a small family of foil-covered rabbits sitting on the cabinet by the door. The Naughty Nephews are coming with their father this afternoon to stay a couple of nights. We're enjoying the quiet while we can. On cue, a flock of tiny bronzed silver-eyes darts through the trees outside my window. And then, the sun breaks through.

Normally I try to avoid Easter. It's usually pretty easy because there's always work on and people to see and stuff to do, but here it's different. Here, there's lots of time to think.

Easter makes me think of my mum.

She died just after Easter, eleven years ago after a long and hideous battle with breast cancer. We had our Easter eggs around her bedside in the hospice at the Mater Hospital. In fact, one of her last real mouthfuls must have been my father's Cadbury Caramello Egg which she got via devious and duplicitous means. He had obligingly held it up to her nose. 'I just want to smell it,' were her exact words.

My mother was a Christian, a Catholic Filipina (her daughters got half the Filipina and all of the Catholic), but later as the cancer kicked in with steel-capped boots she felt the need for stronger stuff and joined the charismatic church. It was some form of Baptist with lots of testimonials and earnest guitars and lots and *lots* of expat Filipinos with names like 'Baby' and 'Angel' and 'Cherry'. Mum had a strong soprano voice and I could always pick her voice among the various church choirs she joined. Years later, I still hear her voice whenever I hear a church choir.

The Easter before that last Easter, Mum had been sure her cancer was going into remission. She became positive that Jesus would cure her as he rose from the cross.

He rose.

She fell.

I ignored Easter for a long time. For me, Easter was a bitter time, a time of resentment and grief. It was also a time of guilty relief because the cancer was so long and drawn out. I spent weeks listening to her every breath thinking it was the last, hoping it was the last and then hoping it wasn't.

That sort of screws you up a little bit.

The kids have changed that.

This Easter, as Christopher and I prepare to have our mountain peace shattered by the joyful shouts and glowing faces of our much loved Naughty Nephews, I am no longer ignoring. I am taking notice. I am thinking about Mum and eggs and death and birth and forgiveness. I am thinking about story and history and about passing things on.

It is a great sadness to me, a deep sadness, that if the miracle of miracles should occur and Christopher and I *do* have a child that my mother is not here to hold that child, to sing that child a lullaby in her own language, Tagalog. My mother never became a grand-mother, she was only forty-eight when she died and my sister Amanda was six years away from having her first child.

But I guess if it *does* happen, then Mum will be there in me, and in the sister-aunties.

Although I can't sing that Tagalog lullaby, I do remember the tune, so I could hum the melody as I rock my baby to sleep. And though I never learned my mother's language—suburban Australia in the early seventies preferred English—there is one phrase I *do* remember and I could whisper it over and over, again and again.

Mahal kita.

I love you.

30 March

I think I boasted a while back when I quoted Naughty Nephew the 2nd, who referred to me as 'my favourite aunt'. (Which makes me sound quite posh and formal and about ninety in the shade with mad wiry hair pulled back in a bun, crepey neck, cameo brooch and lavender scent. Also I say 'back in my day' ... a lot. Also I cackle like a witch ... okay, killing this ridiculous tangent now.)

So here we are, favourite aunt, Christopher and his brother Keith, and the three Naughty Nephews. The lot of us are having a lovely romp through the Blue Mountains. Over cliff-path, under rock face, skipping stones in picturesque ponds, standing about chatting on sweet little bridges over meandering creeks ...

It is on the sweet little bridge that it all goes pear-shaped. One moment, Naughty Nephew the 2nd is bouncing beside me trying to get my hat (I really am that short) and the next he manages to bounce off the bridge, sideways under the useless barrier, and down into the meandering creek, hitting his head with an almighty crack on a huge rock.

You know how those moments are so short but you can dissect them down to the thousandth part? There he laughed and there he leaped and there he grasped at my sleeves and there he slipped and there I grabbed and there I missed ...

and those eyes watching me the whole way down ...

and that sound ...

Thank God and Goddess and everyone up there who's looking down and says 'That kid's got no sense of caution and his favourite aunt's got butterfingers but it ain't time yet ...'

Naughty Nephew the 2nd screams and cries and quickly gets to his feet (the water is freezing) and his dad (with admirable calm) wades into the creek and picks him up. Christopher rallies the other two, blithely unaware, Naughty Nephews. I stare and tell myself firmly not to jump in and not to say anything because I would probably cry and become a wee tad hysterical and Naughty Nephew the 2nd is perfectly capable of doing it all himself.

He seems to have got off with a very ugly ear. Quite squashed and bruised looking.

Nothing on his head. A bruise on his bum. When he finishes crying, his father re-dresses him in his jumper and slings him on his shoulders with a leftover hot-cross bun.

Christopher, who has a first-aid certificate, does special brain injury checks (squeeze this hand etc.).

Favourite aunt carries the wet clothes.

That night I find it hard to sleep as all kinds of awful scenarios play out in my mind, all accompanied by that horrible sound.

Next morning, still dark outside, I wake to the sound of the boys chatting and laughing. I creep into their room. Naughty Nephew the 2nd is still in his sleeping bag on the bottom bunk.

As soon as he sees me he smiles and puts out his arms for a hug. And when, thankful and grateful, I bend down to him, he gives me a beautiful big kiss on the forehead.

There are a few lessons for me here.

No playing on bridges.

Always watch small children closely, especially in mountainous landscapes.

Do not boast about being such a top aunty.

And above all, just give the kid the damn hat.

THE BEST THINGS IN LIFE ...

In our lives as feckless artistes, Christopher and I have had a variety of intriguing and amusing jobettes. These days my work is more of the writing variety and Christopher actually has had a proper full-time job for a few years now. But in those whimsical bygone days when we thought we were brimming with fertility and the world seemed a kinder, prettier place, we had a regular gig at the annual Royal Easter Show.

For around seventeen days each year, I would enter the hallowed gates of the showground with a thermos of coffee and a pack of sandwiches. Going into the shipping container-like atmosphere of the 'Entertainers Area', I would re-emerge some fifteen minutes later as that doyenne of country hospitality and rustic charm: Mrs Merino.

How I sweated to bring joy to the children in my thickly padded and crisply wholesome Beatrix Potterish frock, my rubber hoof gloves and boots and my enormously heavy fibreglass and real wool head.

Alongside my dungaree-clad husband, Mr Merino (played variously by Christopher and another feckless artiste friend whom I will mysteriously refer to as 'George'), we would meander through the byways and highways of the showground pushing a stroller which contained our adorable twin lambs—one holding a fairyfloss stick to its outstretched open mouth and the other seemingly expired with the sheer excitement of it all.

Our task was to simply blend in. We were employed to be a 'family' (how ironic it all seems now) who had come to see the Show. It was not our job to deliberately court attention. Not for us the out thrust paw and amiably nodding head of, say, the Paddle Pop Lion or (shudder) the distribution of sweets and stickers like poor, manhandled, overwhelmed Mr Jelly Belly.

We had dignity. We had backstory. We liked to think we evoked a little landed gentry respectability.

And we were photographed every step of the way.

Sometimes we were buggied through the grounds, for maximum exposure, and I would proudly seat the twin lambs on my lap and make the one that looked still alive wave at the children, while Mr Merino radiated paternal strength and nodded knowingly at the young dads.

Christopher hated the Show, every aspect of it, from the loathsome 'Cheese on a Stick' to the stupid blow-up hammers that teenagers used to give us a whupping behind the Dagwood Dog stand.

Peripheral vision being non-existent, we strolled with a minder in tow who could give advance warning of 'big boys at two o'clock'. If spied, we would trot speedily in the opposite direction towards the relative safety of 'Gardens' or 'Arts & Crafts' where no Big Boy with a blow-up hammer and a Cheese on a Stick would be seen dead.

Christopher especially hated the showbags, aka bags o' crap, so beloved of younger showgoers. In the old days, of course, the showbags were free. I distinctly remember as a kid, my grandma giving me a Bank of New South Wales bag containing a pencil, a wooden ruler, a little notebook and a moneybox. But by now, these had long gone—Grandma, the Wales and above all, the notion of anything being free at the Show.

Anything that is, except a photograph with the delightful Merino family.

Still, showbags held a special delight for me. They were mysterious and bulging and contained tiny sample versions of the real thing. Also chocolates. Luckily, being those famous Show celebrities, the Merino family, we could often scavenge up a couple of real showbags to add to our lamb stroller 'to make it look more authentic'.

Often when casually examining an exhibit, running a hoof over some crystallized ginger or cocking our big woolly heads with interest at an emu oil spruiker, we would be showered with little treats and samples—mainly because our very presence brought the kids running, over-sugared eyes rolling back in their heads, and with them, their stoic parents.

Luckily, 'George,' the other feckless artiste and part-time Mr Merino, was also a great lover of bags o' crap. In our breaks, while Christopher took calls from his agent and rearranged his casting sessions, 'George' and I would divvy up spoils and bicker over who got the last Choo Choo bar.

On the train going home one day this led to an enormous and shocking public brawl between myself and 'George', luckily not in our Merino costumes. Sardined in between exhausted showgoers, we had started arguing over a shared Banana in Pyjamas showbag that contained, most impressively, a Bananas clock. Who wouldn't fight for such a prize? Bickering became shouting became me shrieking and flinging the showbag down the length of the train, then crying all the long walk home and having to be put to bed by Christopher. But I got the clock.

Eventually, we were moved up the entertainment foodchain (we became Vegetables and Dancing Chickens) and Mr and Mrs Merino were relegated to the 'kiddy parade'. There they sat, stiff and disinterested, on the back of a flat-bed ute that was slowly driven around the grounds. They followed the local school band and were in turn followed by a wild-haired old lady in a spangly blue frock covered in plastic dolls, who 'performed' every year for free because she loved the Show so much.

Without proper out-of-work actors to animate them, Mr and Mrs Merino were no longer charming models of good parenting. With a couple of waif-like secretaries or bored work experience kids stuffed inside the suits, they appeared sullen and dirty. The once crisp and wholesome Beatrix Potterishness was reduced to grimy white trash.

Mr Merino looked like a wife beater and Mrs Merino was a crack whore who let her little lambs do whatever the hell they wanted. The fake fairyfloss stick was lost and so the first little lamb, eyes still half shut, lips still parted, seemed ready to suck up a bottle of Mummy's methadone while the second little lamb looked like Daddy had rolled over him when he was on the nod.

Spotting them go past, I could only shake my big fibreglass Miss Broccoli head. It was the end of an era.

I thought of all this yesterday when visiting a friend who has decided to 'go IVF'.

As she whipped open her fridge and brought out her delightful tri-coloured cooler bag I felt my stomach flip. My mouth dropped open as she showed off the matching freezer brick, the smart boxes containing the needle tips and hormones, the cunning little black pencil case for her nifty injecting pen.

'You've got an IVF showbag,' I gasped.

'I know,' she grinned. 'They gave all this cool stuff to me when I started the program last week. It was free! Check out the pen ... aren't you jealous?'

Was I jealous?

Jealous that she's been brave enough to do what I'm afraid I'm going to have to do?

Jealous that she isn't afraid of needles?

Jealous that soon she might be pregnant?

There was a long pause.

'No,' I said, finally. 'It doesn't have a clock.'

2 April

Today the Chinese Fertility Goddess wore knee-high brown suede boots with buckles, a groovy sixties-looking miniskirt and a totally mismatching eighties-looking blouse with appliquéd people all over it. She looked fab. When I told her so she shrieked with joy and dragged me up the stairs and into her office.

'I buy this in Shanghai! Boots first but then my mother says ... what you going to wear with that? Buy more! Buy more! When you have time to look in Sydney? So I buy whole outfit. This morning ... first time I wear it all. I come down ... my daughter, she having breakfast, she look at me and say ... Mum, that makes no sense.'

'Oh no,' I protest. 'It looks great. Kids these days are so conservative.'

I am suddenly reminded of my teenage disapproval of my own mother when she started a Bachelor of Arts degree at Newcastle University, bought a selection of chunky knitted natural-fibre waistcoats and kept getting her hair permed.

'Yes,' she says, 'but when I come to work, no one say anything to me about my clothes. So I think ... my daughter right! It makes no sense. But *you*, you like. I trust you. It makes sense!'

It makes total sense. Unlike my inability to conceive, which makes no sense whatsoever.

But in jollier news, I have a job. Well not a job really, a jobette. Three weeks full-time research for a new TV show.

And here's the thing ... the stories I have to investigate are interesting. And relevant to Australian society and especially where we're at politically.

And the producer told me to write the interviews up as short stories rather than page after page of typed-up transcripts, because they want to investigate the narrative potential. And because it's more interesting for the writer and also the reader!

Could it be so? Passionate storytelling and important stories and television producers who care about character and narrative? And about writers and readers?

Now *that* makes sense.

13 April

The Chinese Fertility Goddess is off on holiday today and Christopher and I are her lucky last patients.

We sit at her desk, enthralled by her description of how much she really needs a holiday. A friend of hers, a prominent doctor, has told her that she works too hard. That she should see fewer patients and charge more.

We smile fixedly.

'I say NO! I can't do that!' CFG pouts and shakes her head. 'My patients need me! This doctor—I don't tell you her name—she say: "I used to be like you, but no more! Fewer patients! More money!" And I think hmmm ... you not very nice doctor.'

The CFG then tells us about how sick she's been. She's been tired and stressed. She screws up her face and does sick dog impressions and describes how she feels like crawling into a corner.

She laughs at herself and we laugh too. Yep, we say. You need a holiday.

Later on she gives us our acupuncture and we lie on our twin beds and think pleasant, calming thoughts. I try to do my visualization but it all seems a bit too much like hard work and I let myself drift. It's been intense for both of us lately. The TV research is pretty full-on; it's all about crime and there's only so many racially motivated bashings, kidnappings and drug wars I can take.

Christopher's work has also been tumultuous. Last Saturday he and a youth support worker were scouring the streets at four in the morning looking for a missing fifteen-year-old girl.

Christopher does a lot of work with an arts company that sometimes creates shows with 'troubled' kids. This particular troubled kid had absconded from the youth hostel where the rest of the cast were staying and was found hanging out in a flat with two twenty-two-year-old guys she had met in the street. She was successfully brought back in the wee hours of the morning, but everyone was a little strung out.

I wake after a while, listening to the sounds of the city and notice how dark the rooms have become.

It's nearly night. As I float in and out of consciousness I realize I can't hear any of the usual fertility clinic noises—the bang of the machines that boil the herbs, the phone downstairs.

It occurs to me that maybe the Chinese Fertility Goddess and her staff have gone home and Christopher and I will be locked in for the next two weeks.

It won't be that bad, I think, we won't starve—I know they sell blocks of tofu here and propolis candies and rice crackers along with the dried twigs and seed pods and chopped up bits of surfboard. And they have a toilet.

And we can probably pull our own needles out.

And I drift like that a bit longer, hearing Christopher gently snoring in the background until finally there is a soft step on the stairs and the CFG turns on the light.

She grins at me and says softly, 'holiday!' I smile back. I notice she has her coat on.

'Oh,' I say. 'You're all packed up to go.'

'Yes,' she says. 'All ready. I wait downstairs and read magazine awhile. Let you sleep longer.' I pause a moment, taking in what she has just told me. I try to imagine Professor Caveman 'reading a magazine' when he's ready to go home, just to let me sleep longer.

'Thankyou,' I say. 'Happy holiday.'

And I feel lucky.

16 April

Christopher and I had our first go at split ejaculation the other day.

(laughs hysterically)

Having another go tonight.

(sighs)

17 April

Christopher and I are having brunch in a beachside café today. This is a very nice moment for the Barren Two and we do lots of smiling goofily at each other, entwining fingers over our plates (a vegetarian no-fat thing for me because I'm good, and eggs and bacon for him because he can) and enjoying the ambience.

And then gradually I realize that a song wafting from a next-door radio is invading that ambience and lo that song is the Bee Gees: 'How Deep is Your Love?' But worse, I realize that *I know all the words*. As the familiar lyrics uncoil from deep within my brain I nearly choke on my soy decaff latte. The *Bee Gees*? How could this be?

To my horror, I realize I have a whole mental playlist of ghastly old songs I could sing in the shower at the drop of a hat: Billy Joel's entire *Stranger* album, Barbra Streisand singing with Kris Kristofferson, Bee Gees ad nauseum, The Beatles, Bread ... I'm talking words, people. Not just bits of chorus and a la de da da. I'm talking *lyrics*! All of them.

This is not me bagging these artists per se, it's just the shock at recognizing how deeply they had penetrated my consciousness at a young impressionable age.

And who is to blame for this evil musical seepage?

My father.

It was those bloody cassettes my sisters and I were forced to listen to on long car trips as kids. Dad's Music was drip-fed into our delicate, developing minds all the long drive from Sydney to Melbourne. Or Newcastle to Sydney. Again and again and again until we knew them off by heart, could sing along with them and, worse, made up little actions.

I think I managed to turn the tide a little by the time I got to high school with (gulp) Meatloaf's *Bat out of Hell* and, variously, a range of New Romantic delights. But by the time I was into the big guns of The Clash, The Specials and The Jam, it was way too late.

I had all but left home. Those long family car trips of the seventies were a distant memory.

I share this with Christopher as he polishes off his crispy bacon and scrummy poached eggs (bastard) because I want to help him be a good non-musical drip-feeding father, if and when the time comes.

'Well actually,' he says, 'I think I had that Bee Gees album myself.'

I stared at him a moment and then ... I let it go through to the keeper.

It was still a very nice morning.

But you can bet your bottom dollar, my dad didn't spend it sitting in a café with a worried look on his face, humming 'You Took the Words Right Out of My Mouth'.

ABOUT A FROG

We lost our frog.

I'm not sure when it happened. Everything seemed fine. We didn't see him every day but we could usually spot him on our verandah at night, all big eyes and straining forearms. At times he climbed the-plant-that-looked-most-like-a-tree and we felt proud because he was doing just what the big tree frogs do.

In the daytime he kept still, often crouching on a leaf with half-shut eyes and a 'don't mess with me' expression.

His colours changed to match his background, so when he sat on the rim of a terracotta pot he turned a muddy green and when he sat on the bromeliad leaf he turned a pale jade green and once, when he sat on the edge of the Larsen 'Chicken of Depression' mug I'd accidentally left by the glass doors, he looked confused.

He was small but feisty.

We called him Neddy but he could just as well have been a Nerida. He was an illegal immigrant as far as frogs go; as a tadpole he'd hatched in my youngest sister's tank a couple of hundred kilometres north and then metamorphosed into a teeny version of himself in my stepmother's bromeliad-filled garden, and finally travelled down the F1 in a jar to our flat in Sydney. In those days he had a friend, Rupert. (Who was possibly a Rose.)

Rupert/Rose left after only a few days. We suspected the bromeliad wasn't big enough for the two of them. We felt Rupert might have gone to 'a better place' aka the verandah of the flat downstairs which had a full complement of potted bamboo and crazy orchids.

But Neddy stayed.

In the morning I would peer, squinting, through the glass doors of the verandah because a day that started with a Neddy-spotting was a Good Day. Just as a night that ended with a final light on (to attract insects) and a Neddy-spotting was a Good Night.

We bought a special red watering can from Ikea because we felt its long spout allowed us to water Neddy's bromeliad and potted palms and the-plant-that-looked-most-like-a-tree with minimum disturbance and also because the fire engine red showed off his neat lush greenness.

He braved horrible ghastly weather, driving rain and Wuthering Heights-*type storms so fierce one might reasonably expect to see Kate Bush swaying one-handedly along the road. Through the glass I would sometimes see him looking cold and wet and hunched on the edge of the potted palm. This, my tadpole-breeding sister Kerry informed me, with just a hint of impatience, was entirely normal. 'He's a frog,' she said. 'He likes getting wet. Stop worrying.'*

Recently, my middle sister Toni went to France to live.

She sold everything she owned to make the trip except for our mother's guitar. This she left with us. She also hadn't eaten since the day before, she was so stressed about travelling. There had been passport shit, and bill-paying shit and saying-goodbye-to everyone shit. And she would be living with a man she had met the year before while surfing at Byron Bay. He was an Aussie who lived and worked in France and had family in Newcastle. He happened to be in Byron for a couple of days break. They had floated around on the ocean together companionably before he recognized her as a girl he once dated in high school.

My sister's hope (and ours too) is that he is the One. And she was going to live with him in France to find out.

She had a few hours before her Air France flight so she was hanging at our flat for a little while. She wanted to see us. But she also wanted to see Neddy, who had made his own long journey from Kerry's tank to our stepmother Dawn's garden to the tiny front verandah of my Sydney flat.

Neddy was not to be found.

We stared hard at every bit of foliage. No Neddy.

I balanced on one foot and leaned carefully out the glass doors to see if he was hiding right down among the bromeliad leaves. No Neddy.

My sister frowned a little. I could see she doubted Neddy's existence.

I tried to excite her by showing off the tiny little Neddy poo that was dotted here and there around the foliage. Not surprisingly this did not satisfy her. She nodded and smiled and made small appreciative sounds when I pointed out the charming little pond I had made out of an old hummus tub but I could tell she was suspicious.

There's no frog, I could almost hear her say. You're making that frog up. I'm going to France, maybe for good, and here you are wasting my time. Some big sister you are.

Then Christopher and I drove her to the airport and gave her some euros for a travel present and she cried and I cried and she said thankyou and I said shut up.

Later, while my sister was winging her way towards Singapore for her first stopover, I wandered out to the verandah again. I hoped Neddy might be there, scaring the shit out of a spider or something.

The palm fronds waved emptily in the sea breeze.

Days went by. No Neddy.

I talked glumly to Christopher about it. Hopeless. 'We think we'll be good parents. We can't even look after a couple of tiny green frogs.'

'Although you know ...' Christopher started.

'... Rupert might be living downstairs,' I continued the thought '... and he might have called Neddy down.'

I thought about this. Rupert, lonely and living in bamboo bliss just a few metres down the wall. Neddy, also lonely and making do with a bromeliad, Ikea watering can and a hummus tub pond. And that maybe it was better that Neddy was going to be with Rupert. Even though it was a long way down, as far as small frogs go.

Maybe for Neddy, Rupert was the One.

I decided that I needed to have a mature response to the situation. Losing the frog did not mean that I would be a bad parent. No Neddy-spotting morning or night was not a signal for a really bad day.

Then I sat at my computer and Googled tree frogs so I could download a tree frog call.

And when we got back from dinner tonight, I stood, sad at heart, holding my laptop out over the verandah and playing the tree frog call over and over.

It sounded like ... gok gok gok krek krek gok.

But what it said was ... Come back Neddy. Come back.

And somewhere in France my little sister started her new life with a man.

3 May

Sunday Bloody Sunday came and went, as did Saturday Bloody Saturday before that, being the first day of another new cycle.

This is usually enough to fling me into a Great Pit of

Depression, but I've been distracted by the prospect of babysitting the three Naughty Nephews all weekend while their parents fly interstate to party on.

It made me think about how long Christopher and I have actually been the Barren Two. Unlike every other event in my life, I didn't write that stuff down. Useful stuff. Dates and things. We call that 'denial'.

How long had we been trying to have a baby?

There were definitely a few years where we were sort of trying without really trying. You know, just 'forgetting' at the crucial moment and giggling like naughty school kids and then snuggling and making up names together for our soon-to-be children.

For the record, we agreed on: Rapacious (girl), Spanky (boy) and Stick (a good either/or name).

Yes. That's *three* children with stupid names.

I guess it was in the last five years, after we moved back from an Australia Council writers' residency in Paris in 2000, that we got down to the serious biz which translated into using the Maybe Baby ovulation predictor (basically a small, lickable microscope), trying to have sex at the right time and doing all that legs up in the air stuff.

I got sick in 2003, for about six months, strange pins and needles numbness that moved up from my toes until I felt I was permanently wearing a pair of thick woollen stockings. We stopped trying during this time, working out instead what the hell was going on with my body. The answer, we discovered, was multiple sclerosis. Which sucked, obviously. But it was a mild case, my specialist told me, early days. Get on with your life.

We got back on the case.

And all this time nothing was happening. And the word 'infertile' did cross my mind but it wasn't something I wanted to dwell on. Why would I be infertile? I wasn't old. I wasn't wrinkly. I didn't have BARREN stamped across my forehead. Impossible.

Around that time we were sharing a house with another couple, Mark and Michelle my friend from uni. They were among our closest friends, and they were 'sort of trying' too. So it was a painful kick to the guts when they came back from their Easter holiday last year and said 'We're pregnant!'

At first we were excited for them and when they said 'Of course we'll have to move,' we said 'No! Why?'

These were the friends we had talked with about buying land and building a house together. And because we were all of the feckless artiste variety (actors and writers) we fantasized about helping look after each other's kids while we variously performed and wrote. Just before I got the residency in Paris we were actually looking at land together. In the country. We wore sensible boots. We discussed permaculture.

So it made sense that we stay in the house together. It was a great house. We were a great household. And *we* were planning to have a baby too ...

And then I got my period.

And it all fell down in a great crashing heap. And I knew that there was something seriously wrong with us and there was no way we could live in the same house as our dear friends and their soon to be born baby. Not if I wasn't going to become a total basketcase. Christopher had also realized the error of our ways, finding me in a bloody, tear-streaked howling mess at the end of the bed one afternoon.

That was the end of the shared household. The start of recognizing that we weren't like all our friends. And the realization that no matter how much we wanted to be like them, how much we wished for it, it might not ever happen.

4 May

Overnight the Great Pit of Depression has mercifully shrunk to a mere Shallow Grave of Discontent.

This is partly because I have work to do, a new draft of a documentary script, and partly because Christopher and I have come down with some sort of low-grade tummy bug thing which we have caught from our weekend babysitting the Naughty Nephews.

The thing is, while babies are generally neat and clean and disinfectable, small boys are, frankly, rather dirty.

Even funny, charming, cute small boys like the Naughty Nephews.

Of course it was Naughty Nephew the 2nd who did the damage, the very same one who slipped off the bridge in the Blue Mountains. Naughty Nephew the 2nd is precocious as all get-out and entirely loveable.

He is also a grot.

The tummy bug thingy had already struck him down on the Saturday. A jolly stint in the park with scooters and tricycles and so forth had suddenly led to a mercy dash home to the toilets.

Too late, sadly.

As the others kept their distance, he kept up a running commentary of the contents of his underpants as we screamed through red lights.

'It's only a bit ... no, there's a bit more ... yes I am hanging on ... but I think it's all in one piece ... do you want me to check?'

'NO!' we shouted. 'Keep your hands in the air where we can see them! Do Not Check!'

Luckily for me it was Christopher's turn to deal with Nephew excretion, since I'd had the joy of Naughty Nephew the 3rd's surprise night nappy.

As I was putting the scooters away, the toilet flushed and out came Naughty Nephew the 2nd, cheerfully explaining exactly what had gone down the pipes.

I bent down to undo his sandals and he obligingly put his hands on my head to balance. I had a sudden horrid thought.

'Wait ...' I said. 'DID YOU WASH YOUR HANDS?'

'Oh,' he said. 'I forgot.'

'THEN YOU'VE JUST PUT POO HANDS ON MY HEAD!'

'Oh yes,' he said. 'Oops.'

Memo to self: Google and see if the story of Typhoid Mary comes in a picture book.

20 May

When I was in Year 12, my favourite teacher said I needed to have a bomb put under me. This seems a harsh statement and possibly a little inappropriate in this post 9/11 climate.

These days I don't think she would make that statement (in fact I know she wouldn't, she chucked in teaching to become a naturopath) but at the time it seemed fair enough. I was one of those slack, eleventh-hour students, the kind you used to see draped over the essay box at uni, still scribbling the final paragraph.

Lock me in an exam room for three hours with a pencil shoved in one fist and a lucky Gonk in the other and I was happy as a bunch of Larries.

Give me six weeks and a bibliography and I'd spend five and three-quarters deeply immersed in university revue rehearsals or student politics. (My best friend Lucy and I once campaigned jointly for the prestige position of Intercampus Liaison Officer under the slogan 'Indamoira Grime—because we're the best ever.' Unsurprisingly, we lost.)

Deadlines are awful things. Horrid little shiny round bodies and long clicking feet. Big red accusatory eyes and tut tut voices. But long after I grew up and put aside childish things like lucky Gonks or sketch comedy scripts, the deadlines remained.

At the moment I seem to have a cluster of the little buggers nestled on the edge of my desk. There's the short film one and the doco script one and the new play one and a really *ugly* one wearing a wristwatch who keeps pointing at my nether regions and whispering 'tick tick tick'. I keep expecting one of them to sneakily reset the clock on my computer so I totally lose track of time and feed them a plate of leftover chicken after midnight.

And anyone who's seen the film *Gremlins* knows what happens then.

Deadlines are very much in my mind at the moment, both biological and on paper.

The doco script deadline, originally looming at the end of this month, has been abruptly changed. Person who changed it told me not to worry, that network doesn't want to see script at end of this month. Naturally, I went into long deadline mode. Sadly, Person was a git. Turns out, network *does* want it at end of this month. Now I must go into *short* deadline mode. Naturally this will include loads of pfaffing about until I move into *perilous* deadline mode.

Also, my friend, whose IVF showbag I briefly coveted, just finished flushing away the failed results. She was extremely calm about it, even though it was basically her one and only chance. Deadline done.

'I'm so sorry,' I told her, aware of how inadequate the words sounded. She nodded.

'Don't leave it too late,' she said.

So yesterday I finally picked up my second referral to a fertility clinic. Looks like I'm going back to Professor Caveman's stomping grounds.

Next month, the ugly deadline with the ticking watch gets a little more ugly.

I'm turning thirty-seven. I may need to bring back the lucky Gonk.

MORE THINGS IN HEAVEN AND EARTH

I said yes because Simone told me people see fairies.

'What do you mean they see fairies?' I asked. 'Surely they just think they see fairies.'

'Of course they just think it,' she said. 'But the thing is, they believe it. They truly believe they can see them. And then they pick them up and they talk to them and their faces just light up with joy. It's so sweet.'

I stared at her. She was serious.

'I want to see the fairies,' I said. 'I want my face to light up with joy.'

'I know you do,' said Simone. 'And I'm going to tell you exactly how to do it.'

Simone and I became friends when we worked as actors for a theatre company in Newcastle.

We performed in several shows together over three years, doing thousands of performances to countless schools around the country. With the rest of the team we became friends in the same way that hostages held captive in dark, airless surrounds or Big Brother *housemates become friends: we forged deep bonds because only the other person could truly understand the horror.*

We spent long distances travelling in our shaky yellow van and shared hotel rooms in half-star motels where famously, once, the beds were full of mouse shit. We received hernias, lugging ridiculously heavy and overcomplicated sets, and suffered near heatstroke as we performed at the height of summer swathed in heavy all-in-one costumes made from layer after layer of Dacron.

We performed to kids who adored us and were inspired by us but we also performed to kids who hated us and showed their feelings by spitting, heckling and throwing bits of broken pencil.

At every show you could be certain of two things.

Firstly, a teacher, who was meant to be watching and supervising, would sit at the back of the audience marking books and barely lifting their head except to murmur ineffectively 'sit on your bottoms please', or if it was a high school 'next person who spits will get a detention'.

Secondly, at the discussion following every performance a student would raise their hand and ask 'Has any of youse been on TV?'

To this day I will think back to my halcyon theatre-in-education days whenever I catch a whiff of that special combination of meat pies, wax crayons and pissed-in pants. I count myself among those lucky few actors who never forgot their lines on stage or contracted headlice.

Post-acting, I began to concentrate on my writing but Simone, crazy, romantic, idealistic Simone, kept trying for acting gigs and she'd landed herself a beauty. After extensive auditioning she got the plum role of Assistant for the Magnificent M (not his actual name), Australia's fifth most popular hypnotist and current darling of the RSL and bowling club set.

As I sat among the half-tanked crowd at Newcastle Workers' Club I realized that it was not too dissimilar to our long gone theatre-in-education gig: the travelling, the substandard accommodation—Simone put her foot down at actually sharing a hotel room with the Magnificent M (she was secretly afraid that he'd hypnotize her into having sex with him)—the performing to a potentially hostile crowd. The main differences were that instead of spitting, this audience threw beer bottles, and Simone had to provide her own costume.

'Now the way it works is that the Magnificent M will call for volunteers. Get up immediately. If you wait, you'll miss out because as people watch the show and get into it, they'll want to be on stage too. If you're there at the beginning and as long as you don't get sent back, you'll be up for the fairies.'

'Sent back? Why would I be sent back?'

Simone sighed. 'Well,' she said, 'it happens every night. He can't hypnotize everyone. Some people, deep down, just don't want to be hypnotized. They just don't believe.'

I wanted it so bad I could taste it. I was the kid who had grown up on Wishing Chairs and Faraway Trees and magic worlds at the backs of wardrobes, down rabbit holes and via bedknobs. I counted the days till I could get my hands on the new Harry Potter. I wanted to see those fairies. I had been waiting all my life. I believed. I had always believed.

When the Magificent M, with a leer and an oily wave of his hypno-hands, asked for volunteers I leapt up and ran down the aisle. My enthusiasm shocked a few people into action; perhaps suspecting I'd get a free-drinks voucher, they also ran onto the stage. The Magnificent M was only slightly taken aback, he'd no doubt expected to have to do a little more persuading, and he smiled and joked about how eager Novacastrians were to lose their inhibitions.

Inhibitions? I suddenly realized I could be in trouble. Ah yes. Hypnotist show. People thinking they were chickens. Kissing strangers. Showing their bums on stage. I waved these irrational fears away. Frankly, during my years on tour, I had done all those things, mostly at the Adelaide Fringe Festival club while pissed on Two Dogs alcoholic lemonade. With Simone, funnily enough. Tonight I was here for the fairies.

The Lovely Simone (as she was known on the Workers' Club stage) sat us down in a row facing the audience. The lights were incredibly hot and bright and we blinked like bunnies in the spotlight. Relaaax, I told myself, belieeeeeve. You waaant to be hypnotized.

The Magnificent M's voice had become soothing and restful and, well, hypnotic and I felt my eyelids flicker. As he passed each of us he grabbed an arm and pulled gently. As he grasped my hand I felt a moment of tension but I had done too many drama trust exercises not to know that I should 'go with it'. My arm rebounded floppily and the Magnificent M moved on with a nod. I had passed the first hurdle. Three or four of my eager compadres had not, however, and glumly returned to their seats for more alcohol and with a promise that there would be a need for more volunteers later.

Now the Magnificent M's voice had changed, his tempo urgent and instructive. We were getting uncomfortable on these nasty hard chairs, we wanted to get off.

Why yes, my relaxed mind affirmed, these chairs are nasty. They are hard. I do want to get off.

'You want to sit on the floor,' he suggested.

Why yes, my mind affirmed. I am comfortable on the floor in front of the telly. Why not on the stage in front of the audience?

'But,' the Magnificent M paused, 'you are also ... itchy. A little itch has begun on your back. Your back is covered in ants!'

Around me, a frenzy of scratching had begun. I paused to assess myself. Was there really an itch?

The Magnificent M hovered menacingly. My eyes focused on the Lovely Simone, who was watching me intently. Her lips moved almost imperceptibly. 'Scratch.'

I scratched like a fiend. My back itched in sympathy. I imagined an army of ants marching up and down my spine and chanting cootchie cootchie coo. In a burst of improvisational brilliance I began to scratch the back of the girl on the floor beside me. Soon we were all scratching each other like a cage of insane chimpanzees.

The Magnificent M waved his arms again in a gesture we had come to know as 'Sleep'.

I tried to sleep. God knows I did. I tried to focus on the fairies and yet not focus on the fairies since I realized that this thing only worked if I could keep my brain in soft focus, as relaxed and floppy as my test arm.

My face must have given me away to the Magnificent M. As he kept talking he reached over and grabbed my arm again, a sort of pop quiz of hypnotize-ability. Once again Drama 1 trust exercises kicked in and he dropped my limp and heavy limb like a clubbed baby seal.

I want to be hypnotized, I told myself slavishly. I want it. I want it. I put my faith in the Magnificent M. Honestly. I believe.

If only he'd blindfolded me and told me to run towards the nearest wall, trusting my colleagues to stop me before I hit, I would have been home and hosed. Those damn fairies would have been mine. My face would have lit up with joy to the power of infinity. Instead he told us that we were (pause) hot, no (meaningful pause) very hot, no, boiling hot and (snicker) we'd probably have to remove our clothes.

(Roar from a 70 per cent pissed audience.)

As the group began with their bad 'I'm getting hot in here' acting and the first of the flannelette shirts began to peel off, I stood up. Simone dropped her stage smile and raised her eyebrow at me, the universal theatrical survivor sign for 'What the fuck?'

I shook my head sadly. It wasn't to be. There were no fairies for me. No magic. And, I realized, I didn't want it, not at the oily hands of the Magnificent M anyway. I didn't wait to be dismissed. I walked offstage and returned to my seat.

By the beginning of the second act, the audience were 80 per cent pissed and the people on stage had variously become chickens, strippers, pizza delivery guys and impetuous stranger-kissing Adelaide-Fringe-Festival-like sluts.

And then ... the fairy bit began. Spooky tingly music started. The well-trained group went to 'sleep'. 'And when you wake,' said the Magnificent M 'you will see fairies on stage.' Cue raucous homophobic jeers from audience. Cue cheeky grin and reproving finger from the Magnificent M. 'The tiny magic variety with wings,' he chuckled.

As the lucky onstage fairy-witnesses began to hop and jump out of the way of the thousands of purportedly dancing fairies I wondered why I hadn't fallen under the spell. It couldn't be that I didn't want to, because I did. It couldn't be that I wasn't relaxed, because I was. The stage really was as familiar to me as my lounge room floor in front of the telly. At any moment I could have taken off my bra through my sleeves, trimmed my toenails or rung my friend Simone to see how her new crappy stage job was holding up. It's true the Workers' Club wasn't my natural habitat. The flanno was not my fabric of choice and beer was not my preferred drink. But it didn't matter. This was a club I wanted to be a part of but I had failed in some way and for some unknown reason.

This week I received two letters of rejection in the same mail from two theatre companies. They were for the same play. The literary assistant who penned one of the letters offered some 'constructive criticism' in the form of suggesting that the material was 'a little too sentimental at times' and that 'the frequent change of scenes might prove rather too difficult to stage'. I'm kind of proud of my rejection letters, they prove to me that I manage to finish my work and send it out, but they perplex me as well. And eventually, they depress me. I do believe in my work, and I do believe in the stories I tell on stage but sometimes it's hard to keep the faith. Too many other people don't believe, and mostly they run the theatre companies I want to stage my plays.

This week also, my girly internal organs are playing some strange sort of 'hide the ovulation' game. Every day I take my temperature and stare at my charts but I can't seem to work out the rules.

On the days that Christopher and I thought we could work out the rules we had great sex. Beautiful, loving, babymaking sex. And Christopher brought out of hiding the holy water. This half-filled plastic bottle was given to him by a Muslim friend he works with. It had been brought back from Mecca and was extremely precious to her. She gave it to Christopher because she knew how long and how hard we had been trying and she wanted to help. 'Just believe,' she said.

It tasted faintly of apricots and rose petals.

Back at the Newcastle Workers' Club, the fairy sequence ended brutishly with the Magnificent M suddenly joining the enchanted throng and stamping the fairies to a pulp. The onstage group was initially taken aback but then they joined in, Lord of the Flies-*style. One girl among them, her face aghast, tried unsuccessfully to pick some fairies up. The bloodied stage became littered with crumpled wings and broken wands. Bright glittering specks of spilled fairy dust floated in the beams of the stage lights.*

And the crowd, now 100 per cent pissed, laughed and laughed and laughed.

2 June

This month I'm booked in for my first ever ultrasound session, in the hope of discovering why my left fallopian tube is such an abject transport failure. It's the same test Professor Caveman tried to send me to, so I just know it will be unpleasant and invasive. And indeed, I discover, it is both these things. Christopher and I take to calling it 'having a date with the Dildo-Cam'.

I'm hoping they'll discover something spectacular like a tonsil or a tiny malformed kidney or perhaps some other wandering organ. I remember when I was a kid getting a splinter in my foot and it mysteriously disappearing, only to impressively re-emerge some weeks later through my knee. So who knows? That peanut I shoved up my nose as a toddler? That biro lid I swallowed while chewing my pen over a last-minute essay? That drunken night when Christopher suggested we 'spice up' things up in the bedroom? Dildo-Cam will reveal all.

Also this month, my short film is finally being made. Hoopla!

This film got funding, through the NSWFTO Young Filmmaker's Fund, but obviously it's not enough. Actors and crew work for love and credits. No one gets paid until it's made and earning squillions. I'll rephrase that: no one gets paid.

The past few weeks have seen a procession of earnest young arty types traipsing around our flat, discussing filters and gaffer vans and vegetarian catering. I think of them as the Fresh Faced Film Brigade and usually I make the tea and then run away quickly. They scare me with their clear shiny eyes and fresh hopeful faces. They exude enthusiasm and optimism and ready-to-be-fulfilled potential, all that stuff Christopher and I used to wallow in just a few short years ago.

They are shooting at the end of this month and currently don't have a full cast (the main character is a six-year-old girl), nor do they have a location—in this case, a caravan. With an ocean nearby. And surfers. And did I mention there are scenes in cars? With traffic? Also, key members of crew are having 'problems'.

'We need a little girl, and soon,' says one of the crew as I hand out the mugs and I bite my lip to stop myself saying 'Actually I don't mind what sex it is as long as it's healthy.'

It's a bit of a load on our minds, what with Christopher having signed up to be producer because, it seems, his days aren't full enough.

So not only do I worry about whether my script will turn out on screen, I worry about Christopher worrying about caravans, oceans, surfers, actors, traffic-safety officers and on-the-edge artists.

Sadly, there are some things the Dildo-Cam *can't* reveal.

9 June

My Sex Life. A Short Play.
Scene One (11 pm)
    ME: I'm going to bed, I'm knackered.
    CHRISTOPHER: Wait ... aren't you on Day 10?
    ME: *(sighs)* Oh God.

Scene Two (11.05 pm)
    Some perfunctory foreplay ensues. Christopher notes the clock.
    CHRISTOPHER: Bloody hell, is that the time?
    ME: Just whack it in will you.
    CHRISTOPHER: I can't just *whack* it in. We need some lubrication.
    ME: *(half asleep)* Spit on it.
    CHRISTOPHER: I'm not spitting on anything. I'm going to seduce you with the sheer persuasive power of my tongue. *(slight pause)* Darling, wake up.
    ME: *(abruptly coming to and wiping drool off the pillow)* Mmmf gnnnn.

Scene Three (11.06 pm)
    ME: *(cheerfully)* Oooh. That's lovely darling.
    CHRISTOPHER: Do you think I'd look good with a beard?
    ME: Shut *up*.

Scene Four (11.09 pm)
    Proceedings abruptly halted.
    ME: Stop ... stop, I have to turn over, it's better from behind.
    CHRISTOPHER: You sexy ...
    ME: Oh shut *up*, it's not for *you*, it's so the sperm gets to the egg quicker. Or better. Or some damn thing.

Scene Five (11.11 pm)
    ME: *(stifling yawn)* Are we there yet?

CHRISTOPHER: *(appropriate noise)*
ME: Great. Pillow.
CHRISTOPHER: Pillow?
ME: Pillow! Under butt. Legs up for twenty minutes ... darling? Wake up.

Scene Six (11.31 pm)
CHRISTOPHER: *(whispers)* Darling I just slipped out.
ME: *(tenderly)* Yes, but never from my heart.
Kiss lovingly then fall immediately into a coma.
I wake at three in the morning with a backache.
ME: *Stupid* pillow.

10 June

We were arguing about whether or not to have sex. Or more precisely whether I had ovulated and hence whether sex now might have the desired effect, i.e. up the duffness.

I was trying to work out when the two lines on my LH test had occurred, taking into account the fact that my temperature had shot up the day before. I found myself saying: 'Don't worry about it, I think it's useless anyway.'

Christopher seemed to have started the washing up at this point but he stopped to say 'It's not useless, I think we *should* do it.'

So back to bed I went and waited.

As I did, I thought about how shitty it was that our once healthy sex life had become such a dreary tool of conception. Do it this day. Do it that day. Do it for three nights in a row and then don't do it for the next three weeks. Do it from behind, do it and then stick your legs up in the air for twenty minutes, do it ... but make sure he pulls out mid-ejaculation. And for God's sake don't shower afterwards.

Sex had become something to tick off on a long line of do's and don'ts. It was part of the routine, just like my thermometer and my LH tests, with the main difference being the thermometer got way more oral action.

At this point the distant clanging of cutlery brought me to my senses. He really was doing the washing up.

I got up and headed for the bathroom, shouting 'DON'T FUCKING BOTHER THEN.'

Christopher came charging into the bathroom and the argument briefly started up again, him with his hands dripping with suds, and me naked except for my spotty shower cap. Thinking back, it was a perfect scenario for a Paris Hilton home video but in our sad reality it ended with him simply leading me back to the bedroom. I only bothered to take off my shower cap when my head hit the pillow and then I started to cry.

It was killing me that our previously sexy lives had been so completely upturned by the fight for our fertility. Bit by bit, the routine, the alternate hope and disappointments, the practical, clinical, mechanical nature of each seemingly futile attempt was wearing us thin. And how long before we start to rip at the seams?

Like many couples, our relationship started with sex. We met while performing in a production of *A Midsummer Night's Dream*. There was no instant spark, no secret admiration for each other. He thought I was aloof and I thought he was a big-city wanker. We had dinner together, accidentally, when the rest of the cast and crew failed to turn up, and discovered that he came from a family of four boys and I came from a family of four girls. It was an interesting moment although not the basis for a long-term relationship.

But on this one night, crazy night, midway through the run of the show, something happened.

I wish I could say it was all in the stars or it was the magic of the show we were performing and maybe it was those things too, but predominantly it was the joint we shared with another cast member in the theatre bar after the show.

Emily, a statuesque blonde, had replaced the alcohol in her life with marijuana, which she combined with fragrant clove cigarettes to create neat little joints that she stored in an antique silver case.

Christopher and I got absolutely rat-faced and within half an hour were rolling on the floor of the bar, laughing hysterically and shoving ice down each other's pants. Thankfully there were few people left and they were all actors. Christopher distinctly remembers hearing one say: 'What do they think they're *doing?*'

We only stopped laughing an hour later when we started kissing. We kissed down the stairs and onto the street and down to the ocean. We walked hand in hand in the moonlight by the ocean baths and I showed him the large circular pool that was rumoured to have a mosaic map of the world beneath its sandy floor. More kissing followed at the water's edge and the moon seemed to drift at our feet.

When the sex finally happened it was fantastic, luckily, because, after such an extended build-up, if he had turned out to be a dud root I probably would have drowned myself in the mosaic map pool.

That was nearly eleven years ago. Today I feel that same glow, that same intense love and desire. We love each other fiercely, passionately, totally, and I hate that all that love is still not anywhere near enough.

I cried this morning because very soon we will put our bodies into the hands of scientists and doctors. We will move into the next phase of trying to conceive, beyond the herbs and the acupuncture and the holy water.

And beyond love.

In the show, Christopher played one of the lovers, Lysander, and I played the mischievous fairy, Puck. This meant I had to hang out with Oberon the fairy king and basically do his bidding.

I tortured lovelorn humans, bullied the fairy queen's minions, stuck donkey heads on 'rude mechanicals' who had wandered into our magic wood, made milk go sour, scared the bejesus out of old ladies and threw things in their drinks. Same old, same old.

I also squeezed the juice of magic flowers into various characters' eyes (including Lysander's) so that when they woke they fell in love with the first thing they saw.

I didn't mind doing this shit, it was cool being on the winning side, and me and Oberon had some laughs when he wasn't sending me up and down, up and *down* the frigging world picking weed and abducting changeling boys.

Oberon gave me explicit instructions for finding his magic flower ... *before milk-white, now purple* etc. etc., *where the bolt of Cupid fell* ...

What*ever*.

What he didn't mention was that growing just nearby was a bunch of other flowers, all much more useful, all squeezable. Mortgage flower, career flower and brightest of all—the baby-making flower.

If I hadn't been such a feckless, in-the-moment type fairy, and if I hadn't been totally Oberon's bitch so that I had to throw a girdle round the earth in *forty frigging minutes* (don't get me started on *that*) I'd have stopped and lingered a little.

Picked some for later. For me.

I mean look at the facts. All it really takes to fall in love with someone is a good joint and a mosaic map of the world.

But that other shit ...

This morning, in that crucial twenty minutes after sex time, butt on the pillow, legs up and not laughing very much at all, I prayed a little, hoped a little ...

And dreamt.

But only a very, very little.

17 June

So last night Naughty Nephew the 2nd rang to say that the planet Neptune was visible next to the moon and it appeared in this position only once every two hundred years.

Christopher and I bounded out onto the verandah to witness this rare miracle of Blessed Nature and lo, there was a bright shining star next to the moon and yea we confidently called it Neptune.

As Christopher continued chatting with Little Mr Precocious I leaned against the wall and gazed up at the heavens, imagining what brave new world might witness the next two hundred years hence appearance of Neptune.

I wondered if Christopher and I, through some other kind of rare miracle, might actually manage to produce a dynasty of progeny, a whole truckload of descendants and maybe one day, one of them might even lean against the wall of *their* dwelling, and look up at the sky and marvel at the future.

Then I stopped because it was cold and the bricks were hurting my shoulder.

As I went inside I heard Christopher asking Naughty Nephew the 2nd if he knew why the planet Neptune was called Neptune. The answer apparently is: because the aliens who live there like to play tunes.

I then phoned everyone I knew to tell them the glad cosmic tidings and to hurry up and go outside, to witness a sight they will nevermore see in their lifetime.

That's *everyone*, even my Grumpy Grandad who has to walk with a stick and sometimes spends the whole day in his chair listening to talkback radio.

This morning, I discovered it was not Neptune. It was Jupiter.

And it was not 'once every two hundred years'. It's just easier to see at the moment.

And finally ... there is *no evidence at all* of tune-playing aliens on Neptune. (A Russian probe did find what appeared to be a rudimentary harpsichord during a recent exploration, but there was nothing to prove anything more than a few basic scales had been played.)

Today's lesson is not to take astronomy lessons from a five-year-old.

20 June

I think infertility can drive you mad.

I expect there have been studies done on this, but I can add my own evidence to indicate a resounding YES, COMPLETELY BARMY.

That regular bloody reminder of age, of failure, of mortality, each month, every month, is doing my head in. Today was the start of yet another cycle.

In one week I turn thirty-seven.

This morning, as I moped on the couch, I started playing that counting game. That's the one where you count up *all* the people you went to school with who are now parents, *all* the people you went to university with who are now parents, *all* the people who attended your wedding who are now parents.

Then I worked back the other way and counted up anyone I knew from those groups who wasn't pregnant and unlikely to become pregnant.

Then I tried to imagine me and the rest of the infertile or childless-by-choice gang getting together for coffee and having a great old time. But I couldn't so instead I thought about those late-thirties, early-forties movie stars who suddenly pop out twins and how much better it must be to be rich and infertile.

Then I took off my pyjama bottoms because I was sure I could feel blood seeping down my leg.

Then I told Christopher I felt like a dried up old prune.

Then he told me it was probably his boys that weren't jumping.

Then I said I wasn't providing anywhere good enough for them to jump.

Then he told me I was beautiful.

Then I cried.

Today, Christopher and I sat down in front of the doctor who will be overseeing our IVF.

We're finally ready to head down that path after six months of Chinese herbs and acupuncture and restrictive diets. We'll be going private so it will be expensive. But the clinic has good results and a good reputation.

The new doctor himself is crinkly, leathery and smiley. He reminds me of Doctor Who, the Tom Baker one minus the stripy scarf.

One day, I hope, I'll reread this and say *there*. That day, a week before my thirty-seventh birthday, when I was about to have my period and felt like I was going mad and told Christopher I was a prune and he said I was beautiful.

That was the day it all began to get better.

24 June

I have just had my first blood test in preparation for IVF. Woo hoo! *(hi-fives self)*

As is my wont when anything vaguely sharp and pointy approaches me, I did my 'heavy controlled breathing', which sounds very probably like a hippopotamus in great distress. Or in heat.

In fact, with my expectations of many and varied sharp pointy things stabbing at my flesh, I hope to perfect an entire range of exotic animal snortings. If I never get work as a writer again I shall have a new career as a voice-over artist for animations, featuring animals either mating or being eaten alive.

Today was extra special because it was the first blood test I had endured alone since I was in Year 7 and all the girls in my grade were being tested for rubella. Rather than being automatically vaccinated (as happened at most schools) at *my* school we were all given a blood test first. It didn't pay to be needle-phobic because every one of us, including the teachers, received at least two injections a year. First cholera, and then cholera/typhoid. Needles were a regular part of life and you learned to lie about when they were due because, along with the rousing school song (*The ocean's at the doorstep, the mountains too are near* ...) and the all-white uniform, getting your 'jabs' arm punched was unique to the RAAF School, Penang, Malaysia.

We lived in Penang for six years all up. Three years in the early seventies, three years a decade later. My youngest sister, Kerry, was born there. My mother first discovered she had breast cancer there. I started both primary school and high school there. And I had twelve cholera or cholera/typhoid needles there, plus assorted tetanus, TB and smallpox.

My sisters and I developed long, complicated routines to stave off the pain of injections.

The most important one was to stop yourself smelling that ghastly alcohol smell, as you made the long walk up the stairs of the RAAF Hostel to the first-floor medical clinic. No matter how many Tiger Sticks or Jolly Lolly icy poles your mother tried to bribe you with, no matter how many salty plums you could stuff into your mouth, if you couldn't stop that insidious smell, that *needle* smell, you were gone.

Luckily for me, Malaysia being a land of *many* smells, I had already trained my olfactory senses to shut down on command.

Once up in the clinic, breathing only through your mouth, with a stern nurse at the ready, you had to relax your 'jabs' arm as much as possible. You could, however, use your other hand to clutch your mother in a vice-like grip.

Then, as the metal sank into your skin, your sisters had to

distract you by pulling monkey faces or pretending to dance on the spot or waving arms frantically like a demented octopus.

Needle over, your place would be taken by the next sister and you were put onto distraction duty.

At university I went round for weeks with suspicious bruises on my legs and an unfilled blood test request before my friend Lucy dragged me into a clinic and held my hand, as much to stop me running and screaming as for comfort.

Fast forward several years to the moment when I, aged thirty, and quite a big girl now, told my then doctor that I wanted to have a baby.

'Well,' she said, 'in that case, I'll send you for a blood test.'

'A needle?' I gasped, feeling my face pale in horror.

She looked at me, askance, and I blushed in embarrassment at being caught out as a Big Wuss. I wanted to have a baby but I was too scared to have a blood test.

Sometime after that I decided to try to turn the needle phobia around. It wasn't easy.

I learned to love the little butterfly needle with its gentle dripping tube and relaxed filling of the plastic vials, with their natty coloured tops. Christopher would come with me and while he didn't dance or do the demented octopus he *did* try to engage me in banal needle-distracting conversation.

But today he's busy working in Canberra. Also, I'm a grown-up.

On that tropical Penang day at the RAAF School, so many years ago, I was one of the first in line for the rubella test, thanks to my surname. When I went into the room, I asked the nurse if I could scream because I knew there was a line of nervous girls waiting just beyond the door and in those days I was a sadistic little smart-arse.

She laughed and said yes. I screamed, there was a satisfactory murmur of discomfort from behind the door and then she shoved her whopping great needle in.

I felt what seemed to be the entire contents of my body being rapidly dredged through the point of the needle and up into the syringe. While I still had my vocal chords I asked, faintly, if I could scream again. Not for the girls outside, for *me*. Because it *huuuuuurt*.

'No,' she said, grimly. 'You only get one.'

29 June

Yesterday I had *tw*o dates with the Dildo-Cam. Could it be love?

At first, the setting seemed right. Cosy room for two, dim lighting, gentle hum of the air conditioner. There was an ensuite for 'freshening up', clean sheets on the bed and a whole box of condoms by the computer to ensure a sterile experience.

First encounter was fine, legs up, brief introduction, lots of lube, deep breath and we were away.

A big monitor was set up in front of the bed so I could see all my squishy bits. It was slightly disconcerting at first because the image from Dildo-Cam's previous romp hadn't been cleared away and there was definitely a baby going on in there. But a quick flick of the switch by DC's handmaiden and there was my own uterus in all its barren glory.

DC's handmaiden was very sweet, pointing out all the features of my womb with a view. A thirty-second Cuntiki tour, as it were. At one point, in an effort to sound appreciative I even said: 'Wow, that's amazing.'

'Yes,' she said. 'And it will be even better when you have your baby in there.'

She was being nice but my instinctive reaction was to scoff, laugh loudly, or weep hysterically. None was appropriate so I did some controlled breathing. Just then, the handmaiden said 'Hmmm'.

Hmmm can have many meanings.

Like: Q. Does this dress suit me? A. Hmmm.

Or: Q. Does this chicken taste all right to you? A. Hmmm.

Or: Q. Palestine, Israel ... any bright ideas? A. Hmmm.

In this case, the Hmmm was in response to an object that was showing up in my uterus.

Something spooky, something mysterious, something potentially evil that may well have come from the spirit world.

A possible Polyp.

Polyps, of course, are NOT ON for IVF. In fact, in the IVF playground, Polyps are frowned upon and ostracized and made to sit pathetically by themselves, with their stinky sandwiches and their Coke-bottle glasses held together by sticky tape. No one asks them to come home for play dates or to stay over and watch scary eighties videos.

'The thing with polyps,' said Dildo-Cam's handmaiden suddenly, shattering my schoolyard metaphor with accompanying Cat Stevens soundtrack, 'is that they can prevent implantation. You don't want to go through all the hassle of IVF and then have problems like this.'

Well, no.

'You'll have to come back this afternoon and let Dildo-Cam have his wicked way with you again, but *this* time with bonus saline catheter so we can have a really good look. We call this a *sonohystogram*. It will be like having the hysterosalpingogram, but better. There'll be no semi-pleasurable genital scrubbing, but, due to the unpleasant heavy period sensation, you *will* get to employ your patented woo-hoo controlled breathing method.' (slight paraphrasing) 'What do you think of that?'

I stared at her. I wanted to say I thought it was unfair and not right and that it SUCKED BIG TIME.

'Hmmm,' I said.

'Are you worried about the price?' She wrenched the Dildo-Cam free from my evil Polyp-possessed cavity. 'Because it's all included. And it's better to know now so that you can have your entire womb stripped, scraped clean and sugar-soaped.' (more paraphrasing)

'What you want, is a *pristine uterus*.' (exact quote)

There are many things I want, I thought as I wandered off into the rain. I want world peace. I want another couple of inches in height. I want a hit play. I want a healthy Australian film and television industry. I want to own the place we live in. I want my mother back. I want to be well. I want a baby.

It had never occurred to me to add 'pristine uterus' to the list but there you go.

Three hours later I was back in the arms of Dildo-Cam, but with a doctor present. When she arrived there was a flurry of glove sorting (too small) and catheter selecting (not the one she wanted). Something about … can she have the one with streamers and a glittery hat and a little clicking beetle … no, my mistake, she actually wanted the balloon catheter which would hold its position in the uterus nicely.

Enter the balloon catheter (sadly with no party bonus bits) and pretty rapidly after that enter the saline solution AND my pal Dildo-Cam, who seems totally unmoved at seeing me again so soon.

Soon it's a full house down under. I'm *all about* the controlled breathing and wooing and hooing like crazy because that 'unpleasant' heavy period sensation is just plain nasty.

The saline solution is not pleasant for the uterus either, which expands, in horror presumably, at its cold salty touch. Cleverly though, this allows for good Dildo-Cam viewing and any Polyps will be revealed in their full, unloved clompy school shoes and daggy-socked glory.

Today, I was blessed.

No school shoes.

No stinky sandwiches.

No Polyp.

Though earlier viewings had suggested otherwise, close-up saline-assisted viewing revealed that the Polyp was no more than an 'irregularity of the lining' and that indeed, my uterus was pristine.

Out came the catheter.

Out came the Dildo-Cam with a wink and a promise we'd meet again.

Out drizzled some of the saline solution. (The rest would run down my leg later that night during a viewing of quite possibly the worst play I've seen in a good long while. Every organ's a critic.)

In the aftermath of the sonohystogram, the air seemed electric. The walls of the examining room shrank back to normal. The wailing sounds subsided as did the hellish controlled breathing/animal snorting. A gooey blob remained on the bed which looked like ectoplasmic residue of a paranormal disturbance, but was later revealed to be Dildo-Cam lube.

'There,' said the doctor in her strange and squeaky voice, 'my work here is done. There is officially No Polterpolyp. Feel free to scurry along to the next stop in the Great Big Fertility Ride. This house is clean.'

(slight paraphrasing *and* plagiarizing)

SMILE

Like two runaway buses ploughing through the city streets, mowing down sk8er kids and buskers and people who shout on their mobile phones, so too do my scripts hurtle ever uncontrollably forward, leaving so many mangled corpses and metaphors in their wake.

Today those corpses include nineteen little girls between the ages of six and eight who auditioned for my short film.

Although my standard practice is to hide from the Fresh Faced Film Brigade as much as possible, on Monday I skulked down to the casting session near Sydney Harbour because Bronwyn, the director, told me they needed help with the Mother Wrangling.

Apparently it is not just about casting the daughter, you need to cast the mother as well, because no matter how good the kid, no one wants a Mommie Dearest lurking behind the camera, snapping their fingers and saying 'Look at me sweetie! Sweetie! Smile! SMILE!'

I was given a list so I could greet the children by name and, more importantly, make special notes on the mothers. It was an easy job, but as the day wore on I began to focus on the children, figuring I could give helpful comments to Bronwyn, who would obviously be delighted at my input.

As each Mother/Daughter Duo approached, I smiled nicely, shook hands and introduced myself as the Writer. This seemingly benign action was actually the first in a series of complex testing devices.

A firm handshake with direct eye contact indicated confidence and professionalism, but too hard a handshake could chalk up a mark in the overbearing category. Coy sideways glancing scored poorly, as did sudden shrieks of laughter at the way my hair was being whipped about by the brisk Sydney Harbour breeze. Staring hard at the huge, ugly pimple that had cropped up on the side of my mouth was an immediate disqualification.

For a promising few who passed the first test I would launch into the second: retelling the story of the film. Any child who glazed over at this point or looked away yawning, was firmly crossed off.

I asked about previous experiences—other short films, commercials, special tiny tots drama school concerts and whether these had been 'fun'. Answers to these crucial questions showed me if the child was irritable or sarcastic or, worst of all, cynical, and earned a big fat NO because these qualities are alien and abhorrent to me and have no place in any of my fictions.

There were little girls who scored high on confidence but low on experience or high on enthusiasm and low on concentration, and many who I crossed off because they didn't show proper gushing excitement at meeting the Writer.

In the end, only one little girl managed to get my full tick of approval.

She was the one who told me I wrote a really good story.

She was also the little girl I decided I would most like to adopt if her parents met with a terrible accident.

To their credit there was only one obvious JonBenet-type Mother/Daughter Duo among the group. They had the same piled-high hairdo with matching earrings. The mother wore a shiny jumpsuit. The six-year-old had bright red shoes I would kill for, and a grin which the mother must have charged up in the car on the way over because man ... the kid never stopped SMILING. Now and then she would also bounce excitedly on her tippy toes and let out tiny squeals of unspecified glee.

This little girl didn't do too badly in my own 'special' casting session, but in front of Bronwyn's camera, it would be a different story. The little girl character in the script has a solemn outlook on this vale of tears we call life. She barely shows her teeth let alone the acre of gleaming pink gum that Smiley was flashing around.

I felt sorry because she was basically a cheerful kid having lots of fun. As they walked, hand in hand, up the ramp (or at least as Mum walked and Smiley bounced) and into the audition, I wondered if they would still be such great pals in ten years time. I thought about my friend who, as a teenager, made her mother walk several paces behind her whenever they went to the shopping centre, in case she saw anyone she knew. And of me railing at my own mother, the shouting and the whining, the 'you don't care', 'you don't understand', and most vehemently of all: 'I wish I was adopted'.

It was starting to get dark when the sound of clippy cloppy red shoes came bouncing back down the ramp. She was still smiling and still emitting squeals of glee. Her mother was happy with the experience and thought Smiley had done brilliantly—'she's always so happy, and everyone loves that, don't they?'

It was late and I was feeling irritable. Yup, I thought sarcastically with just a touch of cynicism. Everyone just looooves that.

There were a couple of other Mother/Daughter Duos still waiting their turn.

As Smiley and her mother bounced happily back down the path towards their car, I heard one of the waiting mothers say rather snarkily to the others: 'Does anyone else recognize her?'

One mother said: 'She's very confident isn't she? Is she on TV?'

'Oh, I'm sure you see each other at these things all the time,' I said jovially.

The first mother shook her head and muttered darkly: 'She's the reason we had to leave the drama school.'

I opened my mouth to ask her more, hoping for tales of pre-teen backstage bitchery, slap fights over spotlights and children made up to look like baby prostitutes, but I realized she was now staring at my pimple.

Instead, I smiled tightly and turned to make a note on my list, pulling at my wind-blasted hair in a vain attempt to keep order.

4 July

Although I grew up in a number of different places, it's Newcastle I consider to be home.

Newcastle was an industrial city, a university city, a working-class city with an artistic streak, a theatrical bent and a dirty sense of humour.

It was famous for its steelworks, its pub riots and the dickheads in cars who rode up and down what was arguably the longest main street in the country. It had two professional theatre companies and a host of fringe and cabaret groups.

It was, as they say, more arse than class. Today the steelworks are closed and the pubs serve boutique beers. The dickheads survived but the professional theatre companies didn't and the fringe and cabaret groups are thin on the ground.

These last few days I've been back in Newcastle, visiting my grandad in hospital. One night two weeks ago, he was felled, like some ancient worm-eaten oak tree. The combination of a dodgy bladder, numb feet and a large glass of whiskey for medicinal purposes saw him first struggle to get out of bed, then stumble, then fall, arms outstretched in a crashing heap. One flailing arm smashed through his bedroom window.

My grandad is a big man, a slightly deaf, booming foghorn of opinions and anecdotes, timetables and bowel motions, shopping lists and war stories.

He was in the British army and drove a tank in the D-day landings. At various stages of his autumn years he had been active in the Returned Services League but changed clubs a number of times, usually after he 'did his lolly' with other members.

At the last RSL Christmas dinner he attended, they mixed up his dessert order and he shouted at the waiter, who insisted he was right, to 'TAKE THE STRAWBERRY GATEAUX AND SHOVE IT UP YOUR ARSE'.

It was strange to see him now, shrunken, stooped in a chair by his narrow hospital bed. Without his glasses his eyes seemed small and watery. Without his teeth his cheeks drooped towards his chin. It was as if his whole face was flying at half-mast, in mourning for what had passed.

During my visits I told him about the short film that is being made this week and a little about how Christopher and I are going, 'healthwise', a euphemism for the IVF process.

In return, he read out all his blood sugar levels for the past week, listed on the back of his hospital meal menus. He noted how they dipped up and down 'LIKE A WHORE'S DRAWERS' and described how the doctor had recently installed a catheter which let him 'TURN ME OLD FELLA ON AND OFF LIKE A BLOODY TAP'.

I told him that Kerry, who works as a nurse at another hospital, was having trouble with her new work shoes. He told me he'd had similar problems during the war with his new army boots.

'TELL HER ALL YOU HAVE TO DO IS TAKE 'EM OFF EACH NIGHT AND PISS IN 'EM AND AFTER A WEEK YOU'LL GET A LOVELY SUPPLE LEATHER.'

Over the last few days his blood sugar levels have stabilized, he can walk with his cane again, and, thanks to strict hospital rationing, he has lost some weight.

The worry for all of us is what will happen next. Where will he live?

He can't feed himself, he can't keep his house clean and he could easily fall again.

He doesn't want to leave his house, he's made that clear.

'I WANT TO KEEP SOME INDEPENDENCE,' he said and though he boomed as loudly as ever, the bluster was gone.

Ten years ago I went to see a psychic who told me that an older man in my life was sick. 'That's my grandfather,' I said, 'he's just been diagnosed with diabetes.'

'Don't worry about him,' she said, 'he'll be a long liver. But he'll wish he wasn't.'

Later I was able to tell my grandad that the psychic had predicted he would live a long time. He seemed pleased with this. I didn't tell him the second part.

Heading back to Sydney, I thought about the way things had changed.

With the steelworks gone, the theatres closed down and the university losing funding and staff hand over fist, Newcastle has become more businesslike, full of homogenized blocks of harbourside apartments and polished-floor cafés. It has lost much of its old bluff and bluster.

And arse.

Just then my mobile phone rings. It is Grandad.

'WHERE THE BLOODY HELL ARE YOU? YOUR VOICE SOUNDS STRANGE.' He is so loud I can hear him without holding the phone to my ear.

'I'm on the train Grandad,' I say.

He tells me his news. He will be sent home soon—but with some modifications in place: meals-on-wheels, a community nurse and a weekly cleaner.

I am relieved. It isn't a permanent solution but it is a reprieve and for a while at least, Grandad can stay living at home.

'Isn't that wonderful Grandad?' I ask him. 'It's just what you wanted.'

He agrees.

'I KNOW ALL ABOUT MEALS-ON-WHEELS. I USED TO BE A VOLUNTEER.'

It warms me to think of my gruff, grumpy Grandad helping other less fortunate souls.

'I think that's great,' I say.

'YEAH. UNTIL SOME CRANKY OLD BASTARD COMPLAINED ABOUT HIS FOOD GETTING COLD AND I TOLD HIM TO SHOVE IT UP HIS ARSE.'

6 July

This morning, over health-giving porridge and caffeine-free, super-antioxidant rooibos tea, Christopher and I read through the wad of IVF information and consent forms that Doctor Who has slung our way.

I point out the bit about shooting up hormones derived from animals and he waxes lyrical about lost generations.

We both talk about 'embracing science' even though we're actually more of the au naturel semi-hippie type. Like ... Christopher built a house, literally, out of wood, and sometimes I can go weeks without shaving my legs. Also, we eat tofu. Or at least we did until I read somewhere that soy was BAD for conception, so now we eat lettuce.

Tomorrow morning, bright and early, we are off to the IVF clinic so Christopher can give yet another sample of the Boys

With Bodgy Heads Who Can't Be Hurried and to meet with the Fertility Sisters.

Yes, that is their actual name. The Fertility Sisters.

This pleases me because they sound like a support act for a Bob Dylan tour. I don't like Bob Dylan as such but tomorrow I hope to see beads, headbands and a shed-load of flower power.

9 July

Our inaugural visit to the Fertility Sisters bodes very well indeed, beginning as it does, bright and early, with Christopher and I just missing the 7.14 am bus and running desperately up the hill with the remnants of last night's sake (be happy!) whizzing through our bloodstreams.

Bus drivers are fickle things, they can be kind or they can be complete bastards and there's really no knowing which way they'll lean on the day.

I once had a bus driver slam the doors in my face after watching me run hopefully towards him. I have also had another bus driver shut the doors on me because the old lady in front was taking too long to get her ticket in the machine and I was politely waiting on the steps behind her.

Anyway, on this day, in this moment, the bus driver is lovely, stopping at the traffic lights to let us get on the bus. Not only that, he waits till we have hauled our panting, heaving bodies to a seat before he starts driving again.

On arrival at the IVF clinic, or, as I shall now refer to it, the House of Groovy Love, I note the surprising absence of headbands. No acoustic guitars, not even a whiff of patchouli. But there's a whole ashram's worth of very nice, very efficient nurses, one of whom has some quite hippie-ish dangly earrings, and a pleasant waiting room and a bunch of magazines that has nothing to do with babies.

First up is Christopher's trial sample. This is to give the House of Groovy Love Scientists some tadpoles to practise washing and blowdrying before the actual event.

Christopher wants me to come with him and regretfully I put down my Very Expensive Magazine and follow him into his little room. (I mean it's a wank for God's sake, do you really need me to show you what to do?) Christopher says something about making sure we try to make it all as loving and 'natural' as possible.

Snort. *Hippie*.

The room is pretty much as I expect it to be, which is several galaxies and a whole lot of hyperspace away from Yoda's make-do facilities. This room has a comfy chair with leg rest, tissues, sink and a pleasant pastel décor, just right for getting in the mood. There is a Saucy Video on a loop and a stack of 'gentlemen's magazines'. There is also a slightly amusing but quite sensible 'What To Do if You Spill Your Sample' step-by-step guide.

What I do not expect is a friendly little printed notice encouraging clients to relax and help themselves to a refreshing cold drink from the fridge or perhaps even *a glass of whiskey*. Sure enough, there is a bottle of Johnnie Walker under the cabinet and a stack of cups. A shoe shine and a head massage could no doubt be provided if one simply rang a little brass bell.

Christopher looks at my face. 'Don't be jealous,' he says. He knows me so well. Then we have a little squiz at the film.

Sadly, we've missed the beginning of the story but I think it's something to do with an infertile couple; some male factor, possible endometriosis, age-related problems ... (although Mrs Infertile looks about twenty-two).

I'm not entirely sure because we left the sound down but I *think* we were up to the bit in the story where they were providing their sperm sample—oddly enough, down at the beach. Despite a promising start, Mr Infertile sadly missed his collection cup. Luckily Mrs Infertile cunningly managed to catch it all on her breasts, which is not, I hasten to add, encouraged in the step-by-step guide.

There was some artful humping among the waves and it all ended with a gentle cuddle on the shore because that's the kind of movie it was.

And because Christopher and I are the kind of people we are, we watched the credits because we appreciate that it takes a whole team to make a movie. That's how I know that *this* movie appeared to have been made by a bunch of Maltese terriers or at least people who like to be known as Mopsy, Popsy and Muffy.

Then Christopher turns the video off and says that he doesn't need porn, just his wife.

So we do a bit of that natural hippie loving and he doesn't spill a drop.

Later we meet our own Fertility Sister, she of the dangly earrings. I will refer to her as Moonbeam. She is kind and understanding and shows me lots of charts and cartoon uteri and practice needles as well as the protocol for my array of tablets and injectables.

We go over everything and talk about administering two needles a day, into my belly, and Christopher blanches slightly beside me and takes my hand. I can tell that he thinks I'm an absolute legend to go through all this and, frankly, I'm happy for him to keep thinking that way, BECAUSE HE'S BLOODY RIGHT.

Before we leave, Moonbeam gives us each a blood test. I am allowed to have the lovely gentle butterfly needle but Christopher requests, and is given, a Big Needle. Not only that, he decides to watch it go into his vein. He tells me it is the least he can do.

I start to laugh at this but then I shut up because, really, there's not a lot else he can do. So I seize the moment and say that for the duration of treatment I want us *both* to completely abstain from alcohol so we can be in top condition. He agrees immediately.

It's up to us when we start the treatment and it looks like it will be at the end of August.

Christopher and I are quite cuddly as we leave the House of Groovy Love. It could be that hippie magic or it could be that we are about to embark on something that feels very very big.

I think this IVF caper might be a bloody steep hill to climb. But I'm glad that, as I go running to the top, chasing the baby bus with my hormones whizzing through my bloodstream, my lovely boy will be puffing and panting right beside me.

15 July

So Christopher and I are walking briskly along the path near our local beach and I spot a mother and son walking up the path towards us. The son is about four and he's talking nonstop and his mother is nodding and half smiling.

Anyway, they're walking up the path and we're walking down and I do my usual thing which is to stare and then look away as they get closer so no one suspects I'm some mad, child-napping, staring-too-long infertile, and then I realize the mother is doing that 'I'm uncomfortable please hush darling' thing (which isn't working) and *then,* as we pass, I hear what the kid is chanting and I *swear* this is it:

> *We're going on a Daddy hunt! We're going on a Daddy hunt!*
> *We're gonna get a big one! We're gonna get a big one!*

Now see, if that was *me* walking up the path with Christopher and I was chanting: 'WE'RE GOING ON A BABY HUNT!' I'd be given compulsory 'quality time' in the quiet room.

Is all's I'm sayin'.

22 July

There was a strange end-of-school feeling about going to see the Chinese Fertility Goddess today.

As Christopher and I settled in the waiting room, we chatted comfortably with Mr Chinese Fertility Goddess who lives behind the counter, and rummaged through the newspapers as if they were our own. And I remembered back to our first visits, how hopeful we were and how sad and desperate we felt. And now, six months later, we're a little sadder in some ways but not nearly as desperate, or hopeless, or helpless.

We tell the Chinese Fertility Goddess about our last visit to Doctor Who and I also give her a quick rundown on the Fertility Sisters.

We have one more wafer-thin opportunity to fall pregnant au naturel—the drugs start on Day 19 of my next cycle. So once more the CFG orders up great bags of nasty Horrid Tea. I will have the convenient vacuum-packed pre-made brews (all twenty of them, since we'll soon be going away on holidays). Christopher will have the inconvenient paper bags of sticks and koala paws to boil up in the ceramic pot.

The CFG checks out our tongues and draws little pictures on our charts—Christopher gets the 'beautiful clear' notation and I get the 'have you been eating sugar?' question.

(Answer: Yes. Nougat. Drool.)

We have decided to continue seeing the CFG and drinking our Horrid Teas throughout IVF. The CFG has many patients who do the Chinese Medicine–IVF combination. Henceforth we shall be among them. ChiVF I think I shall call it. It is not the sort of thing that IVF clinics tend to recommend and indeed the House of Groovy Love rather sternly suggests against it, but I don't care. I'm not ready to let go of the CFG yet.

Finally, it's acupuncture time. It's all very peaceful and I nod off to sleep and when it's over I fold up the woolly blanket and the towels and put them neatly on my bed.

And as I leave, feeling nostalgic and a little teary, I fight an enormous urge to turn to the Chinese Fertility Goddess with a thick texta and ask: will you sign my shirt?

30 July

So late last night Christopher says: I'll get the Horrid Teas darling, you stay tippy tapping on the computer.

And I say: thankyou darling.

Then we have some amusing banter about how I'm having an 'A' tea tonight and he's having a 'Y' tea. Usually, of course, it's an hour of cooking up all manner of dried and skeletal beings in the ceramic pot for Christopher and horrid clouds of stink wafting through the flat. But every now and then he is allowed to have his own prepacked, easily heated Horrid Tea. I have A, B, O or H, depending on where I am in the cycle, and he has Y.

Five minutes later Christopher appears with our lovely, specially bought for the purpose porcelain cups. I take a big swig of mine and nearly spit it over the keyboard.

'This is not my tea,' I say.

Christopher gives me a *what the?* look and sips daintily at his cup.

'Yes it is,' he says.

'No. *This* tea is bloody awful. *My* tea is bloody *disgusting*. You've mixed them up.'

We swap cups and sample the other's steaming brew.

'Mmm,' I say. 'That acidic-armpit-deodorized-with-a-mouldy-lemon taste? That's mine. I know it anywhere.'

'No,' says Christopher, 'it's not armpit. It's nowhere near armpit. It's more sort of decayed-rat-sweetened-with-rose-petals. And that's *mine*.'

So then we start doing that sip one, sip the other thing and sniff one, sniff the other thing until we're both completely confused and wouldn't know our armpit from our composting rodent, and we head into the kitchen.

Now we have to dig the empty plastic packs out of the bin, and we sniff those and run our tongues into the cracks and then we milk the final dregs into teaspoons and line them up and compare the colour with a teaspoon of tea out of the cups and we sniff those and taste those and finally thirty minutes later we decide that yes, without a doubt, Christopher *mixed the teas*.

So we swap them and drink them and head off, finally, to bed.

'The thing is,' says Christopher, 'either we got them right, or I'm about to ovulate and you'll be waking at three in the morning with an enormous erection.'

RIDING THE CAVY TRAIN

I have not always felt my world was a dry and arid desert.

There have not always been tumbleweeds aplenty rolling across the sterile tundra of my barren existence.

In truth, my life has not always been perpetually winter.

There was a time, long ago, when reproduction was rife, when every step would find a fecund stewing mess behind closed doors, each corner filled with the potential for new life in all its abundant, fruity, full-bellied glory.

I call these: The Guinea Pig Years.

It began when my sister Amanda brought home one guinea pig. One small, sweet, long-haired female guinea pig who shuffled her way from carrot scrap to lettuce leaf. Our mother was a little taken aback at first, but she was soon won over by the gentle snuffling 'eep' noises and a pair of shiny, limpid brown eyes.

The animal seemed slightly neurotic, constantly trembling and twitching when we picked her up or gave her food. I suggested we call her Harriet and our father made a little wooden cage for her with a clever indoor/outdoor arrangement. But soon we felt that Harriet was lonely. She would call forlornly, pressing her nose through the chicken wire and twitching her whiskers.

'She needs a friend,' our mother decided, and so the next day my second sister, Toni, brought home another guinea pig.

Because I was the oldest sister and studying Shakespeare at high school, and also because I was bossy and demanding, I convinced Amanda and Toni that the new guinea pig should be called Ophelia. The two rodents eyeballed each other briefly before they began their customary twitching and trembling.

'Isn't that sweet,' said our mother. 'Let's close the door and leave them to get to know each other.'

After a few weeks, Harriet had become considerably fatter. 'It must be the food,' we all said. 'It can't be anything else. After all, Ophelia is a girl.' I still remember picking up Harriet and marvelling at her enormously enlarged figure. 'It's so strange,' we all mused.

Then I realized I could feel things moving in Harriet's belly. Four of them.

Ophelia and Harriet begat Cuthbert, Hamlet, Rosencrantz and Guildenstern. Hamlet and Cuthbert (we still hadn't learned to sex them properly) then begat Cordelia and Portia.

And so it began.

There was a Polonius in there, an Edmund and an Edgar, a Miranda, Desdemona and a Viola and then, when I started university, my youngest sister, Kerry, who was six at the time, took over the guinea pig naming and a succession of Fluffys, Charlies and Bobbies followed. There were babies nearly every month. For some reason, we never gave the guinea pigs away or took them to the petshop. Our father simply extended the cage and then built another.

We were delighted at first, of course, but as the months rolled on and the babies continued to slide out, we became alert and then alarmed. Sometimes my sisters and I tried to conduct hurried conferences about the situation, but it seemed as if every time we mentioned the words 'guinea pig' or 'must stop this madness', another guinea pig was born.

A couple of these babies died and this was sad, and once, a mother guinea pig (it could have been a Fluffy) chewed the feet off her baby and our mother had to drown it in a bucket as we all wailed hysterically around her.

When a guinea pig died it was given to Kerry to deal with. Even at that tender age she had all the sensible and practical qualities of the nurse she would one day become. Along the side of our house she had created an extensive pet cemetery. Each guinea pig was given a grave and a stone with their name written in liquid paper along the top. The first ten dead guinea pigs even received a short funeral service.

Soon, we stopped naming them, unless one was particularly winning or handsome or neurotic or perhaps even reminded us of an early ancestor, so that a whole new round of Cuthberts and Harriets and Hamlets and Ophelias appeared, to skip and tremble and twitch, nibbling at the grass that grew around the graves of their namesakes.

The guinea pig colony grew, unfettered. There were too many for the cage, even for two cages, and so they were left to breed and flourish at the bottom of our backyard. At times we would see them from the kitchen window, a great rippling herd of them running from the grevillea bush to the upturned wheelbarrow to the neat pile of concrete breeze blocks our father had stacked in preparation for a retaining wall he planned to build.

There was a certain majesty in the herd all racing together, a grandeur. Much as I imagine early North America must have looked with all those buffalo.

Early in the morning the guinea pigs would gather expectantly, trembling and twitching together, a seething hairy mass of nibbling incisors and sharp scrabbling little feet. If our mother came to the back door they would pause and look in her direction and then, as one, begin to eep and eep until she threw them the day's scraps.

Our sister Toni, she who had brought home the second guinea pig which we all agreed was The One That Caused all the Trouble in the First Place, would be sent to vacant lots, small parks and untended gardens within a five-mile radius with a flour bag and a pair of garden shears to gather enough fresh grass for the herd. This worked well until one day she discovered a red-bellied black snake, curled up in the drawer with the garden shears. Toni wasn't bitten, but she did touch the snake and that was enough. From then on, it was lettuce and whatever backyard grass managed to grow.

There were casualties of course.

Baby guinea pigs would disappear into the mouths of cats and the claws of eagles who took to perching on our back fence. Our cocker spaniel, Christy, was useless at protecting them. She was loveable and affectionate, but also slightly retarded. Early in the Guinea Pig Years, when we still named them and actually cared enough to send out search parties for missing animals, we found a succession of baby guinea pigs in Christy's kennel. She would gently carry them there in her mouth, settle them beside her body like puppies and then basically lick them to death, no doubt trying to purge them of their loathsome guinea pig scent of cut grass and rotting lettuce. They died in a shock of saliva and maternal affection. God knows how many she may have accidentally swallowed.

When it was finally begun, the breeze block retainer wall took its own dreadful toll. Our backyard was originally a steeply sloping hill. Through the magic of the retainer wall, our father managed to create a two-tiered yard effect. The top part, just beyond the back door, was kept neatly trimmed, for human use. The bottom part was freely given up to the guinea pigs. The retainer wall itself was at least eight blocks high. The blocks were hollow, creating long deep chasms, and our father had not yet filled them with concrete or covered the exposed holes.

One terrible day Kerry discovered that at least two of the guinea pigs had ventured up into the human terrain, run over the edge of the retainer wall and fallen through the holes right to the bottom, where she could still hear them faintly eeping.

Kerry tearfully begged, to no avail, for our father to tear that retainer wall down and release the guinea pigs within. She tried to fish them out with long sticks, with mop handles, with pieces of carrot tied to fishing lines. Nothing worked, and that night it started raining. It was the beginning of several days of hard rain, and when the skies finally cleared and the herd came out to graze, muddy and bedraggled, there was no more eeping from within the retainer wall.

In the end, natural selection (give or take a few eagles, cats, murderously maternal cocker spaniel forays and retainer wall tragedies) took its course.

By the time I had left home for the wider world of university, the guinea pig herd had dwindled to a few grizzled inhabitants that were rarely spotted in the open. A couple of years later, Kerry was the last sister at home, Grandad had moved into my old room, Mum was dying of cancer and Dad still hadn't finished the retainer wall. The liquid paper had all but worn off the rocks which still studded the side of the house. One was faintly inscribed, 'Christy'.

Possibly unrelated to these events (or possibly not), my mother chose to be cremated.

When our father remarried, the house was put on the market and sold. Kerry, never one to be sentimental, held an enormous garage sale and managed to make a tidy profit from our family memories. Even the garden shears were sold. We spent a last day gathered at the house, talking over old times. We remembered the guinea pigs and we laughed when we talked about the surprise in store for the new owners if they tried to dig all those rocks out of the yard at the side of the house.

Kerry insisted there was still a single mutant guinea pig survivor, skulking in the compost. We went to look for him but saw nothing.

If it was true, I thought as I drove away from my family home for the very last time, in him was all that was left of his entire herd history. I wondered what he would think of his Adam and Eve forebears, with their fancy cage and their Shakespearean names. What would he have made of the incredible luxury of all that fresh, sweet, hand-cut grass?

Did he appreciate the great fertile river that had carried his genes through the years?

Perhaps it would have pleased him to know that for a short glorious era, that river had widened into a lake, swimming with a multitude of twitching noses and tiny sharp claws, echoing with a chorus of a thousand eeps. But in time, like all things, the lake had begun to recede, the waters evaporating, the shores encroaching. It had declined into a stream, and then a puddle, and then a trickle, before finally ending behind the old compost heap, the last wet drops in a pair of shiny, limpid brown eyes.

3 August

Christopher and I had been invited to attend the Kindergarten Performing Arts Night at the Naughty Nephews' public school. Naughty Nephew the 2nd, he who is deeply in love with all things Potter, was performing, nay starring, as that loveable rogue, Papa Bear, in the fifth item of the evening, 'Goldilocks and the Porridge Professors'.

Last time we attended a concert in the same venue (featuring Naughty Nephew the 1st) there was an absolute shit fight getting a seat. It reminded me of when Christopher and I picked the wrong spot to watch the Sydney Gay and Lesbian Mardi Gras one year and were nearly crushed against the barricades in a surging wave of sequined crowd frenzy.

Packed into the assembly hall, there were no marching boys in silver G-strings or dykes on bikes but there *was* the same hysterical crowd mentality, camera-as-weapon strategy and bloody-minded determination to get the best possible seat. Christopher, the in-laws, the non-performing Naughty Nephews and I, were scattered to the four winds, eventually finding small rocks and half bricks on which to perch.

This time, my sister-in-law Neâ rang to let us know a queue had already formed ONE HOUR before the doors were meant to open. We hurried down to find she had managed to reserve the second place in the queue, having camped out since play-lunch. As a result, we were able to form a solid cheer squad along the first row of seats, where we amused ourselves as we waited for the show to begin by watching an errant toddler throwing himself repeatedly at the stage.

'Oh dear,' whispered Neâ, 'that's Harold.'

Harold had managed to climb up to the first tier of staging and was now dancing happily to the pre-show music.

'And that's Poor Harold's Mum,' Neâ added, as a tired-looking woman with a wan smile made her way to the front and carried Harold away.

Soon, the audience was in place and the kindergarten kids entered the hall.

Cute? I could have had them on toast they were so adorable. Everyone wore a costume, as made by Mum or Dad. In some instances, this meant a couple of cornflakes boxes stapled together and a few gum leaves taped to the top to represent a 'tree'; in others, there were extraordinarily accurate renditions of kangaroos, emus and koalas. Neâ's costume duties, luckily, had involved a red bow tie, a smart shirt and pants, and a pair of brown furry ears made by another parent.

'I think you got off lightly,' I said to Neâ. 'Check out the detail on that frill-necked lizard.'

'Yes,' she said. 'Guess whose father is wardrobe supervisor

at the Opera Centre?'

The show started with Miss Popular, director and much-loved drama teacher, seating herself in the front of the audience. Her task was to prompt both words and actions, and to shush any noisy children seated in the audience around her. Miss Popular took her drama/directing duties very seriously and the kindergarten children had learned all about blocking, projecting, stage right and stage left and the very important 'no talking in the wings'.

I'm not going to lie to you. There were mistakes. Lines were whispered or dropped or muttered. There were loud calls to 'SPEAK UP' and 'SAY IT AGAIN' and many gesticulating arms by the frenetic Miss Popular as, half blinded by the brand-new, ultra-strong spotlight, children dressed as teddy bears or mad professors or Australian native animals crashed from stage right to stage left or simply stared, mesmerized, at the audience.

There were wardrobe malfunctions, as tails, kookaburra beaks and even our very own Papa Bear's ears variously dropped, drooped or flapped in the wrong place. One poor student was dressed from head to toe in her teddy bear's costume, including a full face mask with only two poorly cut eye holes. Among her more lightly clad peers (Panda Bear, Grizzly Bear, Black Bear etc.) she was like Taliban Oppressed Full Burqa Bear suffering bravely as she struggled to call out 'Yum! Is that honey I see before me?' at Miss Popular's cries of 'LOUDER PLEASE'.

Halfway through the Australian Animal story, a dramatization of a popular Aboriginal children's tale, a familiar small shape leapt onto the stage, beaming happily among the koalas. 'Who is that child? GET HIM OFF!' Miss Popular's arms waved frantically and, slightly confusingly to her cast, she added 'KEEP GOING, DON'T STOP'.

It was Harold, of course and, as before, he was happy to caper and gambol under the gently swaying cornflakes-box tree or with the anatomically correct frill-necked lizard. As the child actors around him muttered their lines ('SPEAK UP!'), Poor Harold's Mum made her second tight-lipped appearance for the night, dragging a protesting Harold back behind the barricades.

My how we laughed, but soon it was time for Naughty Nephew the 2nd to shine and, as if pulled by strings, we all sat up proudly on the edges of our seats.

Although we had predicted it might happen, there was no startling improvization, no 'let's pretend I'm Harry Potter and this spoon is my wand'. There was also no repeat of a performance at the preschool Christmas concert, when blood sugar levels had obviously gone down and he fell asleep in the midst of singing 'Rudolf the Red-nosed Reindeer'. We had spotted him yawning just before he stepped onto the stage, but this time the smell of the face paints and the roar of the crowd weaved their wake-up magic, with good old Dr Footlights being as effective as crack cocaine.

Other grown-ups may have laughed at Papa Bear's obsessive porridge stirring or his declamatory style or his Miss Popular-like wide-arm gestures, but we thought he was simply marvellous. He was hilarious and witty, with just a touch of ironic poignancy as Goldilocks and her Porridge Professors cunningly tricked Papa Bear into giving up his entire store of porridge and recipe books in the name of science.

His job done, Naughty Nephew the 2nd took a modest sideline position, half hidden by the cornflakes-box tree, as the cast came together to sing a rousing chorus of 'Friends'. All too soon it was over and there were last bows and flowers for the wonderful Miss Popular and cries of 'Encore!' from the audience, which Miss Popular wisely ignored. As we left the hall, children and teachers lined up to say 'Well done Papa Bear'.

It was hard to say who was grinning more, Naughty Nephew the 2nd or his Terribly Proud Family including his uncle and his aunt, but sadly the magic quickly began to subside.

In the world of grown-up theatre, Christopher and I (seasoned old luvvies that we once were) would wind down with a few cold bevvys or one of Emily's infamous 'special cigarettes'.

Naughty Nephew the 2nd, on the other hand, had his own post-show rituals of Supper, Bath and Bedtime ahead of him. All good wind-down activities.

And for a last little magic before bed, a chapter of *Harry*, of course.

15 August

A holiday means many things. Time for family. Time for friends. Eating sugar.

A holiday can also mean the chance to apply the most famous cliché of all: We Went Away to Relax and Came Home Pregnant.

Our holiday is a whirl of catching up with Christopher's parents and brothers and their wives and children, usually scattered from Sydney to Fremantle to London.

We reunite in Fremantle in honour of their parents' seventieth birthdays. There are picnics and barbecues, dinners out and strolls by the harbour. We are to spend several days at the family holiday home, a Little House in the Aussie Bush, four hours south of Perth, where we will roast marshmallows and spot birds and eat and drink and play cricket and soccer and Top Trumps with four nephews and a niece.

Before the Sydney gang arrive, and before we head to the Little House in the Aussie Bush, Christopher and I get a few days to play with Le Nephew (aged six) and La Niece (three and a half), the children of Christopher's eldest brother, Nick, and his French wife, Valérie, who live in London.

Le Nephew and La Niece are bright and charming. And bilingual.

La Niece, the youngest, is quiet, with a delightful giggle. For someone so short, Le Nephew is very loud and can be quite ferocious.

'The PLAN! What is the PLAN?!' he shouts at his parents, who wave their hands distractedly and shrug. They're on holidays, there is no plan.

Holidays are for relaxing.

Le Nephew is particularly strict with badly pronounced French words randomly slipped into the conversation by uppity Australian relatives. The rules are simple. Some people are meant to speak French, like Maman or French Grandparents back in Paris. Others are meant to speak English, like Papa, Australian Grandparents and New Uncle and Aunt.

Attempts by designated non-French speakers to speak French are halted by Le Nephew's outstretched disapproving hand and his stern direction to 'Speak English!' Le Nephew and La Niece are allowed to speak both French *and* English because they can. Maman may also speak English at times, especially to poor unilingual Papa. ('Papa does not have a French head,' La Niece has sorrowfully observed to her mother.)

Of course this does not stop Christopher and I mercilessly calling out *bonjour* and *à bientôt* at the drop of a *chapeau*. Five years ago we lived in Paris for six months and learned enough French to apologize for not being able to speak more. Hearing it spoken around us once more is setting off a frenzy of nostalgia.

When Le Nephew's mother lets fly a string of orders I listen in and manage to comprehend *les chaussettes*.

Socks!! She was telling him to put on his socks. He didn't of course, choosing instead to fling them across the room. His mother was cross but I was delighted to pick up this one lovely word like an old friend.

Later when reading Raymond Briggs' *Father Christmas* to the children, I point out that Father Christmas likes his *chaussettes* to be *rouge*. La Niece and Le Nephew look at me, alarmed, as if I have linguistic Tourette's and have just spasmed in French. Le Nephew is so horrified he is lost for words.

Next day, in the park, Le Nephew tells me that if I went to France without him I should be completely lost because I do not know how to speak French.

'Actually,' I say, 'I would be fine because I would just ask someone to help me.'

'But they only speak French!' Le Nephew shouts triumphantly.

'*Oui*,' I say. 'But I should be very polite and say ... *Excusez moi Monsieur, je parle seulement un petit peu Francais. Parlez vous Anglais?*'

Le Nephew stares at me, knitting his brows, face aghast. 'Yes,' I say, trying not to laugh. 'And because the people of France are so lovely and polite they will not mind that my French is so bad and they will say yes, of course we will help you.'

'Well ...' Le Nephew fights back '... what if they don't speak any English at all?'

'Then, we will make conversation using only our eyes and hands and little grunting noises. Because you don't need words to communicate.'

Le Nephew stops and gallops on the spot, rolls his eyes back in his head and churns his arms up and down.

'Do you understand that?'

'Sure,' I say. 'You want to go to the playground.'

'And play on the swings,' he says.

'*Mai oui*,' I smile.

We enjoy these first few days with the two children and they enjoy us and cling to us and demand to ride in our car and hear stories. Le Nephew has no interest at all in 'arry Potter and La Niece is so pleased to have an adult listening to her (so often in the shade of her louder, assertive brother) that she chats quietly and happily in English. She is far less strict than her brother and allows me to point out a *chien* or a *chat* and gives me patient instructions on pronunciation.

One day, strolling through the streets of Fremantle, a painting in the window of an Aboriginal art shop causes La Niece (hanging off my hand) to stumble slightly. She points at the figures in the painting, with their staring eyes and spiky heads, and mumbles to me, 'They are the Naughties.'

'The Naughties?'

'Yes,' she tells me. 'The Naughties come in the night and they kill you. With their gun.'

Le Nephew hears this and adds to the story. He knows the Naughties, oh yes, he knows all about them and their wicked ways.

'They come in a ... ' he searches for the right word in English, and we discuss the possibilities of clouds, rain, mist ... 'that's it, they come in a mist. At night.'

'Also, they wear a costume. They wear a costume like a ... a person nice. So you don't really know that they are a Naughty. But, you are wrong ...' he says to La Niece, 'they do not kill with their gun. They use the ...' he hesitates again, '*explosion*. Yes, they put the explosion in the buses and the trains. And they hide them in bushes. But normally they don't do a sound. They do not want that we recognize their voice.'

'And they are everywhere,' his voice becomes shrill and fearful. 'In London. The Naughties are everywhere.'

Later, I describe this conversation to their mother. 'Yes,' she says, 'it is very bad. I left the television on all that day. I have traumatized my children.'

Holidays are for escaping.

Instead of Naughties, very soon three Naughty Nephews and their parents arrive, and we all head south.

Among the gum trees and the Western rosellas, the Naughty Nephews teach Le Nephew and La Niece to shout 'Good one mate!' and introduce them to the joys of cricket and, of course, Harry Potter. Many hours are devoted to setting up a miniature Diagon Alley around the ashes of the campfire, where jarrah-twig wands are purchased with gumnut galleons—luckily the ground is so thick with them, everyone can be as rich as Harry Potter.

Meals are loud, joyous communal affairs on the verandah or around the fire and nights are full of silly dice games and lots of wine. It's highly tempting but Christopher and I stick to our no-alcohol rule. Instead, I eat all the sugar I want. This mostly takes the form of toasted marshmallows on a jarrah-twig wand (four gumnut galleons, a bargain) held over the campfire.

The Little House in the Aussie Bush is equipped with a shower and a generator but when nature calls our choices are less luxurious.

There is a 'drop toilet', 500 metres from the house, in a three-sided tin hut overlooking the bush (no flush but a bucket of water to help speed the path of persistent poo down a metal chute and into a deep drop).

There is also a 'worm toilet', inside the house, a sort of wooden vat with toilet seat on top. Also no flush—one sprinkles grass clippings over Number Twos. This assists with composting. Somewhere in this steaming poo mountain is meant to lurk a colony of shit-eating worms. But somehow, sometime, these turd-loving invertebrates died and the pile began to grow. I send myself cross-eyed trying to use the toilet without looking at what lies beneath. I feel I know my in-laws quite well, but the worm toilet offers way too much information.

Years ago, when I first came to the Little House in the Aussie Bush, I was scared of the drop toilet, assuming it to be infested with tiger snakes and red-back spiders. This time, after three days of eight adults and five children warming the seat of the indoor worm toilet, I discover the drop toilet is my friend.

Holidays are for reflecting.

For a few days Christopher and I actually thought we might be the Cliché Couple.

Not only are we On Holidays and Relaxing after all, we are also on the brink of starting IVF, which is the second most common pregnancy cliché. My temperature shoots up like a NASA shuttle until our very last day in the bush.

'But we've got a PLAN,' we keep telling ourselves as we stand in a little private clearing and weep together. 'We've got a PLAN.' I blow my nose loudly and a kangaroo bounds past.

Driving back to Fremantle, we stop as soon as our mobile phones come into range and ring the Fertility Sisters to activate our

IVF cycle. The Sister I speak to is enthusiastic and encouraging. She gives me our date for starting—30 August. And we feel better.

Holidays are, for a short time, forgetting—the night fears and the Naughties and the infertility woes.

It's good to be on holidays.

But it's very good to come home.

And it's very *very* good to sit on a toilet and look down to see only your own *merde*.

26 August

I found myself in a toy shop today, playing with rag dolls, waving elephant-shaped rattles and stroking plush toy penguins. It was not an unpleasant experience.

A couple of years back I had a jobette in a gorgeous toy shop in the centre of Sydney that prided itself on traditional and educational toys. I enjoyed working there, arranging the shelves, assembling the toys, showing customers how to play. This was the kind of toy shop that sold hand-carved chairs in the shape of dolphins with polished shell eyes, or rocking sheep with real wool and curved horn handles. There were no Barbies or Thomas the Tank Engines or plastic toys based on currently popular children's literature. 'I'm sorry,' we would say to enquiring customers, 'we don't carry Harry.'

Today, after judicious squeezing and rattling and stroking, I settled on a stuffed fish. It had rattly bits, scrunchy bits, shiny bits, counting bits and boggly eyes. In short, everything you might look for in a fish, bar the actual breathing underwater bit.

The recipient of the fish, or at least, the recipient's mother is not a friend, more a friend of a friend. But I have followed her pregnancy with interest.

Every now and then when I ask for a progress report, I get a message back as well: *don't give up.*

In her early-thirties, shortly after ending a disastrous marriage, this woman had discovered with a shock that she was experiencing menopause. When she told her mother the news it was revealed that both her mother *and* her sister had gone through early menopause at the same age. It seems no one had thought it worthwhile mentioning to her.

Yesterday I saw the Chinese Fertility Goddess to plan our ChiVF strategy.

'From now on, my role is to support you and support the IVF!' said the CFG.

She waved her hands assertively and peered through her fashionably rimless glasses at me. 'Blood tests, ultrasounds ... you speak to me anytime, understand? If you overstimulate, I treat you, quickly, herbs, acupuncture ... '

She screwed up her face and pinched her thumb and index finger together as she mimed jabbing a needle into my overstimulated flesh.

A bag full of Horrid Teas and a gutful of needles later, I stood at the counter waiting as Mr Chinese Fertility Goddess processed my credit card. On the wall beside me were countless photographs of beautiful smiling babies and children and grateful thankyou cards and letters.

'I like looking at the photos,' I said casually, 'because I like to pick out which baby I want.' Mr CFG is used to comments like these and he nodded calmly.

'Which baby you like?' he asked as he pushed the receipt across for me to sign.

I pointed out the one that made my heart flutter. A little girl, half Chinese.

Mr CFG smiled. 'Yes! She's beautiful. Little Eurasian girl.'

This week Christopher and I have taken to early-morning walks along the beach and one morning I saw a toddler sitting in the sand. She was surrounded by seagulls, perched like sentinels around her and stoically looking out to sea. They nimbly skipped out of her reach as she laughingly rolled towards them. She was Eurasian; her grandfather sat nearby, and although I try not to look at babies (so hard to contain that snatching urge) I couldn't help but look at her.

And she looked up at me. For a second our eyes locked. I quickly looked away but I could still feel her staring at me, expectantly.

And the thought came into my head: she thinks I look like her mother.

And though I wasn't her mother, I felt comforted that, to someone whose opinion I valued, I looked like *a* mother.

Although she was heartbroken, my friend's friend reconciled herself to life as a single, childless woman. But in her late-thirties she met a man who adored her and married her. And wanted children.

So, the donor egg search began ...

... and then the IVF started ...

And yesterday, at the age of forty, she gave birth to a healthy, beautiful little girl.

I cried when I heard the news.

In a few days, I start taking my IVF drugs. I'm hoping they are as carefully and individually prescribed as the brews whipped up by the Chinese Fertility Goddess (minus the twigs and pods and bits that look like they broke off someone's surfboard).

I will have Provera tablets, followed by daily Lucrin injections (eek) and then, from the first day of my period, these will be in tandem with daily Puregon injections (not quite so eekish thanks to that handy pen, simply press against tummy and click). This is along with regular blood tests and dates with the Dildo-Cam to check that, firstly my ovaries are growing eggs, and secondly my ovaries are not exploding.

This morning, walking by the beach again, I saw the same toddler. Her family must have been holidaying at the nearby hotel. This time her father was with her, a kindly looking, tall Anglo man. And her mother.

Short. Dark. Eurasian. Hair in a ponytail.

And, yes, she looked like me. And no, I'm not giving up. I want to play at being Mother for a little while yet.

OPENING NIGHT

A ripple of excitement spread through the theatre as the audience took their seats.

'I hear they don't know the ending yet,' one patron said to another as they turned off their mobile phones.

'That's the same with all these shows,' her companion replied. 'You don't even know if they'll get to the final scene. Show down the road's been cancelled twice before they even got to the end of the first act.'

Backstage, the familiar butterflies were fluttering through every stomach. In dressing room one, the box of tablets known as Provera finished the last of his vocal exercises as he stared at himself in the mirror over a sea of flowers and good luck cards.

'Minny-minny-ma ... minny-minny-moo' he chanted.

There was a knock at the door and the stage manager looked in. 'It's Beginners, can you make your way to the wings please?'

Provera nodded. 'Thankyou darling.'

Picking up his box and with a final check in the mirrors, Provera shimmied along the corridor, passing some of the chorus and a few cheeky stage hands.

'Chookas!' they whispered, and he smiled and nodded his thanks.

A young Blood Test, not due for several scenes yet, was polishing her tubes in the wings. 'Are you nervous?' she asked. 'I'm scared I'll lose my vein.'

Provera chuckled kindly. Of course he was, he was shitting himself, but it was bad form to tell the young ones that.

'A little,' he admitted 'but dear old Doctor Footlights will put me right.'

On stage, in the darkness, Provera's co-stars were waiting. Well, not his real co-star, he told himself. This was the Bowl of Porridge and Fruit Salad that did the scene immediately before his. The real co-star was ... he peered into the blackness of backstage ... where?

The mutter of the audience had fallen quiet. There was an air of anticipation. Provera could feel the energy through the red velvet curtains. The music swelled, the lights came up and the curtains opened to reveal the Breakfast Club. They got a laugh almost immediately with their gag about sowing your oats, and Provera breathed a sigh of relief.

'It's a full house,' the stage manager whispered to him. 'The entire dress circle was booked out.'

'Party booking?' Provera massaged his cheeks as he spoke.

'Don't know,' said the stage manager.

'Sweet baby Jesus ... not a hen's party?'

The audience was shouting with laughter. Provera made a mental note to ask the writer to cut some of the opening jokes. Makes it hard for the next actors, he thought.

Provera waved his hands impatiently and the SM withdrew. Touchy arty types, she thought. She looked at her watch—yes, everything going to time. Except ... there was something not quite right, something missing ... She mentally began going through the props list.

The music changed and suddenly it was time. Provera pressed his nostrils and did some quick yogic breathing to settle his nerves as the Breakfast Club rolled off the stage (to riotous applause, he noted sourly) and then it was his cue, his moment! His time! On ... On ... On ... !

Stepping onto the stage he was momentarily blinded by the spotlight that illuminated his four corners. He smiled at the audience. There was an odd silence.

Provera blinked. The music for his duet, he realized, hadn't come up. What the hell was wrong with that stupid orchestra? Last week it was a bulimic flautist hurling into the tuba ... where did they find these people, he thought angrily. This is a professional show, is appropriate behaviour too much to ask for?

There was a cough from the conductor; Provera looked down to see him pointing at his co-star with his baton. Provera turned towards her to see ... nothing.

What he should have seen was a thirty-something Eurasian woman, standing, post-breakfast, glass of water in hand, ready to break open the security seal on his box to pop the first of a week's worth of pills.

What he saw instead was the pale face of the stage manager gesturing frantically from the wings and mouthing something at him.

'IMPROVISE!'

Provera turned back to the audience with a faint smile. They were silent. Up in the dress circle, the tinkle of martini glasses indicated that the crowd upstairs were happy to wait, but those in the stalls were not quite so patient.

'A funny thing happened on the way from the pharmacy ... ' he began.

Backstage was utter chaos. Anyone who had feet was running hither and thither, checking dressing rooms, toilets and props cupboards.

Sitting unconcerned in the green room, a syringe full of Lucrin and a Puregon pen ('Just click and stab!') sat over their poker game and poured themselves another glass of wine.

'She's probably off with the fairies,' Lucrin said, speaking through the cigarette perched at his lips. 'Deal again.'

Puregon shook her head. 'She's not so keen on fairies after that nasty incident with the hypnotist,' she said. 'I think she's got cold feet.'

The stage manager put her head in the door. 'You're on call, you two, don't go anywhere.'

'But if there's no star, what are we meant to do?' Puregon fidgeted with her dial-up knob as she spoke. The stage manager clucked her tongue in annoyance.

'Firstly,' the stage manager said, 'she's just late, she hasn't cancelled. Secondly, you're not on till next act anyway. Thirdly, you've been told before, don't fiddle with your costume.' And with that she was gone.

Puregon looked towards Lucrin, who was adjusting his plunger.

'Can I ask you something?' she said. Lucrin raised an eyebrow. He had a very bad reputation, Puregon recalled. Something about his rakish charm and piercing wit. The young blood tests were forever saying that he'd 'pinch an inch and take a mile'.

Puregon stood up and turned around. 'I just want your opinion,' she said. 'Does my bum look big in this pen?'

Several hours later, the missing star opened her dressing room door to find the stage manager waiting with her costume in hand.

'What's going on?' asked the star. 'Is this a surprise dress rehearsal?'

'No,' said the SM, grimly. 'It's a surprise opening night. And you're meant to be on.'

There was an audible gasp. 'I thought it was tomorrow,' she said, with a quaver in her voice.

'No darling,' said the SM as she pulled the frock over the star's head and ran a brush through her hair. 'Today's Tuesday the 30th, remember? First day of your Provera pills? Blood test on Friday the 2nd, Lucrin on Saturday the 3rd ...'

'Oh my God,' came the moan as the SM led the star swiftly through the backstage corridors. 'How could I forget? And the audience ... '

'The audience are fine,' said the SM. 'Your pals from the hen's party or wherever they came from have run a charades competition, a trivia quiz and an eighties music singalong. Everyone's happy.'

Through the curtains the familiar strains of 'Tainted Love' were being given a good working over.

'But I haven't eaten,' said the star. They stopped just shy of the curtains. 'I mean, I ate dinner hours ago. It's 11.30 at night. I can't take the Provera tablet unless I've eaten something!'

'We've arranged a stand-in for that,' the SM assured her. 'She only just missed getting into the fruit salad this morning so she was thrilled when we rang her agent. Chookas darling ... you're on.'

Cue music ... cue lights ... and onto the stage stepped the star. Warm applause greeted her apologetic smile and Provera gave her a hug that made them call for more. 'But never do that to me again ducky,' he whispered into her neck. 'I nearly dropped my progesterone—not a pretty sight.'

Hovering stage left was a pretty strawberry, nervous but determined not to show it.

The music swelled for our number and then ... they began to sing.

And so, our IVF show finally starts. A little late, a little sloppy in the entrance, a few fluffed lines and a lot of nerves.

But it's finally here.

Cue fear.

Cue strength.

Cue hope.

2 September

The Fertility Sisters have assigned me a special IVF card which lists my drugs and the amounts I have to take, and my tests and what days they fall on. They've also asked me to come into the House of Groovy Love today for a blood test, to check that I'm not pregnant (as if) and to make sure that I had actually ovulated this month.

As I sit on the bus among the early morning commuters, I cling to the card like a talisman. It has calming words on it, I notice, pleasant thoughts like *We're Here For You* and *Ring Us Any Time*. Just holding it makes me feel a little less anxious. It is almost the equivalent of that one-nostril-at-a-time breathing you do in yoga, or of chanting *I am in control* and *I know exactly what I'm meant to be doing.*

There are a couple of reasons for my anxiety.

Firstly, I picked up my Lucrin from the local pharmacy yesterday. But as Pharmacy Girl got my stash I saw that it was sitting on an open shelf. Immediate panic. I was sure that the Fertility Sisters had told me Lucrin *had to be kept in the fridge*.

'Oh my God,' I thought, 'now I shall have to Speak Firmly.' I felt the blood rush to my face because, frankly, I hate confrontation, it makes me cry.

ME: (*speaking firmly*) I understand that this drug must be kept refrigerated.

(*Subtext: Why don't you just shoot me up with chicken soup?*)

PHARMACY GIRL: Um, no I don't think so.

ME: (*face reddening*) I believe the IVF clinic sisters indicated that Lucrin should be kept in the fridge. In which case I'm wondering why this is at room temperature.

(*Subtext: I'm going to cry.*)

As I speak I suddenly see that the box says 'store below 25 degrees'. Nothing about 'keep refrigerated'. I take a step back. Meanwhile, Pharmacy Girl is rifling through the box for instructions.

PHARMACY GIRL: It says to keep it below 25 degrees Celsius.
ME: (*flustered*) So, ah ... what temperature is this room?
(*Subtext: I have been an idiot.*)
PHARMACY GIRL: Um ... I don't know.
ME: No, neither do I. That's the problem, isn't it? Because you know, this stuff is expensive ...
(*Subtext: I want to go home now.*)
PHARMACY GIRL: (*firmly*) I think it's 20 degrees.
ME: Really?
(*Subtext: I'm actually a very nice person.*)
PHARMACY GIRL: I'm pretty sure.
ME: ... I don't want to spend six weeks injecting myself and then find out that it's crap.
(*Subtext: Please be nice to me.*)
PHARMACY GIRL: ... Yeah 20. Definitely.

Later I ring Christopher, who is away for work, and he assures me that the room would have been no hotter than 20 degrees. 'If it had been 22,' he says, 'you would have felt it. Twenty-five is hot.'

Well okay then. But still, as I sat on the bus this morning, it niggled.

My second reason for anxiety is that my temperature practically flatlined this month. It didn't bother going up at all. Could. Not. Be. Arsed.

Did this mean I hadn't ovulated? And if so what would *that* mean? When I ask the Fertility Sister who siphons my blood she says if I hadn't ovulated they would keep me on the Provera tablets for another week and hold off on the Lucrin. And after that if I *still* hadn't ovulated they would stop the Provera. After that, presumably, I would enter IVF Purgatory, where I would float in great torment for aeons until enough prayers had been said for my soul to be released or I ovulated, whichever came first.

Later I drive to the airport to wave off my dad and stepmum and the gang of friends who have decided to tag along with them to Malaysia and Vietnam—including my sister Kerry and Troy, her beloved—because Dad and Dawn are so the Experts on Where to Eat in Penang and these people will go anywhere for the promise of a perfect Hokkein Mee.

At the airport I park the car and then fall in a heap because I am sure I've left my phone and house keys back in the flat. And then there is much gnashing of teeth. And tears. And swearing and yea verrily there is shaking of fists at God and also pouting of lips, which sometimes helps.

Then, miraculously, the keys and phone are found in a hitherto completely secret pocket in my handbag that I swear I had no idea was there.

I run as fast as I can towards the airport terminal and then immediately run as fast as I can back to the car because I had forgotten to lock the stupid thing and then I feel a bit sick so I walk the rest of the way.

Later, coming back to my car I say to myself: 'What is that thing on the road in the car park?'

For there, before me, was a flattened card covered in dirt.

'Hmmm,' I say, 'surely that is not my special IVF card?'

And so it is. And lo the tyremarks are legion.

So then there is more gnashing and stressing and also a bit of repeated knocking of my head against the bonnet of the car.

In the afternoon a Fertility Sister from the House of Groovy Love rings to say that it is all perfectly fine. I was *not* pregnant (well duh). I *had* ovulated.

And I can start injecting the Lucrin on the morrow.

And also that it is fine to have the Lucrin at room temperature, at least until it has been opened.

It's true, I feel a little stupid. However, I don't feel that today's worry has been wasted. I'm sure it was good practice for when I've *really* got stuff to freak out about.

When the shit *does* hit the fan I can be assured that I'll be *totally* in control and I'll know *exactly* what I'm meant to be doing.

5 September

> *... this time she found a little bottle on it ('which certainly was not here before,' said Alice), and round the neck of the bottle was a paper label with the words DRINK ME beautifully printed on it in large letters.*
>
> *It was all very well to say 'Drink me', but the wise little Alice was not going to do that in a hurry. 'No, I'll look first,' she said, 'and see whether it's marked "poison" or not'; for she had read several nice little stories about children who had got burned, and eaten up by wild beasts and other unpleasant things, all because they would not remember the simple rules their friends had taught them: such as, that a red-hot poker will burn you if you hold it too long; and that if you cut your finger very deeply with a knife, it usually bleeds; and she had never forgotten that, if you drink much from a bottle marked 'poison', it is almost certain to disagree with you sooner or later ...*
>
> Alice's Adventures in Wonderland

The first day of injections loomed and things looked very grim and lonely. Christopher was still away on work. Sister Kerry, who is of course a proper nurse in a proper hospital, was on holidays, sister-in-law Neâ (ex-nurse) was away for the weekend and even the junkie on the corner had gone into rehab.

The problem with trying to inject yourself is that you know, intrinsically, it's just plain wrong. Like holding a red-hot poker or cutting your finger with a knife, sticking a needle through your skin seems a silly, nay, downright stupid, thing to do.

And of course the thing is, when the Fertility Sister was giving us the rundown on How To Inject Yourself, I was staring at her jingly earrings and wondering where to have breakfast and in the back of my mind (the bit that wasn't taken up with jingly earrings and breakfast) I was thinking: but it's not me doing the injecting anyway, it will be somebody else.

For a few days it seemed that there was nobody else. Thankfully, at the eleventh hour, Neâ decided to stay home that weekend, study and also 'help with the stabbing'.

Unlike Alice, *my* little bottle comes with a neat blue cap, on which are embossed the words:

Flip Off.

Flip Off is not welcoming. It is not encouraging. It seems like a sort of buttered-crumpets method of telling someone to leave quickly. It certainly doesn't make me want to plunge a needle through the rubber stopper, suck up a neat ten units and then replunge said needle into my freshly inch-pinched, alcohol-wiped stomach.

Inject Me would be a better message. *Or better yet ... You're Very Brave and You're Doing a Great Job.*

On Saturday, Neâ buzzed round on her groovy Vespa and bounced into my flat with an unfamiliar light in her eyes. Unlike me, she was very calm about the whole business, and apart from an awkward ten minutes when she sat patiently holding a loaded syringe and I sat hysterically laughing, weeping and clinging to a handful of my own flesh, it was in and over quite quickly.

Truthfully, it didn't hurt at all. Although it did make a tiny 'pffft' noise as it went in and that sort of hurt my sensory perception of my own stomach.

'I think I can do this,' I told Neâ afterwards. 'I think I can do it by myself.'

'Okay,' she said. 'But if you start and you find yourself ... you know, falling into a chasm, then ring me and I'll come over.'

On Sunday, I stared into that chasm for at least twenty-five minutes.

'Alrighty now,' I said to myself. 'Breathe in, inject, breathe out, remove needle. Breathe in ... '

And then the terrible to-and-fro hovering started. A friend who is also going through IVF had warned me about the terrible to-and-fro hovering, and said that she managed to prick herself four times before she was able to slide the thing in. On my third time I thought of her.

This time it has to go in, I said to myself.

Except then my legs needed readjusting.

And the time after that I forgot to breathe in.

This morning, Christopher is back.

'Would you like to inject me darling?' I say sweetly as I prep up my fit.

'Ahhh ... no no,' he says. 'You're Very Brave and You're Doing a Great Job. How about I take a photo?'

On that first day alone, as I struggled to push that sharp shiny thing where a sharp shiny thing had no business to go, I thought for several moments that I had made a big mistake. I had fallen into that chasm fifteen minutes earlier and not realized it. I should have rung Neâ immediately and begged her to come round and help.

Instead, I stayed frozen on the edge of the couch with one hand holding a syringe just above my stomach and the other grimly pinching an inch. I was one of those silly friends of Alice, the kind who got burned or eaten by wild animals because we couldn't remember the simple rules our friends had told us.

In the end, what finally tipped my hand was the sight of that smug little bottle of pre-chilled Lucrin waiting for me on the side table. I had already suffered the panic of wondering whether the pharmacist leaving it on the shelf would affect it, and the ensuing relief when the Fertility Sister assured me it was fine as long as *it remained in the fridge after it was opened*.

I realized it had been sitting there for thirty minutes. In a room. With a heater blazing.

I saw red.

'Mother*flipper*!' I said out loud. 'Now my flipping Lucrin's getting warm.'

And suddenly, with a push and a 'pffft' it was in.

12 September

We're lurking about at the House of Groovy Love for another blood test and to learn Christopher's results for his most recent sperm test. It's not good news. In fact it's a big red 'F' and a sad-face stamp. Christopher's boys are fast and plentiful but they've been well and truly whacked with the ugly stick, what with their sad little bodgy heads and their feeble little spakka tails.

As if that isn't hard enough, there's also that gang of tough-kid antibodies. When they're not smoking behind the toilets they like nothing better than rushing at Christopher's poor crippled little guys and sitting on them, shouting 'Stacks On!'

We are told that this means, like the tooth fairy, the ICSI Pixie is destined to pay us a visit. Unlike the tooth fairy, though, we will not be finding a gold coin beneath our pillows. Instead, our credit card will be siphoned dry.

ICSI (Intracytoplasmic Sperm Injection) is the taking of one egg, drilling a little hole into it, then the taking of one sperm, squashing it into said hole and thus creating life. In other words, our sex life for the past few months encapsulated. It even contains the same level of joyous spontaneity.

It's a measure of how far we have come that Christopher and I now look wistfully at IVF and see it as being a natural method of procreation.

'What ... you mean they just hook up? Randomly? In a Petri dish? What kinda crazy free-for-all sex party is that?'

On Saturday, Sandalwood, the Fertility Sister, said that Christopher's poor morphology was caused by environmental factors: stress, pollution, little green Toxic Sperm Invaders who fly down from the planet Infertilita and so forth. Then she said that we should all move to Byron Bay and grow our own vegetables, which frankly made me feel entirely justified in making up the whole House of Groovy Love scenario.

Sandalwood tells us that the House of Groovy Love Scientists will be able to explain to us all the hows and whys and wherefores of ICSI. We have never seen the HOGL Scientists. Like Willy Wonka's oompa loompas, they beaver away behind the scenes, quietly testing and peering into their microscopes and IVF-ing some things and ICSI-ing others. The thought of quizzing them about my husband's sperm is tantalizing.

But will they sing? I feel like asking. Will they sing and will all their little friends sing too, and stand on their hands and do somersaults and look sternly and sorrowfully at us and then lead us away to the juicing room?

Sandalwood hands over the famous Puregon showbag for the next phase of the IVF cycle. It contains drugs, needles, the Puregon injector pen, a nifty little chilly bag and ice brick, and a cool sharps dispenser which I have decided to keep my pencils in.

As she administers yet another blood test, the Fertility Sister asks if I'm feeling any side effects from the Lucrin injections.

'Like what?' I ask. I wonder if I should mention the incredible Room Clearing Farts I seem to be managing these days.

'Feelings of worthlessness,' she says.

In my head, a little movie plays at about a billion miles an hour of this whole heartbreaking, soul-sucking, humiliating, dehumanizing, infuriating experience. This crappy bullshit babymaking routine spanning over the last five years, wrenching at every fibre of our courage, humour, creativity and love.

'I feel sad,' I tell her. 'Having to inject all that *stuff* into my body. Every time I pull the needle out I have a little moment of sadness.'

Christopher picks up the showbag and we say goodbye and head for the lifts. We don't say anything for a while, we just stand side by side, letting our fingertips touch.

Do I feel worthless?

Oh yes. But I also feel angry, excluded, weary and generally lost.

The thing is, I know my husband feels like this too. And I don't think I can blame *that* on the Lucrin.

16 September

This night, eleven years ago, Christopher and I first stood on the edge of the century-old wading pool cut into the rocks at Newcastle Beach.

The moon shimmered in the water around us and somewhere at our feet, buried under the sand, was rumoured to be a mosaic map of the world.

If someone had tapped me on the shoulder and said: in eleven years time that man now sticking his tongue in your mouth will be sticking a needle in the fatty tissue around your bellybutton, I would have laughed and laughed, because it seemed so perfect a moment I scarcely dared hope it could last beyond that one night. And then I would have screamed like a girl.

There may be nothing more than this.

No small version of ourselves, no combination of blue eyes and dark hair, Anglo and Asian, blind optimism and fearful reluctance, hot lust and cold wet tears.

A family of two.

But what we hold between us are, if not our dream children, countless shining moments.

Like tiny fish slipping through the tide, bright as the full moon on water or the thrill of a first kiss or the thin flash of steel as it enters my skin.

In the map of our lives, there is the unknown and the unknowable. Here be dragons of fear and heartache and all the grey islands of our grief.

But here? And here?

And all of this here?

Here be love.

19 September

There was an odd moment watching Aussie film *Little Fish* where I found myself sitting back from the screen and thinking ... why look, there's ex-junkie Galadriel, Queen of Lothlorien scoring heroin for stinky, sweaty scag-head Elrond, Ruler of the Rivendell Elves.

Cate Blanchett and Hugo Weaving were doing a marvellous job of respectively angsting and jonesing but it was still weird seeing them in these less than salubrious roles. Cate's world-weary Aussie-battler mum was played brilliantly by Noni Hazlehurst, who did the full range of actorly faces from 'Fiercely Defensive of Ex-Junkie Daughter' to 'Heartbroken at Memory of Deadbeat Son's Motor Accident' and the mandatory 'Pissed as a Fart But Trying to Still Make Sense of the World'.

By coincidence, Christopher and I had also seen Noni on the big screen only two nights earlier.

On that night we ventured into a place we had never been before.

God willing we shall never return.

This was a place of wailing voices and wringing hands. A place where souls were poked and prodded by demons with shiny teeth and nasty, grasping fingers. It had garish lighting and watery orange juice.

And yet we came willingly, because we were also offered a free holiday or DVD player or sound system *just for attending*. A friend had recommended us as potential customers and when the phone call came, with its accompanying free gift, the base animal instinct of getting 'something for nothing' won over our more civilized selves.

Yes, we attended a timeshare seminar.

We, and other recommended couples just like us, were being 'sold' holidays in our choice of 'one-bedroom, two-bedroom or studio-sized apartments' for the rest of our lives.

I had a problem right there with the whole 'lifetime of holidays' theme.

Lifetime? Who's to say what that is? Twenty years? Thirty years? My mother died at forty-eight. If I live to the same age that gives me a whole eleven years worth of apartment holidays on the Gold Coast. Bargain? I think not. The special offer of the night was available for a whopping seventy-five years, but when we looked incredulously at Samantha the Sales Demon she smiled and said we could always transfer the offer or PASS IT ON TO OUR CHILDREN.

Bing! A little warning light went off somewhere to the left of her head.

The evening started innocently enough. For twenty minutes we watched a video with many scenes of rolling ocean and smiling, relaxing couples sitting on the balconies of their one-bedroom, two-bedroom or studio-sized apartments.

Except for the absence of sperm-on-heaving-cleavage shots, I could have sworn it was made by the same people who provide the helpful videos in the 'men's room' of our fertility clinic. Same grainy images, same dodgy lighting.

Marketing idea! Put the two together! Imagine the winning combination of naked women riding horses on the beach below a series of one-bedroom, two-bedroom or studio-sized apartments!

The video was narrated by Noni Hazlehurst. She was sincere, concerned and convincing. When the lights were switched back on at least three-quarters of the room were nodding thoughtfully to themselves. Balconies! Holidays! Apartments with a range of bedroom sizes! I sipped at my orange juice and imagined our pleasantly sunlit, sea-sprayed future. True there was no way we could afford it, but what about those priceless walks on the beach? Two bedrooms would be good, I thought wistfully. Just in case we had (ahem) an unexpected guest.

Having been softened in the video room, we were now fair game for Samantha the Sales Demon in a one-on-one sales pitch. She flashed her little maps and diagrams, she dazzled us with her upside-down writing skills as she made notes for our benefit. She cracked jokes and spun her own travel stories until our ears were bleeding and we were begging to sign up just to make the pain stop. In a brief moment alone, we studied our options.

ME: I like holidays.

CHRISTOPHER: You hate these kinds of apartments. I hate these kinds of apartments.

ME: It seemed a good idea when Noni was describing it.

CHRISTOPHER: Why are you even considering it?

ME: I want to go home.

CHRISTOPHER: Be strong.

When Samantha came back she intensified her barrage. Christopher and I exchanged looks and then, shamefully, we played the IVF card. 'Sadly, we won't be taking up this amazing offer,' we said. 'We're doing IVF. It's expensive, it's all-consuming, we don't know if it will work or how much we'll have after that ... '

Samantha made a tiny pouty face and summoned her manager to 'approve our free gift'. Instinctively, Christopher and I moved closer together.

The manager listened to our story and nodded kindly. 'I too have friends who have gone through IVF,' he said. 'It's very difficult.'

'Yes,' we said. 'Very difficult.'

Praise the Lord, I thought, he's going to let us go.

'BUT what we've found,' he went on to say, 'is that many couples who have DIFFICULTIES CONCEIVING go on our timeshare holidays ... '

Christopher and I stared at him, mouths open, aghast. *Bing!* went the little warning light. The manager had just strayed into dangerous territory. He was about to suggest the Most Hated Piece of Advice You Could Ever Give to an infertile couple.

'... they discover that all they really needed to do was to UNWIND from their busy lifestyles ... ' *(Bing!)*

Oh no no no ... I could hear Christopher moaning beside me. I clutched at his arm. He was shrinking into his seat.

Be strong, remember! I tried to use the power of my mind to shout at him.

'... and spend some time just CHILLING OUT. *(Bing!)* They found when they dedicated just a little time and money upfront they actually managed to CONCEIVE! *(Bing!)* AND ONCE THEY HAVE THEIR CHILDREN, THEY CAN TAKE THEM ON HOLIDAYS TOO!' *(Bing! Bing! Bing!)*

Silence. I smiled tightly at the manager and stared at him, imagining my eyes as laser beams fixed on high and his innards dissolving into custard. After an awkward few seconds he excused himself and moved away.

Samantha sensed a certain tension and looked quizzically at me.

'It's just that *everyone* says all you need to do is ... *relax*,' I explained.

She nodded happily. 'But you know, it's so true ... my friend had two miscarriages but then—'

Christopher looked up. 'No,' he said between gritted teeth.

Christopher is not a violent man by any means, but his face was running through the kind of range that belonged up on the silver screen. There was 'Barely Controllable Rage', 'Grown Man Pleading' and the impressive 'If I Had But a Teaspoon I Would Kill You Now'.

Samantha laughed brightly, little realizing how close she was to death.

'No no, but really, I have to tell you,' she persisted, 'it's a great story because my friend really wanted to have a baby, so she booked herself—'

'NO! STOP!' Christopher cut her off. He was a broken man. 'STOP NOW. IT WON'T HELP. BELIEVE ME.'

In the gift room, the electronic appliances looked second-hand and the holiday vouchers were for two days accommodation in tired three-star establishments. There was no mention of smart one-bedroom, two-bedroom or studio-sized apartments, let alone bare-breasted women frolicking with their frisky stallions. Christopher and I picked a voucher and then shuffled through the door, clinging to each other like a couple of helpless, hopeless, freebie junkies.

'That's two hours of our lives we'll never see again,' we wept to each other, ashamed and exhausted.

It was raining, and as we made our way home I could imagine the sales staff sipping their watery orange juice as they stood at the floor-to-ceiling windows, already scoping the city for their next victims.

But the horrible truth was, they had a head start. Like all the other junkies in the room, Christopher and I were asked to sign a paper before we were allowed to leave.

It didn't give them our eternal souls.

It was much worse.

It gave them the names and mobile phone numbers of our friends.

21 September

I began the first of my return dates with the Dildo-Cam. This time, Christopher was in the room, so it was a slightly awkward reunion—a bit like running into an old boyfriend, where everyone smiles politely and your husband mutters 'Oh right, you're *that* Dildo-Cam.'

At first, Christopher didn't realize what sort of ultrasound I was having and sat himself at the business end of the room, thinking he was out of the way.

'Ah ... no,' said Dildo-Cam's handmaiden awkwardly. 'It might be best to sit up the *other* end. Most people find it more ... comfortable.'

'It's all right,' I assured her, 'he's been up that end before.'

We exchanged early morning guffaws while Christopher, poor lamb, looked bewildered.

'Now,' said the handmaiden as she brandished a condom covered Dildo-Cam, 'a lot of people prefer to put it in themselves ... '

'No,' I said without a second thought, 'I don't mind. Bung it in.'

It occurred to me later that this may not have been the best response. 'No,' I seemed to be saying, 'I do not prefer to insert my own Dildo-Cam, I prefer you, oh gentle handmaiden, to do it for me.' Was this saying that I was lazy? That I was contrary? That I thought she should do the bloody job she's paid for?

Regardless, in it was bunged and we were off and away.

Soon my lumpy bumpy ovaries appeared in all their black and grey glory, like a pair of socks stuffed with marbles. There seemed to be fourteen egg follicles on one side and seven on the other, all in varying sizes.

When we returned two days later, the follicles had grown considerably, the larger of the gang ranging from fifteen millimetres to eighteen millimetres. I felt quite proud of my growing eggs, but this also explained why I had been feeling more and more like a chicken. Lots of brooding, lots of waddling (no wait, that's a duck) a little bit of pecking for scraps.

Christopher has now been primed to meet the Dildo-Cam's sharp, pointy cousin on the day when my egg retrieval will be performed. I keep saying the phrase *foot-long needle* and he keeps nodding calmly.

'Foot-long needle seems rather harsh,' he said at first.

'Yes, but a drinking straw wouldn't have quite the same effect,' I pointed out. I speak with a bravado I don't actually feel. With Dildo-Cam to show the way, this particular mother-of-all-needles will be pushed through the vaginal wall into first one side and then the other, to prick the follicles on each ovary and extract the eggs.

Exactly when this harvest will take place, only the Dildo-Cam will know. But it will be soon, the Fertility Sister assures me, very soon.

Like, maybe this weekend.

Things seem to be moving a tad fast. I'm trying to stay calm and serene even though we've lost Doctor Who (unexpectedly boarded the Tardis and went on holidays), who has now been replaced by Doctor Seventies Rock Star.

I haven't even *met* Doctor Seventies Rock Star; all I've managed to do is chortle and hum the chorus to one of his namesake's hit songs. It seems strange to think that the first time he meets me properly I'll be legs up and hallucinating. He'll have a better relationship with my lala than he will with my face. But then, he's a Seventies Rock Star after all.

More tragically, we've temporarily lost our Chinese Fertility Goddess. *Damn* those school holidays. She will be gone at that vital time when I go for both my egg retrieval *and* transfer of the embryo to my uterus a few days later. The plan was to have acupuncture before and after the transfer.

I'm trying to be sensible and brave about this. I'm trying not to dissolve in a puddle of Horrid Teas and antler horn. It's just one of those dumb, stupid, bad-timing things. It's just how it is.

The whole infertility story is unfair, from the Once Upon a Time right through to the ... well, the end bit. However it ends. And not just for me. I'm hearing about women on their fifth, their sixth, their *twelfth* cycle of IVF. Women who have finally conceived and then miscarried. And then started all over again.

I don't want to think about what we'll do if this doesn't work. It seems to have been going on for so long. I'm partly stunned at how doggedly we keep going, step by step, dollar by dollar, blood test by blood test, drug by drug. Friends and family ask how we are coping and say that we're doing amazingly well, but I don't feel like we're doing well, I don't feel like we're doing anything. We're locked in our little carriage on the Great Big Fertility Ride, hair on end, hands gripped over the rails, knuckles white, rocketing forward. We're not doing anything. It's all being done *to* us.

And driving us, dragging us, forward and ever forward, is this urgency, this desperate need and want.

This desire.

There is one more acupuncture session left with the Chinese Fertility Goddess. I'll get loaded up with teas to drink in those few days between egg retrieval and transfer, and afterwards. The Chinese Fertility Goddess will be positive and supportive and encouraging. And that will help.

But in the end, in that little room with the bright lights, it's just going to be me and Christopher.

Me, Christopher and Doctor Seventies Rock Star of course.

And ... if Doctor Seventies Rock Star drops out—drowns in a pool of his own vomit, say—then it'll be just me and Christopher.

And quite possibly a drinking straw.

29 September

It was Penang, 1979, and the chickens lived in a small house, built by my father, between the coconut palms and the custard apple trees. There were five of them, small, black and cheeping incessantly. My sisters and I had never seen anything as cute, and that included our newly born sister, Kerry.

Baby Kerry lost points with me early, after an unfortunate incident in our lounge room. With two friends from high school standing by, I had confidently jiggled her on my lap, demonstrating my easy and intuitive mothering technique. The friends were impressed at my handling skills but even more impressed when I lifted Kerry high above my head and called her name and she vomited straight into my open mouth.

The baby chickens encouraged our nurturing instincts and gave us unusual fluffy dolls to dress in miniature clothes. We fed them and watered them and hosed out their stinky skanky coop. They grew quickly and soon lost their fluffy down, coinciding with our own loss of interest in their wellbeing.

We hoped for eggs, planned for eggs, considered ourselves deserving of eggs but it became obvious very early on that they were all roosters. At times we would spot them running hastily around the coconut palms and one of us would be moved to throw a handful of feed their way.

Yesterday I spent four hours trying not to clock-watch as I waited for my call from the Fertility Sisters. I was expecting them to haul me in again for another blood test and ultrasound.

I finally rang the House of Groovy Love at ten past four. I was feeling neither particularly groovy nor loving. I was worried about losing the Chinese Fertility Goddess on Tuesday, I was worried about having been handed over to a new doctor for my egg retrieval, I was worried that I couldn't seem to think or work on anything beyond my ovaries.

'Hello!' said a cheery voice on the other end of the line. It was Rainbow. Or Sandalwood. Or Patchouli. One of them.

'So, are you all ready to trigger tonight?'

I gasped. The 'trigger' is the last needle of the cycle. It comes scant hours before the actual egg retrieval.

'Ah, no,' I said, aware that my voice was starting to wobble suspiciously. 'I don't know anything about the trigger shot, no one told me that's happening tonight ...'

'Okay, well tonight you need to have your trigger shot. It's a little more complicated than the other injections. You've got the pack? And you know how to administer it?'

'Nooooo ...'

I seemed to be having trouble stopping my bottom lip from jutting out. I could feel that distantly familiar kindergarten 'I want to go home' emotion welling up inside.

Apparently, this was all told to us at our first meeting at the House of Groovy Love. This would probably be the meeting where

I zoned out, hypnotized by a combination of no food, sheer terror at the word 'injection' and the Fertility Sister's jingly jangly earrings.

'Never mind,' she reassured me, 'we can go through it now and it will be fine.' Patchouli was obviously adept at dealing with on-the-edge-about-to-trigger IVF patients. After I had taken a page of notes on how to break open the little vials, draw up the solution, mix it with the powder and inject the lot into my stomach (or butt or leg), she mentioned that I wouldn't be having Doctor Who at the retrieval. Did I know that?

Yes, this was something I did know. 'I shall be having Doctor Seventies Rock Star,' I said confidently.

There was a pause.

'No, you will be having Doctor Weekend.'

And at this point, my inner kindergarten student fought her way to the front of my consciousness, pigtails flapping, shoelace untied, dirty grazed knee ... and I began to cry.

'Oh dear,' said Patchouli. 'Are you all right?'

I gargled my distress.

'No *(sob)*. First I had Doctor Who and then I was told I had to have (sob) Doctor Seventies Rock Star and now I'm having Doctor Weekend. I just ... feel ... like ... I'm ... being ... SHUNTED AROUND. (snuffle, snort, weep).'

I didn't add that I had lost my Chinese Fertility Goddess too, but that was in there.

Patchouli was reassuring and very nice. She told me that Doctor Who doesn't do retrievals on the weekend, Doctor Weekend always does them so I would never have had Doctor Who on a Saturday, anyway. And, I would not have had Doctor Seventies Rock Star because he's actually an obstetrician. Who told me I was going to be having him?

'Someone,' I said vaguely. I had learned my lesson about naming names after the timeshare seminar incident.

'So, you're okay now?'

'... Yes.' *(sniff, blow nose)*

It seemed fitting that my final injection of this phase, just like the first, should be administered by Neâ. All that nursing experience paid off well as she flicked and whirled the little vials and popped off the glass tops like an old pro.

It was a quick needle, which was good as the stuff inside was thick and unpleasantly viscous. Rather like shooting up a syringeful of snot.

In 1979 my parents were in their early thirties. They were enjoying their second stint of living in Penang and making the most of the tropical lifestyle. This meant free yearly holidays to places like Singapore and Thailand, having authentic curries in dubious eating establishments and a lot of parties.

The party vibe started early at our house, with our father unfurling roll after roll of aluminium foil and taping it up on the wall behind his reel to reel tape recorder. When the heavy metallic lever was slotted into place, the pulsing disco rhythms of 'Night Flight to Venus' would cause his homemade disco light set to flash in time to the music. In an opposite corner, the glowing yellow lava lamp was set to Groovy; in another, the fibre-optic fantasia lamp cast its ever-changing multicoloured spell.

Throughout the day, local vendors would speed up to the house, in their battered cars or on their scooters, balancing trays of curry puffs or bags of chipped ice.

Mary the Egg Lady was a regular visitor in her cheerful blue van and we were always pleased to see her. This day, along with bringing a carton of eggs she also took away our five chickens. Our mother had offered us money for them and we pocketed our thirty pieces of silver with glee. No more guilty feeding! No more stinky skanky chook house! In those days our pocket money was a pathetic dollar a week and we leapt at the chance for more.

That night, Amanda, Toni and I sat on the stairway in our pyjamas, peering through the banisters, mesmerized by the lights, the music and the eye-popping range of batik fabrics. Pointy-collared shirts, boob tubes, wraparound skirts or flared trousers, it seemed there wasn't a garment yet invented that could not be improved by dripping wax on it and dipping it in garishly coloured dyes.

We were not just there for the dancing; our hope was that some kindly adult would take pity on our wan, gaunt faces and hand us a few curry puffs.

And so it was that kindly Aunty Janet, seeing us staring forlornly through the bars of the stairway, handed us each a miniature chicken drumstick. As we put them to our lips, she remarked on how generous we'd been to donate our chickens for the party. There was a horrified silence as we stared at the tiny skinny legs and wings. Only a few hours earlier the entire tray had been happily scurrying and flapping around the coconut palms. Amanda dissolved into loud tears.

'This would never have happened,' she sobbed, *'if they could lay eggs.'*

My own eggs are yet to appear.

Somewhere between this moment and that, between the retrieval and the transfer, between the coconut palms and the custard apple trees, Christopher and I can only hold hands and wait.

24 September

Just got back.

Totally stuffed.

Hurt like hell but I'd do it again tomorrow if I thought it would help.

Seven eggs.

Going to bed now.

25 September

Going into Egg Retrieval, I was calm, I was chilled out, I was relaxed. I knew what was going to happen and I was prepared.

'Pushing', I knew, was something I would experience. Also 'discomfort'. There would be some 'short stinging' first, as the butterfly needle was slid into the back of my hand and later as the local anaesthetic was injected into my vaginal wall. Then there would be 'strange sensations' as the foot-long needle was introduced to my ovaries. Follicles would be drained and eggs removed. Later, there would be some 'cramping' and continued 'tenderness' in the area.

Ha bloody ha.

As Christopher and I slowly approached the room, a nurse was standing at the doorway, smiling. Inside was a scientist, also standing by, also smiling. It was almost as if we were British royalty about to examine a new country manor, except of course the Queen wouldn't be doing it with her undies rolled into a ball and shoved in her dressing-gown pocket.

Doctor Weekend helped me into the big chair and I popped my woolly socked feet into the stirrups. Christopher sat beside me. So far so good.

As Doctor Weekend leaned in towards my lala, speculum in hand, I felt a stab of sympathy. 'Poor Doctor Weekend,' I thought. 'Spends all his days with his head between women's knees, hoovering up their eggs. Can't be very nice.'

This was to be the last warm and pleasant feeling I would have towards him.

Perhaps it was because I was so bloated and pumped full of follicles, but everything he did hurt.

The speculum? Yowsa. The swabbing of the vaginal wall? Ouchy ouchy ouch.

He leaned in and pumped some of the anaesthetic into my hand and for an all too brief moment I floated around joyously, but came back with a jolt as he shoved in the Dildo-Cam.

Dildo-Cam and I have had our moments, our tiffs, our strong words, our little silent treatment games. But during retrieval he was an absolute *bastard*. 'Owwwww,' I winced and Doctor Weekend paused.

'Your bladder needs emptying,' he announced.

'Oh,' I said, 'I thought I did that before I came in here but never mind I can go again.'

'That's fine,' he said cheerfully. 'I'm going to use a catheter.'

I nearly jumped out of my chair. My hands came up in the international symbol for 'Stop Right Fucking Now'.

Catheter?! Sweet mother of God.

For the past two months I have been hearing all about catheters via Grumpy Grandad. Ever since his recent fall our phone calls have begun with Catheter News, where I get to hear about whether it's 'PLAYING UP' or 'AFFECTING ME OLD FELLA' or on a couple of sad occasions 'SPRUNG A BLOODY LEAK'.

Now, here was Doctor Weekend brandishing said catheter and telling me to move my hands out of the way.

'Can't I just use a toilet?' I begged. 'I really don't like the catheter.'

'It's all right,' he said, pumping a little more jungle juice into my treacherously willing veins, 'just imagine I'm standing in a river, doing some fly fishing and I'm about to catch some lovely trout.'

And before I could say *what* are you talking about, it was in and draining away like Niagara Falls into his little green tray.

'Right then,' he said, 'let's get on with it.'

Exit catheter and re-enter Dildo-Cam. Cue more howling and shrieking from me. Also sobbing. Also crying. There was some more pumping of the jungle juice, which seemed to do nothing.

'Egg on one!' The scientist did her best, encouraging us to behold the sight of my ova on her monitor before it was sucked up into the needle. The nurse hovered helpfully at Christopher's shoulder.

'Would you like to see the egg on monitor one?'

He glanced up quickly but turned back at my pathetic sobbing. Perhaps in nine months.

There were some appeals from Doctor Weekend to look at the screen and see my lovely follicles. Beside me, poor Christopher was stroking my hair and whispering sweet, comforting, but ultimately useless, words into my ear.

At one point I did open my eyes, but through my tears I could see that frigging foot-long needle shining away and I lay back and howled.

'Do you want me to stop?' Doctor Weekend paused a second. 'Because you can always ask me to stop.'

'No,' I gulped, 'keep goooooiiiinggggg ...'

'All right,' he said. 'But you need to calm down a bit. Stop breathing like that. Stop curling your legs up like that. Look at your husband. Look at the monitor. Just RELAX.'

Despite my agony I was aware that it was pointless to kick him in the face. The best I could do would be to dislodge his glasses with my woolly socks. Next time: steel-capped boots.

It wasn't the needle part that hurt. Sure, there was a slight stinging and the unpleasant pushing, but frankly I would have had a ten-foot needle rather than that scumsucking Dildo-Cam, because *that* was what was doing the damage. It is so *totally* over between the two of us. I'm not responding to his semi-literate text messages or passing on his chain letter emails. Dildo-Cam and I are THROUGH. I felt as if my pelvis was being crushed. Oddly, it was only on the right side; when Doctor Weekend switched ovaries, the pressure miraculously disappeared.

Now I simply cried in relief and punctuated my sobs with 'I'm so sorry I'm such a wuss.'

'You're not a wuss,' Doctor Weekend called out brightly, 'I wouldn't go through this for quids.'

Seven eggs later, I was wheeled into recovery where *finally* the anaesthetic kicked in and I could truly relax. Doctor Weekend came in to see me a few times and ended up having long, kindly conversations with Christopher about the magic of IVF, ICSI and trout fishing.

To be fair, a surprising number of egg retrieval gals actually *walked* out of their rooms. So it's just *me*, then, with the pain threshold of a blubbering wussypants gnat.

While I was sleeping off my trip to hell, Christopher was summoned to the Little Room of Pleasure to provide his half of the bargain.

Obviously, having seen me arched up in front of him howling like a banshee, the last thing he felt like doing was wanking into a jar, but duty called. Sadly, just as proceedings got underway, the alarm on his mobile phone went off, warning him that the parking meter was about to run out. Quickly he zipped, whipped off his little blue surgical overshoes and ran out to get a new parking ticket. When he got there he found he had to run to three separate ticket machines to find one that wasn't jammed. Finally he returned, sweaty but reshod—and, I think it's fair to say, a little out of sorts—to his room.

Remembering his basic hygiene laws he stepped up to the hand basin. There were some irritating problems with the towel dispenser, necessitating firm manly tugging, before a satisfactory hand wash and dry could be finished. This only added to stress levels. Time was ticking on. Those hard-won eggs were calling. Bypassing the free scotch, Christopher flicked perfunctorily through a couple of magazines and fastforwarded the video.

He told me later that he thought of me and I'm sure he did, because as he finished the job he fell against the offending towel dispenser and the whole thing broke and collapsed off the wall with a resounding crash. Despite this, his boys were good and a little while after this we went home.

As Doctor Weekend was finishing up, mopping away the blood from my thighs, he said, 'Reckon you'd like to do this all again tomorrow?' This was a little joke and no one in the room responded, treating it with the contempt it deserved. But in my mind I wondered, would I do it again?

And I knew, even then, the answer was yes. Not tomorrow maybe. But next week. Or the week after. Or the week after that. If this is what it takes, I'll do it.

Today, Moonbeam from the House of Groovy Love calls to tell me that of the seven eggs, five have fertilized.

Five embryos!

'And the thing is,' I confess to Christopher, 'I think I want them all.'

He looks at me. 'So do I,' he says.

And then we clutch at each other, in awe at the possibility of having an entire family in one Petri dish.

27 September

It can't be bad being an embryo.

You blob about with a few mates, get a bit of energy up, divide, go for a swim across the Petri dish, compare cells with the dish next door, do a bit more blobbing ...

Today being Day Three, I ring the House of Groovy Love to talk to the Fertility Sisters and find out how the Famous Five are coming along.

I expect them to have thinned out by now. To the Fantastic Four. Or the Holy Trinity. Or the Dynamic Duo. Or even just Super Embryo.

But in fact, the Five are still thriving. I take a moment to chat a bit more with Rainbow about how many embryos they might transfer.

Doctor Who originally said it would be one but now Christopher and I are nervous and thinking maybe we should have two ...

Yesterday at my acupuncture session with the Chinese Fertility Goddess I asked her opinion. One or two?

'Could you cope with twins?' she had asked as she efficiently jabbed needles into my ankles and heels.

A very good question. I would rather have one but then I would rather have twins than the risk of none at all. But all this seemed like a stupid and presumptuous problem to have, to be even thinking about the possibility. Christopher and I are so used to being disappointed. It feels as if we have been trying for years just to get close to where we are now. Every utterance, every discussion about the possibility of pregnancy has to be accompanied by the words 'if all goes well' and 'but we'll wait and see' and, on my part, frantic knocking on wooden surfaces.

My conversation with Rainbow continued. 'On the day of the transfer,' she explained, 'you'll talk with the scientist and with the doctor, and you'll be able to make a decision about how many embryos you'd like transferred based on how well they're going. You don't have to decide now.'

Bruised knuckles aside, the Day Three report is: I feel hopeful. Jolly hopeful even, as Ms Blyton would put it.

And in a dish, somewhere in the middle of the city, a bunch of embryos are blobbing and dividing and sculling down their ginger beer as they plan their big adventure.

29 September

In less than two hours, my embryo transfer will begin. It should be over in five minutes, which seems ridiculously short for all that's led up to it.

I went for a walk yesterday along the beach. Christopher and I used to briskly walk this route every morning. This time, still bloated from the injections, I could only mince slowly and carefully. Christopher powered away up the hill, and I ended up at a shrine.

In January 2003 there was, according to the faithful, a visitation from the Virgin Mary just above Coogee Beach.

I'm not exactly sure why she turned up at Coogee; most tourists head for Bondi.

Still, she came, she hovered, she went away again and even though the council took away the fencepost she had favoured, the faithful keep coming back. There are flowers there, real and fake, little statues, holy water, postcards—a contingent of Filipino nuns and priests dressed in white even visit once a month to say the rosary. And enjoy the view, presumably.

It's not a permanent structure and it changes regularly, depending on how recently the local yobs have kicked the crap out of it and how quickly the local believers have restored it. It's obviously not council sanctioned either, which takes its toll on the flowery borders and the framed holy pictures which creep out along the fence. Yet it survives, a tiny subversive altar to resilience and faith.

So this was me, inching up to Mary's place, to have a little chat and make a couple of requests. It couldn't hurt, I figured.

I asked for the women who know the fear, the loss, the hurt, the grief, the gut-tearing anger, the tears. The women who write about their pain, and the women who read about it. And for the women who recognize their story. This story of aching and emptiness and obsession and sacrifice. It gets told again and again, in a multitude of variations. Always the same. Always different.

Like snowflakes. Like popcorn kernels. Like babies.

I know, logically, there can't be happy endings for every single infertility story being told.

But I asked anyway.

30 September

Somewhere in some IVF textbook is a comforting little note that the uterus is not an open triangular box as suggested by the familiar cutaway diagram.

It is, in fact, more like two slices of bread with a layer of jam between them. Inserted between the slices of bread and into the jam, the embryo is like a raspberry seed. Hence, there is no danger of it rattling around and falling out.

Into my jam sandwich we chose to put back one raspberry seed. It was the most advanced of the embryos and beginning to leap out of its shell with excitement.

The others were also in a good state. They will be frozen, in the event that this one turns up its toes, or—and it makes me snort to think of it—if further down the track we decide we want to try for Baby Two. We'll find out today if they all make it to the ice-cube tray.

The procedure was quick and cheerful: a syringe and a catheter, a wave and a prayer, a whoosh and it was over.

Now comes the two-week wait, that mythical magical limbo land where embryo and uterus decide if they want to bunk in together for nine months.

Christopher and I knew it was time to leave the recovery room when we started taking stupid pictures of ourselves on our camera phones and laughing hysterically, but in tiny hushed voices, nudging each other whenever we saw a nurse's feet beneath the curtain.

It was like being in Year 11 again and hanging out in the library study rooms with your boyfriend, where you were ostensibly studying 2 unit economics but in fact were really sticking your tongues in each other's mouths and your hands down each other's pants. And laughing. Every time a teacher walked past you would shut up and stare solemnly at your J-curves and murmur about distribution.

Christopher and I are mature, grown-up people now who have no need of hands-down-the-pants action in IVF clinic recovery rooms and we wouldn't know a J-curve if we tripped over it—but there was no way we could stop with the explosive snorting and repressed giggling.

I suppose you'd call that relief. Or just, you know, idiocy.

RENAISSANCE MAN

In 1999, the first person I knew to organize his millennium New Year's Eve was my father. He and my stepmother, Dawn, had booked tickets for a nudist ball on the North Coast of New South Wales.

I winced when he told me.

'Why a nudist ball?' I asked him. 'Is that necessary?'

'Why not?' He grinned and started to dance around me, shaking a set of imaginary maracas and singing about how when his baby smiles at him he goes to Rio.

These days, I have discovered, my father's holidaymaking in Malaysia and Vietnam has ground to a slight halt. He has always had painful arthritis in his knees and now it's also affecting his hips. According to an email from Dawn, my father has spent most of his time resting in a Hanoi hotel after having cortisone injections.

Before they left I gave my father a small white woven scarf.

'It's a Tibetan prayer scarf. It's blessed,' I said. 'It's to bring you and everyone else safely home.'

'Fair enough,' he said. 'Now, what DVDs do you want?'

'No thankyou, pirated DVDs are illegal,' I said primly.

'It's all right. I know you're a writer. I'll get you something arty. They pirate the boring stuff too, you know.'

'Don't get any,' I insisted. 'Please. I will be worried.'

'Okay, fine,' said my father, rolling his eyes at Christopher. 'I hear you. No DVDs. What about software?'

Remember that girl at school whose father was really strict? She wasn't allowed out with her friends without stringent curfews and conditions and if she was late her father would drive around the streets looking for her. He'd drop her off punctually and pick her up early from parties.

She was paranoid about cigarette smoke in her clothes and alcohol on her breath. He'd complain to the principal about an 'offensive' song he overheard playing at the school dance while waiting for her outside the gymnasium. The complaint would lead to a written apology and a promise to never play the song again. (Ironically, the girl's friends considered the song stupid so as a result, briefly, her father became a sort of accidental hero.)

That was me. That was my father. When I complained to my mother and asked why he had to be like that, she sighed. 'You know why,' she said. 'It's because he cares.'

One night, after too many drinks at a friend's party, I realized I had broken my curfew. I set about trying to convince my friends to run away with me, to Sydney, because it was now obviously impossible for me to ever return home. For half an hour I crouched under a street lamp, arguing the benefits of living on the streets in the big city and completing our Higher School Certificate by correspondence.

'What's the worst that can happen?' one friend sensibly asked.

'I will be grounded,' I said sadly.

'Then we will visit you,' he said, and the others nodded their heads in agreement.

'Yes. Every day. And we'll tell you everything we do so it will be as if you were really there.'

My eyes welled up in gratitude. 'You're such good good friends,' I gushed. 'I really really love you.'

'And we love you,' they chanted back. 'We really really love you.'

'Oh look,' I said, pointing, 'there's my dad waiting for me on the footpath.' And in a small cloud of dust my friends turned as one and bolted into the night.

A few years ago, my father went to watch the Sydney Gay and Lesbian Mardi Gras for the first time. He asked me if I wanted to see his digital photos.

'Oh yes,' I said, 'we've been to Mardi Gras a few times. It's fun isn't it? What did you do, stand on a milk crate so you could get a good view?'

'No,' my father said smugly. 'I looked out the window of the float.' Then he cranked up his computer to show me his Mardi Gras slide show. There, waving happily among the drag queens, was my father. The man who in years gone by had crossly demanded to know 'why do they have to flaunt it?' was now triumphantly riding in the front seat of a supporter's float for a local gay and lesbian radio station. He was dressed in black and white cowskin hotpants and a glittery cowboy hat. My stepmother strolled alongside, in her matching garb, waving happily.

As I flicked through the photos of his night of politically correct debauchery I thought of the time my father reluctantly let me see The Rocky Horror Picture Show *with my high school boyfriend. It was at the RAAF base cinema, so it was as good as supervised, I had argued, and we had other friends going, including my girlfriend Kim, and her father (also in the RAAF) would give me a lift home ...*

My father listened to my pleading and finally nodded.

'I can go?' I gasped.

'You can go,' he said. 'But I'll drive you there myself.'

He paused, thinking it over, and then delivered the horrifying news: 'In fact, I think I'll watch the movie too and then drive you back. It's all right,' he added, seeing the look on my face, 'I don't need to sit with you and your friends.'

My memories of that night are hazy. Instead, burned into my brain is the image of the back of my father's head, sitting ten rows down, alone in the middle of the cinema.

Looking at the pictures of my father, here throwing condoms to the crowd, there arm in arm with a tall man in stilettos and pointed breastplate, I was aware of strange and painful feelings. My father was slightly disappointed with my reaction, thinking me prudish, but in reality I was jealous of his joyous expression as he flung generous handfuls of condoms and sachets of lube to the cheering crowd.

When my sister Toni still lived in Byron Bay, she was often visited by our father and stepmother, who roared up the highway on their motorbike. They would spend an idyllic weekend swimming, chatting and nibbling away on the local dope-infused muffins, a specialty of the region.

When Toni told me this, I was aghast. 'Our father took drugs?' I asked.

'He ate muffins,' she said calmly. 'In fact he liked them so much he bought half a dozen.' When I confronted my father he didn't bother denying it. 'They're in the freezer,' he said. 'Help yourself.'

'Dad ... ' I spluttered. 'Don't you remember telling us if you ever found marijuana in our schoolbags you'd take us to the police?'

'Sure,' he admitted. 'Tell you what. Put one in the microwave and I'll go you halves.'

The change had begun when my mother died. Her cancer was long and cruel and my father gave up everything to care for her. After weeks of sitting by her bed, listening to her breathe, when the end came, I told my father I wanted to leave.

'For how long?' he asked. It had been years since I'd had to ask my father's permission to go out, but I still felt nervous.

'A week,' I said. 'To ... ' I tried to think of the furtherest place I could go.

'To the Melbourne Comedy Festival.'

There was a pause. 'Okay,' he said. 'We'll have the funeral when you get back.' We cried for a while and then fell silent.

'You know,' he said, 'I used to resent your mother, for the social work she did, for her university studies.' I nodded. Over the years my mother had become a sort of one-woman warrior for social justice. I thought perhaps it had started in Malaysia when she organized a group of other nurses to travel to the refugee camps on the borders of Thailand and Cambodia (then Kampuchea) to deliver medicines and to report back to the RAAF on the situation. When she returned home to Penang she organized an enormous fundraising concert for the refugees. A couple of weeks before the concert date she had discovered a lump on her breast but she, a trained nursing sister, decided to leave it until after the concert was over to have it checked out. There was too much else to do. Later, when the cancer went into remission there was no stopping her.

I looked into my father's face. Tiny soft moles were growing on the skin beneath his eyes. It was as if his tears had taken root. 'But now,' he continued, 'I realize that what your mother did was more important than anything I ever did. And maybe my whole reason for being on this Earth was to support her and her life's work.'

I nearly fell down the stairs.

These days my father attends weekly men's workshops, which involve a lot of manly drumming and 'talking from the heart'. He and Dawn attend week-long blues festivals and country music festivals and pitch their tent in the mud. He has long conversations about spirituality and life journeys and destructive patterns.

I love his freedom, his joy in his partnership with his second wife and his relationship with her children Ros and Paul, his new relationship with us, his grown-up children and his grandchildren. I love the way he hugs my husband and sends him his love over the phone. I love that he tries to learn from people and from his own mistakes and that he struggles with his old patterns and rigidities. I love that his eyes fill with compassion when I talk about my fear that I will never be a mother. And the way he tells me, like a father, that it will all be okay.

On the final night of the millennium, I stood at a window of a friend's flat in Paris, gazing fearfully out at the Eiffel Tower. The city was spread out before us in all its glory but I was counting down the seconds till the world came to an end. All the world's computers, I was certain, were about to crash when their calendar thingies failed to compute the year 2000. Or something like that.

Some hours earlier, on the other side of the world, my father had been kicking up his bare heels among hundreds of nude revellers.

Eschewing the obvious, he and Dawn wore costumes: matching his and hers leopard-print G-strings. My father even went so far in embracing the festive mood as to affix a temporary tattoo, depicting a pair of full red lips, to his left buttock. Waving his arms in the air and shaking his groove thang, he felt quite the scene stealer, until next day at the Grin and Bare It Café.

'How'd you like my hot lips?' he asked a fellow nudist as they perched on their hemp towels and sipped at their steaming mugs of chai.

The friend looked confused.

'Oh come on, don't tell me you didn't see it!' My father pointed to his bum. 'My hot lips tattoo!'

'Oh right,' the friend smiled with relief. 'Man, I was going to talk to you about that. We were worried it might be a ringworm.'

5 October

Letter to a bunch of cells six days past transfer

Dear Embryo,

I'm currently in Two-Week Waiting Hell while you make up your cells about whether you want to hang around or not.

It seems like years ago that you got to whoosh right through my cervix and into the amusement park that is my uterus. That was a one-way ticket by the way, you don't get to ride again, and if you leave the park, a big scary man rips you apart and gobbles you up.

No, just kidding, but you know ... stay behind the fence.

Okay, so you're here, you're eleven days old, you're doing that cell-dividing thing you embryos are so damn good at. (I tried just now but we lose so much flexibility after about the age of twelve. I used to be good at cartwheels, too.)

I can't actually see you but as far as I know you have no teeth. Or maybe just the one which you perhaps used to hatch out of your little shell. Like baby chickens!

You're way too young to remember this but your aunties and I had chickens when we were kids! They were so cute! We loved those chickens! And then we ate them, but we loved them first, and my point is that they hatched. And they had teeth.

Or at least a tooth apiece.

Sensibly, I know you don't have feet either. However I feel you may have done a little rolling. Am I wrong? I don't think so.

You've felt the rush of speed from your catheter ride, and it'll take a little while for the adrenaline to wear off, and you're going to be attached to the wall of my uterus for, oh, nine months (hint hint), so roll, little embryo, to your heart's content (or at least the cells that will eventually merge to create your heart) but just be sure to end up on the back wall by my spine (I hear that's best) and STAY BEHIND THE FENCE.

From today on, I believe, you will think about attaching yourself.

I say don't think, do.

I'm always one for procrastinating and I can tell you it leads to disappointment. There are no prizes for pfaffing about, it's not cool or smart to hang back and I assure you there are no other uteri to compare with.

Don't go thinking: I'll wait for that catheter to whoosh me into another one and check out the décor, there are NO MORE CATHETER RIDES, I don't know how many more times I have to tell you.

Don't worry about the whole attaching thing either. I know you don't have fingers to cling with but some sort of cellular stickiness will occur; your cells will mix it up with my cells and there will be a cool bonding experience. Trust me, it will work.

Or I guess you could always hang on with that tooth.

Meanwhile, I'm drinking my Horrid Teas and squirting progesterone gel like there's no tomorrow. These will give you a helping hand (since you have none). I apologize if you're getting any nasty smells in there; it could be the gel backing up around my cervix, or the tea (I'm used to it, but it always freaks other people out) or maybe that asparagus we ate last night. Currently, I have moles that are bigger than you. I think I might have skin pores that are bigger than you (but frankly in this weather that's no biggie).

One day, if you stick around, and you grow and get born and survive your childhood where I nearly love you to death and those angsty teenage years where we have screaming matches and sulk-offs and then you become a big strapping ADULT (which means your genes will have come straight from your great grandparents, because your father and I are dwarves), well then ... I will be able to say to you ... I knew you when you were smaller than this (.)

And oh, oh how I wanted you.

So please stay.

Please stay and grow and keep away from the fence (and that's the third time I've told you now, so that might have to be time on the naughty chair) and let me write more of these stupid letters. Please.

Love (and you would not believe the absurdly enormous amount I have for you, even now),

Vanessa
xxx

9 October

My sister Amanda gave me my first fertility doll. It was from Africa, a wooden female figure with a round, flat head and pointed breasts.

'You hold the body like a handle,' she said, 'and smack the back of its head against your palm, like *this*.' Oddly, this little ritual, while appealing in some ways, failed to bear fruit.

Her fertility doll now stands on a little shrine in my lounge room. Clustered nearby are a Russian fertility doll, given to me by Christopher's mother, a metallic South African fertility doll with wild hair and a prominent vulva, given to me by my friend Hadass, and a tiny bone Celtic doll with a spiral over her abdomen, given to me by my sister Toni. There are the last mouthfuls of a bottle of Mecca Holy Water Christopher received from a Muslim friend, Nada, and an ancient Little Golden Book entitled *Prayers For Children* which I bought from a hospital garage sale three years ago, stoned off my head on whatever that cool anaesthetic is you get given when you have an echocardiogram.

This morning, my friend Mark, who is looking after our flat while we are away, rang to ask if he could also add to our already large pile of hopeful bric-a-brac his Mother Theresa rosary beads and a bag of mandala sand that had been blessed by a Buddhist monk.

'You have a lot of blessings on your shrine,' he said reverently.

'Yup,' I said. 'Whack 'em on, the more the merrier.'

It seems a little sad that the final blood test of this IVF cycle, and I mean THE blood test, the is-she-or-isn't-she test, should happen not at my IVF clinic, the House of Groovy Love, with all its wild-child free-spirited Fertility Sisters, but at another IVF clinic in another city far far away. In Melbourne, in fact.

Last Thursday, many *many* hours of my life were lost to driving along the Hume Highway from Sydney to Melbourne. We drove because someone somewhere said that flying when one *might* be just pregnant was not a great idea, and we came to Melbourne because the arts company Christopher works with is doing a show at the Melbourne Arts Festival. Once we've seen that, we'll be driving on to Adelaide where my new play is opening next week.

You see ... that's the crazy thing about all this. Life goes on. People work, play, travel, live. It's almost unbearable for me to think that the world doesn't revolve around whether or not a cluster of cells decides to stick to me but apparently this is the case. I wonder how long I can actually go without thinking about having a baby. An hour? Twenty minutes? Ten?

It's as if this year I've lost all my concentration, my focus has narrowed, my identity shrunk. Like Alice, I am folding up like a telescope.

Paradoxically, somewhere inside me the beginnings of life may be unfolding to meet me. Or maybe not.

When I read back through my old diaries I am astonished at the expansiveness of my thoughts and words if not my deeds. I wrote this ... I wanted this ... I dreamt this ...

And then, here and there, over the years, a line or two glows from the page like a warning beacon ... *Think we might be pregnant ... would like to have a baby this year ... still not pregnant ... I think there's something wrong with me ...*

Before we left, my sister Amanda rang from her home in New Zealand to tell me that she is having another baby. This will be her fourth child. She told me that she was seven weeks pregnant and she was hesitant and careful of my feelings and sensibilities. She also told me that she wouldn't tell any of our family until after I get my results.

'If you have some good news,' she said, 'I want you to be able to tell it first. I don't want to steal your moment.'

I hate that my infertility has stopped my sister from being able to share her wonderful news right *now*.

I hate that she couldn't tell me the day, no, the very minute she found two lines on her home pregnancy test, which is what I would do if it were me.

I hate that she couldn't shriek with unbridled joy over the phone but had to use careful, quiet, kind words full of compassion and understanding.

And I love her for this.

'If you want, you can write about it,' she said. 'And you can get angry with me.'

'Why would I get angry with you?' I laughed.

'Because,' she said gently, 'it's not fair.'

Tomorrow at 8.30 am I will have the Test. And I've decided to try not to do my own testing before that. No creeping out to the chemist for a home pregnancy test. No, really.

I have never ever seen two lines on a pregnancy test before and I am willing to forgo the possibility of that for my last precious hours of blissful ignorance.

While I don't know, I can still pretend there's some hope.

I can point out every possible pregnancy symptom to Christopher and we can grin wildly at each other. He can kiss my tummy and call it the Baby House and I can toss about names like so much garden salad in my head.

For what it's worth, Christopher, the light to my shade, the fire sign to my water, the sun to my moon, my biggest blessing of them all, is positively glowing with optimism.

He believes.

But then, he always did.

And for just a few more hours, I want to believe too.

10 October

I see.

We've got one of *those* embryos. One of those 'I'll play on the fence if I want to' type embryos.

This afternoon a Fertility Sister rings from the House of Groovy Love (the Melbourne clinic has forwarded the results to them) with my results.

You know how you can tell from their voice?

My beta level is 8. Starlight explains that this means there is *some* pregnancy hormone floating around but nowhere near enough to definitively shout YAY HOORAY.

A beta level of 50 to 100 would be a definitive Positive, for instance, and 2 would be a definitive Negative, but 8 is just, well, fence sitting.

So now I have to go back to the Melbourne clinic on Thursday for another blood test. Just to make sure one way or another. I try to look on the bright side of this. It isn't a definite negative. The walk to the clinic is very pleasant.

That's about it for bright sides.

12 October

When Pandora and her playmates find a box and are told not to look inside, they're naturally very curious. They live in paradise, things are beautiful and amiable and benign and probably a tad boring, and more than anything they want to look in the damn box.

When Pandora finally opens the lid, all the evils of our world are released into the air: war, hate, violence, disaster, pestilence, anger, email spam ...

Pandora manages to slam the lid shut, trapping the last occupant who begs to be let free. Pandora is scared but when she does open the lid again, she lets out Hope. Hope was originally imprisoned with the other beasties as a sort of divine insurance policy. Without Hope, the human race could not survive the despair that comes from living in this world.

The spotting started on Tuesday night. Very faint, very pink, very gentle.

A sort of apology from my uterus for what was to come.

Within a couple of hours, it was definitely over. Christopher and I curled up together on the carpet and hugged each other and wept and hugged some more. I cried into his hair and snot ran down his neck. We made ourselves into a little two-person space pod and closed the hatch on the rest of the world and whispered secret things that made us sigh and nod and squeeze ourselves even tighter.

We were so ridiculously proud of this embryo. Our embryo. Eleven years after our bodies first met, our genetic signatures had finally come together. It was the closest we had ever come to being pregnant. For a few days it had made us Pretend Parents. We wore cheesy grins. We played spot the Bugaboo.

I was almost numb with despair. With the unfairness. With the why-does-it-have-to-be-so-difficult? And with the waste. Along with everything else, I suddenly felt that I had spent all this year and more, working and focusing and yes, obsessing, on trying to fall pregnant. The IVF cycle had, each day post-transfer, wound this thread still tighter and tighter with each injection, each unit of Lucrin or Puregon, until finally it came crashing down with that first drop of blood on a cotton pad.

It was as if this was all I was, a woman trying to fall pregnant, and I had failed. I had lost not just a pregnancy but a year of my life and part of all the years of my life where I had wondered *will this be the year?*

Did it hurt more, I wondered, than all the other cycles where we hadn't used IVF, where we'd simply used temperature charts or Yoda's split ejaculation method or the Chinese Fertility Goddess's Horrid Teas?

I picked at the thought, like a scab. Yes, the answer flowed.

Because we saw the embryo.

Because we were told how well it was all going.

Because we knew people who'd fallen pregnant first IVF cycle.

Because we were closer, we felt the possibility before us; we believed we simply had to reach out and grab it. Because we heard the voice of Hope, and we chose to release her from our personal Pandora's Box.

Because we thought we were special and we deserved it.

And yes, it hurt more than the rest.

Today I spoke to a Fertility Sister. 'It wasn't you,' she said.

I had asked her if there was something wrong with my uterus.

'You had the scans, we would have picked something up,' she said. 'It's more likely there was something genetically wrong with the embryo.'

'But it was a good embryo,' I said. 'They told us it was ... hatching.'

'I know.' She was sympathetic. 'But they only go on how the embryo looks. How pretty it is. They don't test the embryo genetically. It might look like a great embryo but not be able to sustain. Whereas an embryo that doesn't look as good might go on to become a successful pregnancy.'

All being well, and tomorrow's test will help determine that, we can start another cycle at my next period. And transfer one, or maybe two, of the frozen embryos.

But that's twenty-eight days away so we're putting Hope back in her box for now.

We could all do with a rest.

15 October

This week the company Christopher works for presents their show-in-progress, about the experiences of the Spinifex people: the Indigenous Australians who live in the Western Desert. They are the people who were living at Maralinga when the British tested several atomic bombs there in the fifties.

The audience buys their ticket to attend all five shows of the season. Each night they are given a lesson in the Pitjantjatjara language as part of the show.

'*Wai palya?*' the audience is asked as they enter the theatre. Hey you! How are you going?

'*Uwa palya*,' they are taught to respond. Yes, I'm going well.

Once, there were over 500 dialects spoken by the Indigenous population, with about 250 distinct languages. Today, only about forty-eight languages remain intact, many with less than one hundred speakers.

The audience is encouraged to participate in an online language learning program so that next year they will be able to watch the completed show presented entirely in Pitjantjatjara.

This week I have learned to sing the classic children's song 'Heads, Shoulders, Knees and Toes' in Pitjantjatjara. *Kata, Alipiri, Muti, Tjina.*

I have learned the words for water, rock, earth and the place of your birth. I have learned about *Tjukurpa*, which is dreaming and also storytelling.

This week I have also learned that my hormone levels have

finally dropped to an acceptably non-pregnant level.

All done. All clear. All over.

No more pesky pregnancy hormones haunting my system. Start again next cycle.

It's a bittersweet blessing.

Wai palya?

Uwa palya.

I think.

19 October

The Australian Bush is a place of much myth-making. Our films, literature and visual arts are bursting with classic scenarios.

Children become lost in the Australian Bush. Rascals escape there from the long hand of the law and emerge as bushrangers. Victorian schoolgirls in long, pretty white dresses wander about like zombies and are never seen again.

The Australian Bush is full of strange spirits and peculiar beasties. It's alternatively a barren hell hole where explorers and early settlers go to die or a rich fertile Aboriginal All-U-Can-Eat of native foods and bush tucker.

Driving from Melbourne to Adelaide, Christopher and I stop to walk in the Australian Bush. It's spring, and the pamphlet for this area promises wildflowers. Ten minutes into our walk, we find our first orchids. Tiny, orange and gold, delicate lovely things.

'Look,' I point it out to Christopher. 'Isn't it lovely?'

'Hmmm,' says Christopher. 'Yes.'

Then he adds, rather thoughtfully, 'I find orchids to be very ... vulval.'

'Right. Yes,' I say. 'But also, look at the pretty colours.'

Christopher sighs. I have never seen him so moved by nature.

'Something about those ... petals that open and expose themselves like that ...' he murmurs.

For a moment we are silent, contemplating the sensual beauty of the bush. Insects buzz distantly, a gentle breeze wafts against our ruddy cheeks ...

Then Christopher says: 'Orchids are just Genitals on a Stick.'

Thanks to the socks-stuffed-with-marbles ovaries, and the delightful retrieval process and the transfer and the emotional treats that came after, it's been a long time since Christopher and I have been legs up and laughing.

So, what with the tranquil atmosphere and the honey smell of wattle in the air and the fact that it's spring and then those damned sexy orchids, for a moment it looks like we will enact another classic scenario of the Australian Bush, that being the one of Randy Couple Go For it Up Against a Gum Tree.

But a few steps along the track, I screech when I see a rock wallaby with its head ripped off and the stump still bleeding, and a black crow flies overhead cawing in that ominous black crow kind of way, and now we seem to be in that other classic scenario of the Australian Bush, the one where it's also the Home of the Creepy Decapitating Insane Maniac; and the mood is lost.

23 October

Adelaide is wet and cold but my play is hot. It is a fine production. Tonight is opening night and I feel a great surge of emotion as I come out of the theatre. I am happy. And relieved. The words I had set on the page were only words. This group of artists have made it live.

A lot of the audience stay to chat and drink, which is always a good sign. Christopher is grinning proudly and I go to join him, meeting the people he is chatting with and catching the last stages of the conversation.

'Congratulations,' says a girl with a groovy sixties haircut.

'Thanks,' I say. 'I think the company did a fantastic job.'

'Well,' she smiles. 'That's the baby.'

I stare at her. 'Sorry?'

She gestures back towards the theatre.

'That's the baby,' she says. 'You know. All the work that's gone in, the gestation, the delivery. That's the baby.'

Other people in the group nod, knowingly. Christopher and I are blank and speechless. She sees our faces and mistakes our lack of response for misunderstanding.

'I'm not making any sense, I'm sorry,' she laughs. 'It's the vodka. It's a conversation I had earlier and now I'm referring back and it makes no sense. It's okay, I'm going to stop now before I make a complete fool of myself.'

If we weren't quite so tired, I would have rolled with this one a bit more easily. But she's caught me off guard. Is this the baby? I find myself wondering.

Because if it is, it needs to be a really fucking *beautiful* baby, a *huge* baby, the sort that wins awards and tours capital cities and gets picked up by theatre companies overseas.

Even then, I thought, it wouldn't be *enough* baby for me. And anyway, where is it written down that you can't have all the babies you want? Why can't I have *both* babies? The writing sort *and* the sort that vomits down your back?

The next day, after catching up with an old friend from uni, we start to head home. A few hours out of Adelaide we cross the Hay Plain.

This is a huge flat expanse that seems to go on forever. The tallest thing you might pass is an emu. It had been raining in Adelaide and as we left a storm was brewing.

We pass right through the storm and by the time we get to the Hay Plain we are a little way in front of the rain. Because the land is so flat, you can see to the horizon on each side of the road, and the storm clouds have created an enormous bridge. We seem to be driving under the belly of a huge grey beast. And through the clouds burns a brilliant sunset sky.

We brought a stack of CDs with us and are listening to Nick Cave as we make this leg of the trip. We don't talk, we are both quite mesmerized by the clouds and the sky and Nick Cave's dark sexy music turned up loud.

At this moment, an enormous flock of birds surges across the road. We saw them coming from miles away, hundreds and hundreds of long-necked birds wheeling and swooping in formation. Christopher tries to slow as we get closer, many of them have dropped and are flying at car level and I can see many more flying straight at us.

My mouth opens, which might be to gasp or to scream or just in sheer wonder, I'm not sure which, but as Nick Cave sings 'Come sail your ships around me' the birds shift and effortlessly pass overhead in a great rush of black wings and white throats and then they are gone, turning and whirling, patterned across the burning billowing sky.

Christopher and I exhale slowly, painfully, and I realize we have both been holding our breath.

'I think,' I say finally, 'we may have just starred in a Nick Cave film clip.'

27 October

The first attack happened when I was four years old and my sister Amanda was three.

In Penang, circa 1972, a popular family outing involved a stroll through the Monkey Gardens. These were so named for the large hordes of smallish, hairy grey monkeys, with thin red hands and beady eyes, that roamed openly around this pleasant expanse of parklands.

They were free to chitter and play and caper in the trees and simply do what small grey monkeys do best, which is to steal food, masturbate and spread disease.

How we clapped and laughed at their antics.

On this day, as part of our family outing, our parents had endowed us with little bags of hard, dry peanuts with which to tempt our hairy playfellows into providing still more simian tricks.

My four-year-old fist stuffed with peanuts in their shells, I felt heady with the power of largesse.

I have the peanut bag. All monkeys must love and adore me.

I dispensed them sparingly, not wanting to over-value the monkeys' talents and spoil them for the future.

Was that a cartwheel?

Here have a peanut.

Pulling rakishly at your mate's tail and causing an ear-piercing screech?

Two peanuts for you, my friend.

Leaping five feet towards me and baring your fangs in an unpleasant manner?

Take the bag, I want my mummy.

My sister was not so fast. A second fang-baring monkey followed in the wake of the first and jumped up, biting Amanda on the face. That was the end of our family outing. My mother, with baby Toni in her arms, was furious. She complained bitterly to the gatekeepers on our way to the hospital. They were stoic.

These are the Monkey Gardens. Those are the monkeys.

Can you identify the monkey who bit your child?

She could not.

Eight years later, we were back in the Monkey Gardens. This time, there was a new babe-in-pram, Kerry. As we walked, we remembered the attack on Amanda, all those years ago. We laughed gaily as we described how terrifying it had been.

Actually I didn't laugh quite as gaily as all that—those monkeys really were scary.

As a Penang Girl Guide (Patrol Leader, 'Kookaburra') I had now experienced the unique trauma of a 'monkey raid' during a Girl Guides' camping holiday. Along with reef knots, splints and square lashings we were taught that there is no negotiation with monkeys. If they were brazen enough to enter our tents we were to let them take whatever took their fancy. There could be no heroes. Many a can of Impulse Body Spray and jar of instant coffee was lost on that camp.

Amanda was, once again, holding a bag of peanuts and walking in the midst of our family group when the inevitable happened. A large grey monkey came swooping out of the trees to our left. It headed straight for my sister, leapt up and bit her hand.

This time my mother was not so slow.

Dropping the handles of the stroller, she rushed at the monkey, armed with her batik handbag and shouting like a maniac. Lifting the bag, she walloped it hard across the monkey's head. Stunned, the monkey turned a backward somersault and then disappeared back into the trees.

At the time I was full of admiration for my mother's courage and jealous that it hadn't been me who'd caused her outburst. Now I realize that it was simply another illustration of nature at work. Just as the monkey saw food in the peanut bag clutched in my sister's sweaty palm and attacked for it, my mother saw her offspring under threat and attacked in response.

Mothers can be fierce creatures.

This week I learned that Helen, the last of my friends in our tightknit uni group has had her baby boy. Meanwhile, Amanda has finally let my family know about Impending Number 4. I add my own expressions of joy but I can't stop the mean, hard little thought that I wish it was me.

Infertility also has many fierce creatures, so many scrabbling, chittering reasons why my transfer didn't work, why maybe the frozen embryo transfer we'll attempt in November won't work, why maybe none of this crap, Chinese Fertility Goddess included, will *ever* work.

Can you identify the monkey who bit your child?
No.

Time seems to flow effortlessly around us, our friends and family grow and procreate and produce.

Somewhere in that fuzzy grey crowd of beady eyes and reddened hands, in that chattering noisy horde, there might be the reason why Christopher and I aren't parents. But we can't pick it out.

Instead, it feels like we're just standing side by side, getting older, getting tireder.

We're chucking peanuts while the rest of our life seems to walk on by.

30 October

Amanda has had a miscarriage. She rings to tell me and we cry on the phone. There is nothing I can say to help, nothing I can give her.

I am so ashamed that I felt jealous of her and guilty that I wished it was me.

She is devastated.

And so am I.

This is officially the month that sucks.

That is all.

1 November

When did Halloween creep into the Australian psyche?

As a child, for instance, I certainly didn't go from neighbour to neighbour begging for candy and threatening to soap their windows or firebomb their letterboxes if they weren't forthcoming.

I did at various times run wild with my fellow seven-year-old gang members, doing naughty things like knocking on doors and running away (tee hee) or riding my bike through the cemetery (in the daytime, of course), but none of us expected to be rewarded for our hijinks, quite the opposite.

I'm not totally convinced that trick or treating is such a wholesome activity for a stable society anyway. You put on a mask, you knock on a door, neighbour opens said door and is 'scared', you shout your demands at the top of your hyperactive, sugar-stimulated voice, and they hand over the goodies. Then you run away. Aren't we just role playing generations of armed robbers?

Last night Christopher and I took time off from grieving the non-attachment of cellular masses to attend trick or treat with the Naughty Nephews. They had put together their own costumes. Each one had a scary mask to which they added their own special costume flourishes courtesy of the dress-up box.

Naughty Nephew the 1st was a werewolf, for instance, but he also included a garish Hawaiian shirt open at the chest and a rakish straw hat. To up the 'scary' quota, he had his father tie a skull and crossbones flag around his waist. The effect was sort of *Pirates of the Caribbean* meets *Gilligan's Island* in need of a good wax job.

Naughty Nephew the 2nd wore a creepy looking mummy mask but he also wore his Spiderman suit (with built-in padded muscles) and a Spirit of the Sydney Olympics flag as a cape. This is the child who has earned himself a name for peeling off all his clothes in the school playground at the drop of a hat. The mask came off before the first treats had come out, and the cape shortly after.

Naughty Nephew the 3rd began his costume with a lurid green Frankenstein mask and very disconcerting it was to have it roaring unexpectedly somewhere near one's knees. He also wore a green dinosaur tail, a blue pyjama shirt and a crown.

Christopher and I wore shorts and socks with sandals and went as a pair of German backpackers.

Following the paper pumpkins that were stuck on letterboxes up and down the street, the children began their quest for chocolate, sugar and a range of chemical preservatives known only by their numbers. The adults trailed alongside, discussing the outrageous prices of whole pumpkins this week, pretending to be scared when the knee-high Frankenstein let out a roar, and eating mini Flake chocolate bars.

Before too long, anyone over the age of twelve was rendered obsolete. Once they understood the routine the children were off, filling their bags, snatching up more and more, running breathlessly from one pumpkin to the next and shrieking 'Trick or treat!!' at the top of their voices.

It was all the parents could do to hover by the gates and call 'What do you say?' and 'Have you said thankyou?'

As the hordes neared the house of the Naughty Nephews, Christopher and I were sent inside with the basket of lollies.

Foolishly, we were lolling around in the dining room, not camped on the doorstep, because as the heaving mob reached the front door and roared 'TRICK OR TREAT' we weren't quite fast enough and they poured in through the open door and began to *run* down the hallway towards us. It was like Day One of the Myer half-yearly sales in ladies' lingerie, and we didn't have a flashing red light.

Stop, we shouted. Line up. One at a time. Say thankyou. One per person.

Tiny, and not so tiny, arms jabbed away at the basket, voices behind latex masks jabbered and growled unintelligibly. They may have said thankyou but they may also have said 'Your costumes suck big time'.

Later, we sat out on the street with the grown-ups and discussed all the fun stuff we used to do as kids.

In our childhoods, those halcyon days of Australian suburbia, we ran wild and unsupervised, we rode our bikes in the cemetery or for miles along the river and everyone grew pumpkins and chokos in their backyards. Summers were hot (but not as hot as they are now), Paddle Pops were larger and policemen were friendly.

They were the good old days. Before stranger danger or razorblades in apples. You could roam the streets, knocking on doors and running away, any day of the year. Flake chocolate bars actually tasted of chocolate and really *did* flake, and German backpackers were safe to hitchhike here and there across this wide brown land.

It was *all* treat back then, we decided as we watched the first Halloween casualties begin to limp home with cut feet or bruised arms or fingers that had been caught in doors.

All treat.

7 November

One of my friends tells a story of taking her niece on a roller-coaster ride at the Newcastle Show fairly soon after having eaten a steak sandwich.

The niece held up well but my friend didn't. Halfway up (or down) she felt the imminent return of the steak sandwich, which she captured neatly in her new leather handbag.

I was impressed at her sense of civic responsibility. She was willing to sacrifice the handbag rather than spray her niece and various passers-by with her stomach contents.

As Day 1 of my cycle looms it's time for Christopher and I to get our tickets, once again, for the Great Big Fertility Ride.

This time, we won't be riding up front in the shiny new IVF carriage. Instead, we're strapping ourselves into the Frozen Embryo Transfer carriage. It's slightly dented, the paintwork's scratched and there's the unmistakeable whiff of previous failure in the air, but hey, at least we got a seat.

This time round, it's a 'natural' cycle (which makes me laugh hysterically, because when was the last time any of this felt 'natural'?) so I am spared the evils of the Lucrin syringe or the Puregon pen.

I will, however, be inserting progesterone pessaries to help any possible sniff of pregnancy along. Obviously I'm looking forward to these. As a child, one is always told not to stick foreign objects up your nose (baked bean anyone?) or in your ears and certainly not up your botty. No longer! Infertility is like revenge against the Sticking Things in Your Body is Bad brigade.

It seems weird to be hopping aboard once more. The crushing disappointment from our IVF cycle is still with me, shimmering below the surface. I'm trying to ignore the fearful voices that whisper to me, telling me our embryos are crap and my womb a toxic cesspit.

Just before our ride takes off, the door opens again and a familiar figure squeezes in. It's Hope. She's got a big cheesy smile as she tells us This Could be the One!

We nod and smile, warily. The mechanism starts up and our carriage starts to move. Hope gives an excited belch. Steak sandwich.

As we start our first dip, I grip my leather handbag.

If Hope hurls I know who's going to have to catch every drop.

13 November

And then, there are some days when being an aunty is almost enough.

It was bath time and Naughty Nephew the 3rd, aged three, he of the blue saucer eyes and the baby chicken fluff hair, insisted he was *perfectly capable* of undressing himself.

Alrighty, we said.

He took off his T-shirt the conventional way, then decided that he would remove his pants by running from the lounge to the front door and back, to try to make them fall down around his ankles.

When this method seemed a little slow he decided it would be better to jump up and down on the spot.

He was right, but it was even better when he decided to pop some Jumping Up and Down Till My Pants Drop music on the electric keyboard. This turned out to be the junior piano classic 'Für Elise'.

Naughty Nephew the 3rd adjusted the tempo till it sounded as if it was being played by the Chipmunks on speed and then he jumped and jumped like all the chickens in hell were pecking at his heels.

And *then* those pants came down!

16 November

Because nobody can ever have enough fertility magic crap, I bought my friend Fiona a very small, very cheap and slightly nasty 'Quan-Yin With Child' statue.

This uniquely precious piece, carved from solid purple plastic, caught my eye among the Lucky Sumo Toads and the Laughing Buddhas.

Quan-Yin is the Goddess of Mercy. When not being merciful she has a sideline in facilitating childbirth (hence the child).

According to the printed material that came with my extravagant gift to Fi, Quan-Yin is also famous for halting evil thoughts and wicked intentions in dreams.

This is how I know that Quan-Yin and I can never really be friends, because my dreams are rife with wicked intentions and my thoughts are evil to the power of a million. I am constantly cursing people who park outside our flat, for instance, forcing me to park all the way down the road. The selfish bastards gather after working hours to frequent the pub nearby. Damn them for having regular leisure time and the ability to drink alcohol. As I struggle back up the hill I note all the cars that don't have 'resident' stickers on them (which would rightfully entitle them to steal my space) and then I project evilness upon them.

Of course, by the time I reach our letterbox I am not only exhausted, I am smitten with guilt and feebly try to retract all curses and hexes. It's one of the daily difficulties of being both Catholic and Irritable.

Anyhoo, Fiona and I had a very lovely brunch. We don't catch up that often, living in separate cities and all.

Fiona is going through that delightful sphere of IVF hell known as endometriosis, with all the pain and horror that includes. Following her own IVF roller-coaster ride, she is now kicking her feet against the carriage bars and carving her name in the seats with a box cutter while she does her two-week wait.

Over our matching non-caffeinated beverages, Fiona opened the sparkly wrapping paper and we exclaimed delightedly at both the quality of Quan-Yin's purple plastic and the ugliness of the babe in her arms.

'Gee thanks,' she said.

'You are so welcome,' I said. 'And if the bitch doesn't work, let's torch her.'

Yesterday, Fiona sent me an email. In it she said:

> *Two things I'll bet you didn't know about Quan-Yin:*
> *Thing one—if you accidentally go to sleep with her in your hand you will then wake up four or five hours later going 'What the hell is this thing stuck to my cheek?' She leaves quite a lasting impression.*
>
> *Thing two—she glows in the dark!!! Yessiree—what excellent forethought on the part of the plastic carving artisans. You are never groping around in the dark for her because she lights up like a beacon ...*

I am delighted. Glows in the dark *and* adheres to cheek? Truly the gift that keeps on giving.

And finally, in Frozen Embryo Transfer News, this time we're going for TWO. That's *two* embryos to be invited to take up residency in my uterus. Doctor Who has decreed that from here on it will be blood tests each day, with an occasional sprinkle of Dildo-Cam magic, until ovulation.

Five days later it'll be transfer time, also known as Squirty up the Clacker Day. And I'm not arguing with that.

Even though we should know better, Christopher and I are excited.

In fact, it's the kind of excitement that would normally demand that SUTCD be made a public holiday except I just *know* the non-working, beer-swilling bastards would be parked outside my flat all frigging day.

19 November

I think I may be suffering withdrawal symptoms.

My fingers keep straying wistfully to my stomach to pinch an inch. I look through my stash of unused needles, peer through the contents of my Puregon showbag. Yesterday I felt a distinct urge to shoot up 10 units of Lucrin straight into that fatty belly tissue.

Me, who prior to starting an IVF cycle was scared of needles.

Even as I write this I am imagining the injection spot, the cool shock of the alcohol wipe, the strange plunging sensation of the needle, the sting as it withdraws, leaving a bead of liquid shimmering on my skin.

Instead I get my fix of steely penetration from the daily blood tests I have at the House of Groovy Love while they monitor my cycle.

On Thursday I was told that my hormone levels are not rising 'as expected'.

What should they be? I asked the Fertility Sister.

'Well,' she said diplomatically, 'it's still a rise so that's fine, but some people do double.'

Ah. The old doubling trick again. Some people do double. The pregnant ones, for instance.

That was the trouble with our last cycle. I didn't double there either.

I imagined being told our cycle wasn't up to it. That I wasn't going to ovulate by myself. That we would have to wait till the next cycle. And start the whole thing all over again.

Yesterday, I was so busy wistfully clicking on my Puregon pen I missed a phone call. It was Patchouli from the House of Groovy Love.

'Good news,' she said on the voicemail. 'Your levels have risen.' She added, a little coyly, 'We expect to see what we're looking for tomorrow.'

Assuming she's not talking about a cure for bird 'flu, that means ovulation this weekend. And Squirty up the Clacker Day sometime around Thursday.

Maybe I'm just a late doubler, I thought.

I realized I wasn't really jonesing for Lucrin after all. It was actually the sense of control I had been addicted to. And the fear that, left to our own 'natural' devices, we couldn't come up with the goods.

The thing is, Christopher and I are actually great at doubling. We double just fine. It's the addition part we seem to be flunking.

21 November

Once, in Newcastle, I shared a house with a cat called Toby who was a known Malicious Shitter. He was fluffy and cute and light on his feet but he was also bitter, demanding and horribly judgmental. When a new housemate failed to pay homage to Toby in the manner to which he was accustomed, the cat promptly crapped on his bed. A little combined *Happy Housewarming* and *Screw You* gift from the furry one.

I myself once owned a cat that turned out to be a Malicious Ejaculator. On the day I moved out of a shared household in unhappy circumstances, he made a very efficient statement of our mutual displeasure on the doona of the flatmate who replaced me.

Obviously, I was horrified and apologetic but I think I can honestly say now, in the fullness of time and with my advanced maturity: 'Ha ha, serves you right, my cat spoofed on your bed.'

Until last year, Christopher and I shared a house with Dougal, an otherwise lovely dog, who was not a Malicious Farter per se, but *was* arguably a Farter with Intent.

Early on in the relationship a friend came to visit the house. As he waited at the door, both Dougal and I went bounding up the hallway to greet him. When we reached him I called out my customary greeting and Dougal let out his. It wasn't until we were later having coffee and Dougal again chimed into the conversation that Peter sniffed and then admitted he had thought it was me at the door.

'It's not that bad,' he added, 'I actually thought it was nice that you felt so comfortable around me.'

This morning at the breakfast table as Christopher and I ate our porridge, one of us let rip with an absolute corker. There was a small pause and then the non-farter said: 'Do you think you'll do that when our children are sitting at the table?'

The farter thought a moment and then said: 'I shall do it until they are old enough to speak. And then I shall tell them that there will be no farting at the table.'

Potentially, that rule could come into effect in about ... oh, say, 3 years and 9 months.

Ovulation was on Sunday. Transfer is this Friday.

Eek. Christopher and I are hoping with every fibre of our digestive systems.

14 November

When I picked up my progesterone pessaries from the pharmacy I saw they were individually foil wrapped.

'Ooh. They're like little chocolates,' I said.

The pharmacist looked at me sharply. 'Did they tell you how to use these?'

'Oh yes,' I said.

'And you know,' he added, slowly and clearly, 'You have to take them out of the wrapping first.'

I stared at him. He was serious.

'Yeees,' I said. 'I do know. I learned that lesson with tampons.'

My second-last blood test at the House of Groovy Love was administered by Rainbow, a delightful Scottish girl.

'And hoo many embryos are ye transferring,' she asked in her delightful lilting accent.

'Two,' I said.

'Oookay, so we'll thaw tiltoo and let you knoo,' she said, smiling. 'Ookay?'

'Okay,' I said. 'Actually, no ... can you just repeat that?'

'We'll thaw tiltoo,' she said again, a little slower this time for the half-wit Australian. 'Ookay?'

'Yeeess,' I said. I wanted it to be ookay, God knows I did, but I had no idea what she was saying. It was as if she was speaking a whole new language. I screwed up my face and shook my head.

'No. I'm sorry. Can you just explain? What is "tiltoo"? Is that a thawing procedure?'

'You want two,' she said patiently. 'And so, we keep thawing until we get them.'

'Oh,' I said. Understanding began to flow like hot gravy into my brain. I half closed my eyes as I translated her words out loud: 'So ... you will ... thaw them ... until there are ... two ... remaining embryos that are able to be ... transferred?'

There was a pause. She looked at me as if I really was the imbecile I sounded.

'Yes,' she said. 'Till two.'

Tomorrow is the transfer. Tomorrow we see just how fast the Frozen Embryo Transfer carriage on the Great Big Fertility Ride can go.

I'm getting that churning feeling in my stomach as I think about it. It's the excitement you get when you don't want to get excited. It's the nausea caused by that enticing infertility cocktail of fear, hope, dread and faith.

That here we go again, bloody hell I hope this works ookay this time feeling.

It's very similar to the feeling caused by eating a steak sandwich before you get on a rickety Newcastle Show rollercoaster with your niece.

Or swallowing a delicious fistful of progesterone pessaries. Foil and all.

27 November

It is a truth universally acknowledged, that a woman in possession of a good embryo must be in want of an effective shortcut through the city.

On the day of transfer this effective shortcut is not forthcoming.

Many coarse and unpleasant words are spoken during this stressful and painfully slow journey and many calming and soothing noises are made by Christopher in a vain attempt to calm me down as I try to shout out the window: 'Out of our way, *bastards.*'

At one point of complete stasis, I open the car door and step onto the road to try to see just what is holding up traffic and if I can use the laser-burning powers of my Furiously Unimpressed Stare to melt a pathway through. I can't see what the hold-up is but

Legs up & laughing

the staring seems to work because finally we're on our way.

The first part of this transfer is meant to start with the Chinese Fertility Goddess, which is where we are headed now, on our way to the House of Groovy Love. Last time she had been gallivanting on a holiday somewhere, so this time I am determined to take full advantage of her presence. This means acupuncture both immediately before *and* after the transfer.

As soon as we arrive I am ushered straight up the stairs and onto a bed, no appointment, no waiting. I realize that this must be what it is like to be famous, or else to have private hospital insurance. The Chinese Fertility Goddess is lovely and, as if sensing the traffic horrors of the previous half-hour, she rams a pair of needles straight into my fists to calm me down.

Does it work? Well I suppose so. I do know that by the time I walk out I have stopped abusing other motorists and that can only be a good thing.

Christopher drops me at the House of Groovy Love, a mere three minutes late, and goes to park the car. And soon, very soon, my pants are off, my backless gown and terry-towelling dressing-gown are on and my blue disposable booties are in place.

The doctor who will be doing the squirty business is not our actual doctor, Doctor Who, but perhaps this is best. We had seen Doctor Who for a grand total of twenty minutes, during our initial consultation. Every now and then we've received instructions from on high, passed down to us by the Fertility Sisters. Was he overloaded with patients? Was he taking the Tardis for a spin? Whatever. If he actually materializes now I may faint with shock.

Instead, this time we have Doctor Lovely Accent who was originally the Chinese Fertility Goddess's top tip for best Sydney IVF doctor.

When I spoke to a Fertility Sister last week and she told me that I would be having Doctor Lovely Accent instead of Doctor Who I said 'Oh goody, I hear great things about him.'

'Yes,' said the sister, 'and it's all true.'

With Christopher back from parking the car, I am soon in the chair, legs up and waiting.

It begins, as ever, with a quick visit from the Dildo-Cam—we exchange some pleasantries, I ask how business is going, he says he's looking forward to the Christmas break and by the way my uterine lining is looking good.

Doctor Lovely Accent measures my cervix, which, he says, will assist him in knowing where to place the embryos. And, speak of the devil, up they pop on the screen before us. Christopher and I clutch hands and become ridiculously moist eyed.

It turns out that in the process of thawing 'tiltoo' one embryo curled up its cells that might one day be toes and bit the dust. Of the two that made it, one is starting to do whatever that thing is that non-frozen embryos do and the other is obviously still feeling the cold, because it is miserably hunched over itself and telling anyone who will listen to turn the bloody heater up.

Speculum in place, syringe carrying embryos is brought over and all too soon Squirty up the Clacker Day is officially over for me, specifically the part that involves squirting and clackers.

Back we go to the Chinese Fertility Goddess. Mercifully the traffic has eased. This time, not only do I get to go straight upstairs and lie on a bed, the CFG comes out of the consultation she was doing to swiftly apply pins, give encouragement and offer bowls of M&Ms with all the brown ones taken out (slight exaggeration). I sleep for an hour and then Christopher drives me home and I sleep some more.

Just before he'd finished, Doctor Lovely Accent had popped the Dildo-Cam back in. 'Look,' he said, 'there are your two embryos. Or at least the air bubbles beside them.'

There they were, two bright stars in the dark skies of my uterus.

'Go little guys,' I muttered.

And so we begin again. The waiting time. The hoping time. The dreaming time.

I drink my Horrid Teas and swallow my folic acid and slide my progesterone pessaries in and try not to dwell on what may or may not be.

Black thoughts pop up, negative words sound in my ears, fear and grief and depression raise their ugly heads. I grit my teeth and floor the accelerator and shout as we bravely hurtle towards them.

Out of our way, bastards.

29 November

Even with several days to go before the pregnancy test, Christopher and I have started talking about the Twins.

We do this because we are stupid. And greedy.

And also, because we are basically optimistic people, or at least Christopher is and he's managed to infect me with his contagious happy talk. And we do it because without some hope, some small confidence that *this time* it might work, we couldn't go on.

I'm swallowing red ginseng capsules and drinking Horrid Teas day and night. With the night tea I add two spoons from the deer antler soup that looks like thin honey and smells like wet dog.

I don't drink alcohol, I don't drink coffee. Some days, especially those when I can't think of what to write, when words seem as far away to me as babies, I could kill for one cup of pitch black espresso with that crema stuff on top. But I don't have one, not even one, because I'm still hoping.

Denial is such a big part of the babymaking spell. It's as if the more I deny myself the more I deserve to have a baby. I suspect this is my Catholic upbringing. Either that or my eldest child status.

Yesterday I felt sick all day.

No, not sick, more like very slightly hungover or very slightly carsick.

Don't think about it, I told myself. Forget about it.

And so I did. In fact, I managed to do such a good job of

forgetting that I went grocery shopping and then carried the bags home. It wasn't until I was climbing the stairs to our flat that I thought *'Goddamn,* these bags are heavy ...'

Swiftly followed by 'Oh. I'm not meant to carry heavy things. *Bugger.'*

I'm hoping that my genetic make-up—generations of Filipino peasants tending paddy fields—will stand me in good stead here.

PEASANT 1: Ah Maria-Conceptionata, what a good day it is to be planting rice. We work hard from dawn to dusk and yet the mud is cool to my feet, the sun beats down upon our cunningly woven rattan hats.

PEASANT 2: So true, Maria-Immaculata. Life is hard, but I do enjoy watching the water buffaloes gambol and play. Also, I'm about to give birth. Also, we're having fish for lunch.

Gentle splashing sounds as the women move along the row.
Sun shines. Baby born. Rice grows. Fish for lunch.

(As I type this I am listening to the soundtrack of *Amelie*. It's all hopeful chords and wistful melody. I'm feeling waves of yesterday's mini hangover. And now that damn piano accordion is making me cry. Dear God I want a coffee. And a baby. But not in that order.)

LOVING THE CYNIC WITHIN

The invitation described the event as a 'pagan wedding' with the added exhortation to 'please wear fancy dress!'

They were innocent words in themselves but somehow, as I peered at the accompanying happy snap of the bride-and-groom-to-blessed-be snuggling by a rose bush, they sent me into a spasm of rage.

'Why pagan?' I stormed at Christopher. 'And why, for Goddess's sake, must it be fancy dress? There's only one person who should wear fancy dress to a wedding. We call that person a bride.'

It wasn't just the principle of the thing. I'd had plenty of experience strolling the highways and byways of the Sydney Royal Easter Show in a variety of animal and vegetable costumes. In those days, I didn't do it for my social life.

My righteous anger didn't subside when I noted that there was no actual theme to the fancy-dress pagan wedding.

Guests weren't being asked to appear 'skyclad', for instance, or 'to come as your favourite chakra'. Instead, in curly handwriting, was the cheerful addendum 'Your choice!'

Moreover, they didn't want presents, they wanted people to 'donate to a charity—any charity, your choice!' the invitation blithely chirped.

'So ... what, we can donate to the Sceptics' Society?' I railed. 'Or how about the We Hate Pagans Retirement Fund?'

The lack of specificity towards dress code or charity seemed certain proof of a lackadaisical attitude towards marriage.

'Do they actually want to get married?' I frothed. 'I mean ... maybe the invite should say "You are invited to ... a Saturday in the park. We may even get married! Your choice!"'

It seemed to me that not an original thought had gone into the entire event. It was as if the prospective bride and groom got drunk one night, randomly tore pages out of their Wedding Cliché book and then pasted them together with their own saliva into a ceremony. Pagan, sure, eight years ago maybe, but now every man, womyn and their labradoodle dances widdershins under the full moon.

The location was a popular spot for barbecues, picnics and, you guessed it, weddings. And the fancy dress (your choice!) and the donate to charity (your choice!), while sounding wonderfully free and unfettered by convention really meant NO SHOPPING and where was the fun in that?

'Actually,' Christopher chimed in, 'you can give them a present.'
'Really?' I brightened.
'Yes,' said Christopher. 'It says here they'll also accept a bottle of either single malt whiskey or champagne. Your choice.'

A few days later I got a call from the groom. 'Did you get our invitation?' he asked.

'Oh ... yes, it looks terrific, we can't wait,' I lied.

'That's wonderful,' the gβroom enthused. 'And ... we'd really really love it if you would read something at our ceremony.'

I choked. And then accepted. It was a manners thing.

'But that's okay,' said Christopher. 'It will probably be "your choice"'. He was packing his suitcase as he spoke; sadly, due to business, he would be unable to make the fancy-dress-pagan-whiskey-charity wedding. I was going alone.

'It is not,' I informed him, tight-lipped, 'my choice. It is instead Kahlil Gibran's The Hackneyed ... *I mean,* The Prophet.*'*

'At least you'll find that on the internet,' said Christopher. 'No awkward searching through bookshops.'

'That's right,' I sourly agreed. 'In fact, I can probably just read it straight off a tea towel.'

I spent the morning of the fancy-dress-pagan-whiskey-charity wedding worrying about what to wear. Standing naked in front of my wardrobe, I gritted my teeth while trying to cobble together something that could be considered both suitable for a wedding and also 'fancy dress'.

I thought wistfully of my glory days as Mrs Merino, star of the Royal Easter Show and perfectly dressed for a garden wedding with her trimmed straw hat, her pink stripy Beatrix Potter dress and her rubber hooves, but she was long gone to the wardrobe department in the sky.

Instead, I phoned a friend. He advised me to wear my stripy black and white shirt and beret and go as a Parisian.

It is a mark of my desperation that I actually agreed this was a good idea. I could even buy a baguette while I was at the shops picking up 'my choice' of a bottle of alcohol. This was fine until I realized I couldn't find my beret and my stripy shirt was filthy. Suddenly it all began to seem like a waste of good bread. I became more and more irritable as I walked home with a bottle of scotch under my arm.

Eventually I put on a nice dress and a hat and called a cab. I decided that if anyone asked I would say that my dress was clean which was fancy in my books.

I arrived at the gardens with my worst fears realized.

I knew no one.

The designated wedding area was filling up with Jane Austenish looking lords and ladies in bonnets and frockcoats who turned out to be the bride's family. Most of the groom's family seemed to be dressed as extras from a Blues Brothers film.

Distantly, I spied the happy couple. The groom was wearing something shiny and futuristic and the bride was dressed as Marilyn Monroe.

For no apparent reason, both were also wearing crowns.

I stood under a tree for a moment feeling like a complete dick, even though I wasn't one of those guests dressed as a giant frog or Felix the Cat. Fred and Wilma Flintstone strolled past, champagne in hand, followed by Robin Hood and a couple of Merry Men.

This deeply disturbing moment was broken by the groom waving me over with a robotic clink.

I was introduced to Mystery Cornflowers, the pagan celebrant. She wore a flowing lady of the lake type frock, although I noted that in a concession to the marshy grounds she was also wearing sensible lace-up shoes.

Mystery smiled and shook my hand. For such a wafty name she had a firm grip.

'It's marvellous that you're reading,' she announced. 'You can also help me by holding my Booke of Magick.'

I attempted to take a step back but her piercing green eyes had locked me in a psychic tractor beam.

'I've got so many rituals to get through,' she confided. 'Of course, I know most of them but sometimes I get a little confused. It would be a big help.'

'Where should I wait?' I asked, with some misgivings.

'Here,' she said. 'Next to me. In the Magic Circle.'

My misgivings, like an evil hex, increased sevenfold.

As Mystery sprinkled flowers to mark out the Magic Circle she explained that it would become a sacred space containing only her, the bride, the groom and me. Then she handed me a large twiggy broom.

Biting back the horror, I said, 'Actually ... I think this sounds like a very special job—perhaps one of the bride's sisters would like to join the circle?' The bride shook her head. 'You do it,' she said, 'and then they won't fight about it.'

The ceremony began and the guests began to gather. As the bride and groom entered I was instructed to close the circle off with my broom. This was to ensure the energy was held within the circle and also to allow me briefly to pretend to be a member of the Gryffindor Quidditch team.

Mystery Cornflowers pasted a beatific smile of great peace and compassion upon her face and spread her arms to encourage the audience to come closer and feel the power of the Magic Circle, while also being careful not to tread upon it.

Holding aloft the Booke, I took my cues from Mystery and turned to the east, west, north and south, intoning 'Blessed Be' with every quarter spin.

I helped hand out chunks of cake so that the bride and groom could feed it into each other's mouths, I passed over lengths of ribbon so that their hands could be tied together in an expression of their mutual love of S&M or commitment, I forget which.

Hell, I thought to myself, is other people's weddings. But this was a special sort of Hell.

And none of it was my choice.

This morning I woke up and realized that I don't believe in babies.

Or at least, I don't believe in mine.

One of the biggest problems with all this infertility malarkey is that a major side effect, unlisted on any instruction sheet, is extreme cynicism.

Even though I have seen my embryo up on a screen, heard the encouraging words of doctor and scientist, clutched at Christopher's hand and whispered hopefully, the truth is that now, four days after transfer, I feel about as pregnant as a bucket.

As each day of the dreaded two-week wait goes by, it brings me closer to the moment of truth and it seems impossible that this moment can be anything but disappointing.

Back at the fancy-dress-pagan-whiskey-charity wedding, my moment of truth came when it was my turn to read.

Must not sound bitter, I told myself sternly. Must be professional and not let nasty cynical attitude seep into blissful marital universe.

I unfolded my tea towel (no, not really), cleared my throat and began, 'Let there be spaces in your togetherness ...'

As I read on, maintaining my patented Mystery Cornflower's beatific smile, I happened to look towards the bride and groom. They were standing facing each other but as I glanced towards them they both looked up and smiled at me, utterly radiant with happiness. They were so obviously and completely in love, it took my breath away. To my shock, I promptly got a catch in my throat and had a little involuntary sob, mid-word. The audience sighed and smiled kindly at me.

Well there you go, I couldn't help thinking as the tears began to well. Serves you right for being such a mean, cynical bitch.

As the ceremony continued, I looked around the Magic Circle at the guests. The Blues Brothers were weeping black mascara behind their dark sunglasses. Felix the Cat had raised his pipe cleaner whiskers so he could blow his nose. Fred and Wilma and the Jane Austen crowd all smiled beatifically back and I realized that I had been mistaken. Love was the choice all along. Wherever it's celebrated. However it's dressed.

In all its pagan worshipping, multi-clichéd glory.

Blessed be.

2 December

Letter to two bunches of cells seven days past transfer

Dear Embryos,

I've been thinking about you both quite a lot and wondering how it's all going in there.

You've probably noticed that you're not the first to occupy the place. Maybe you even had a bitch among yourselves about being given a used uterus.

The truth is, one of your little mates was in there a couple of months ago. I haven't been in to look myself and nothing's shown up on the Dildo-Cam, but I wouldn't be surprised if he did a bit of tagging round the cervix, a little graffiti by the fallopian tubes. *Embryo Was 'Ere*, that sort of thing. Frankly, I think he was that kind of blastocyst.

But let me assure you both, THE LINING HAS NEVER BEEN USED. I grew that one especially for you.

And anyway, it really wasn't occupied for long.

Embryo 1 decided not to stay. Not immediately. There was a little pfaffing in the womb, a little lounging around the Pink Palace before he finally jumped the fence.

It was enough to leave the faintest hopeful glimmer of a maybe possibility of a pregnancy.

(You embryos can be a little cruel, anyone ever tell you that in the Petri dish?)

I'm not going to come down all heavy, even though I want nothing more than to grab you both in a headlock and staple you to the wall of my uterus. It's important to let you embryos make up your own little minds (or whatever rudimentary cellular brain smudges you've formed) about whether you're going to hang on.

And I'm not going to bang on about keeping away from the fence because look what a fat lot of good it did with Embryo 1.

Instead, I thought I'd encourage you by telling you that a big exciting bonus about sticking around and actually being born is ... meeting your dad. I'm pretty sure you'll think he's the best thing since ... well, since that new jello stuff the House of Groovy Love developed to grow you little guys in, and you know how good that stuff is, right?

He's gorgeous and talented and caring and he's such good fun to play with, ask your cousins the Naughty Nephews.

And I love him more than anybody else in this whole world ... for now.

Here's a little something that no one else knows about your dad.

His head smells like rice pudding with cinnamon on top. True.

And sometimes, like apricots.

And very *very* occasionally like parmesan cheese but mostly it's rice pudding and that's one of my favourite smells in all the world.

And if you come into the world, and I really hope you do, he'll let you smell his head whenever you like. I think I can speak for him on that one. I'm not sure about the rules on watching TV or spitting from the top floor of posh hotels, but the rice pudding head-smelling I think we can say is in the bag.

It might even be genetic, so along with his blue eyes and my brown skin, you could get a scalp that smells like a classic English nursery dessert.

It's your dad's birthday today. The very first present I ever gave him was a stovetop coffee pot. Wouldn't it be cool if this year we gave him the biggest present ever ...

So just mull it over, okay? Think about your gorgeous dad, with his blue eyes and his rice pudding head, who can't wait to hold you and love you and play cricket with you.

That's all I ask.

Well that, and keep away from the fence.

Yours, with ridiculous amounts of love as always,

Vanessa
xxx

5 December

Things you might do during a two-week wait:

You might make a list of jobs that need doing before Christmas.

Sadly you will only make this list in your head and you will only ever recall the entire list once when you are lying in bed and can't be arsed getting up to write it down.

For the rest of the Two-week Waiting Period you will be haunted by vague memories of the List as you determine to put things on and cross things off.

You might decide to get a haircut.

This is because you are attending a wedding on the weekend and you are sick of pulling your hair back into a boring ponytail and exposing your spotty forehead to the world. But on the morning of the wedding you may wake up and go: 'Bugger, I forgot to book that appointment.' But then later, genius may strike you!

'Look, here in the shopping centre is one of those very cheap, very nasty, no booking places! All the hair cutters are standing about waiting for hair to cut. And here I am, practically standing in the doorway and I'VE GOT HAIR.'

Later you will emerge with your hair strangely layered and your fringe reshaped and a lurking suspicion that it's not really a very good cut at all. You will attend the wedding with your hair pulled back in a boring ponytail exposing your spotty forehead to the world.

This will be a lesson learned.

You might tell your sister-in-law that you intend making an entire nativity set using papier-mâché and roll-on deodorant bottles.

To your surprise she may hand you a bag of washed empty roll-on deodorant bottles which she has collected because she is a mother of three children and they Do Craft.

Now you are stuck with this task because you will look like a wally if you hand back the bag of washed empty roll-on deodorant bottles and you would feel guilty if you just shoved them into a recycling bin.

During your Two-Week Waiting Period you might choose to start the Roll-On Deodorant Nativity Set. You might sculpt your Christmas artworks on newspaper so as to avoid mess.

But then a breeze may blow through your flat and in a panic you may be forced to grab precious ornaments to weigh the newspaper down. This will lead to precious ornaments being streaked with flour and water which dries with a cement-like consistency. This will be irritating because cleaning them will be another job to add to the List.

A quick and clever fix, however, will be to put the precious ornaments somewhere people won't see them, like in that spot behind the bookcase.

You might spend long periods of time staring at your nipples in the mirror.

This is a natural thing to do, as you are wondering if they are changing in any way to indicate pregnancy.

Then you might decide your boobs are sagging. Then you might start holding a breast in each hand and wiggle them up and down, pretending your nipples are eyes and your bellybutton is a mouth and it can talk to you. Then you will stop because this is *not* natural, it's just stupid.

You might read that pineapple is good for implantation.

Immediately you will dash out to the fruit shop. However, there will be two kinds of pineapple available and you will spend half an hour weighing them up in each hand and wondering which is best for the embryos.

Unluckily, a fruit-shop man will hear you muttering to yourself about pineapple and embryos, but on the bright side the sheer embarrassment will encourage you to make an immediate choice.

Your sister might ring from New Zealand and chat while you both wait for the phone call from the clinic.

As you chat together she will mention that pregnant women have higher body temperatures. Inspired, you may get your digital thermometer and shove it in your mouth. Similarly inspired, your sister will get *her* thermometer and shove it in her ear.

Strangely, your conversation will flow unimpaired.

You might get a shock when you go in for your blood test and the Fertility Sister asks if this your 'final' blood test.

You may wonder if she means your credit card has been declined or if all the Sisters got together and decided they hate you and your husband with his rice pudding head and they never want to take your blood again.

On your way home you and your husband might feel moved to hug and embrace a large piece of public art because it reminds you of a pair of enormous ovaries and hence it could be lucky.

You will need to do this surreptitiously, because the artwork is in a public space surrounded by offices. This will make you feel like Harry Potter trying to run through the wall at Kings Cross station without anyone noticing. Except, of course, you will not be carrying an owl.

6 December

Letter from two bunches of cells on the day of the pregnancy test

> dear vanessa,
>
> got your letter.
> have decided to stay.
>
> > love, us.
> > ps. when we say 'us', that might mean just 'me' in which case i'll love you twice as much.

7 December

Can one be hysterically calm?

When the Fertility Sister calls and tells me that I am definitely pregnant I thank her politely, but then find my voice shaking and wobbling when I ask her to confirm the beta.

Four hundred and ninety? That's substantially more than 8, I think. And then I catch hold of Christopher and tell him the news and after that there are not many words either of us can say, either hysterically or calmly.

With a great screech of brakes and clunking of gears the Great Big Fertility Ride pulls in at the station. Christopher and I gingerly step out of the carriage. Hope's already brushed off the vomit and darted off to climb into someone else's carriage and start the ride all over again. She's such a roller-coaster tart.

We feel exhausted.

We feel incredulous.

We feel very very lucky.

It's the earliest of early days but to get to this point, for us who have never ever been pregnant, seems an incredible achievement.

Christopher and I stagger shakily past the ticket booth and make our way towards the exit. In the background I can hear the crazy music start up again, the gears clunk into place, the doors on the carriages slam shut, the babble of excited voices.

I'd like to watch, wave them on their way, maybe buy a Cheese-on-a-Stick for old time's sake but then I remember that Roll-On Deodorant Nativity Scene isn't going to papier-mâché itself and so we hurry on home.

11 December

Bogong moths live in caves in the mountains for most of the year. They're small and dark brown and apparently are chock-full of protein with a delicate nutty flavour. Now and then you see them braving it in the big city, dashing themselves against car headlights or street lamps.

One year, they all went absolutely ape shit and every single Bogong Moth in the Known Universe came to Sydney. Like some sort of evil entomological Schoolies' Week, they came, they bonked themselves stupid and they made a big bloody pest of themselves.

One evening, they started flying into my flat. I hurriedly closed the windows but then they started crawling in through the ventilation shafts. There were hundreds of them.

At first I tried to scoop them up and throw them out the back door but soon the whirring noises and the furry wings and the way their feelers poked through the slats first, closely followed by their brown bogongish heads, began to freak me out and I turned on the vacuum cleaner and began sucking them straight off the wall.

Vacuuming up live bogong moths is not something I'm proud of and it would never have happened if Christopher had been home, because he is like Saint Francis of Assisi to invertebrates and what he can't catch with an empty yoghurt pot and a piece of cardboard isn't worth catching. In fact, it's probably not an insect at all, it's probably a piece of cheese or a raisin or something.

The joy at learning that I had finally been struck over the head with the preggers stick lasted for about forty-eight hours and then the Niggling Doubts started creeping in.

I tried to shut them out, I tried to say to myself … *feel the queasiness … witness the extreme fatigue* … but eventually they won.

Why should you be pregnant? The beta was wrong. It's like last time when you were pregnant for a minute and a half. This time you'll be pregnant for an hour and a half but it'll still end the same way … ooh, what's that? Your period??

On the weekend I gave in and called the House of Groovy Love.

'I'd like to come in for another blood test,' I told them. 'I got my beta last week and it all sounded very good but now …'

The Fertility Sister was calm. 'Of course,' she said, 'you want to make sure it's all progressing the right way.'

'That's it,' I said. 'Because the thing is I have Niggling Doubts.'
Mmmm.

I could hear the scratch of her pen as she wrote 'Nutter Incoming' beside my name, but her voice was soothing.

'If you want to come in and check that's fine, we understand. You want to put your mind at rest.'

The problem with vacuuming up bogong moths is that you don't actually kill them. Instead, they rustle about inside the vacuum cleaner. Eventually you start to catch one or two, horribly mutilated, crawling out of the nozzle.

Niggling Doubts are much harder to kill. Another beta test will help, for now, but there's no vacuum cleaner on Earth big enough to suck them all up.

And it's not as if I could fry them up and eat them. Unlike bogongs, Niggling Doubts have zero nutritional value.

And of course, as everyone knows, Niggling Doubts taste like *shit*.

15 December

Last night I dreamt I gave birth to twin boys. As can happen in dreams, Christopher and I imaginatively decided to name them Gary and Barry.

Gary died at birth and at first I was very upset, and then I decided that we should change Barry's name to something nicer starting with B. Except we couldn't think of anything and then I accidentally left Barry in a restaurant.

End of dream.

I'm still pregnant. When she rang to give me the news, the Fertility Sister was brisk and efficient. She made suitable reassuring noises, encouraged me to call whenever I had questions and then ... she was gone.

I feel strangely bereft. My life has revolved around early-morning blood tests or daily injections or dates with the Dildo-Cam. All that poking and prodding, all that *attention*. It was addictive, I now realize. And it made me feel that, even though we didn't have a clue what was wrong with us, someone, somewhere, did. Which is pretty much how the medical system works, really. Put yourself in our hands, don't ask questions, we'll make the decisions for you, you'll get better. Maybe.

The House of Groovy Love was like a second home. A weird expensive sort of home where most of the inhabitants sit around reading magazines, waiting to have things poked into their fanoirs, but a home nevertheless. And now, I've been evicted.

My ultrasound is booked for 30 December. Here, if Everything Goes Well, we should see a heartbeat. Or two.

In the meantime, Christopher and I are working on a new show that will be performing in January. There are deadlines to be met and scripts to be written. Christmas is upon us again and that means a few days of hanging out with family and seeing some old friends and swimming at the beach a lot.

It means playing with Naughty Nephews and laughing with my sisters and listening to Grumpy Grandad update us on his catheter and how he's invented a way of keeping it from sneaking out his enormous underpants by sewing an elastic loop into his Y-fronts.

And it means delivery of the Roll-On Deodorant Nativity Scene. It's starting to take shape, although the angel's wings are still a little wobbly. I'm up to my arms in flour-and-water paste and strips of old newspaper.

'But will it be ready?' Christopher asked, a little sceptically.

'Oh yes,' I assured him. 'It will be *great!*'

As I spoke there was a familiar, faint fluttering behind my head but I quickly thrashed about with a rolled up newspaper and the sound disappeared.

WATERBABIES 2

Phuket, Thailand, 1980. On this day Dad and Amanda and I go whooshing into the ocean, leaving Toni on the sand to look after new baby Kerry, while Mum organizes things, as mothers do, way back in the cabanas.

I swim and I dive and I marvel that I can see all the way to the bottom.

The sand is so white and the water so blue. And everywhere I spy the saucer-sized shell-like sand dollars, each with a star etched over one fragile, crispy thin surface.

And it's great until we all try to swim ashore and discover that we're caught in a rip. And my sister and I discover that no matter how hard we try we can't get in to the shore.

Amanda starts to cry but I feel calm; as I look over at the beach, it all seems so peaceful, with my youngest sisters, far away, playing in the sand.

And then Dad calls out to Toni suddenly. 'Bring a rope!'

I laugh at this and say no Dad, we don't need a rope, but then I feel how the water pulls at my body no matter how hard I swim, and how I can't seem to get anywhere.

And Dad calls again and I realize Amanda was right, we're in trouble, but how can that be when the water is so blue and the ocean floor so pure and sandy white?

Now Dad alternates between telling us not to panic and calling out to my sister on the shore. He starts swimming behind us, trying to push us in towards the beach.

Toni, standing on the sand, is looking at us; she knows something's not right but she can't quite hear us and anyway she knows she can't leave the baby alone.

'Help.' Amanda's scream is thin and high pitched. 'Bring a rope!'

Dad, patient, persistent, keeps trying, pushes first one daughter into shore and then the next. But as quickly as he pushes one in, the other gets dragged out again and he has to swim after her, and then while he's pushing her towards the shore the other one is dragged out again. It's this, seeing my father swim from Amanda and back to me, over and over, that makes me understand the danger we're in and finally I too call out to our sister on the sand.

'Bring a rope!'

I realize, when I think back on this time, that although our father could save himself and perhaps save one of us, he couldn't save us both and I wonder what he must have felt. Did he even start to make that choice or did he crush that thought down and just keep swimming, keep pushing in one daughter after the other.

Twenty-four years later, thousands of people will die on these beaches, and in total there will be many many thousands lost. The tsunami, on Boxing Day 2004, is a shocking and fearsome event. My father rings me and tells me of a girl, a family friend who I first knew as a child and then later when she went to the same university as I did, who is missing. I spend many hours online, compulsively looking for news, going through hospital lists, thinking of her family doing the same, searching hopelessly for her, at first among the hospitals and then among the dead. I can't believe the devastation I see on my TV screen, in the newspapers. How can this happen? When the water is so blue and the ocean floor so pure and sandy white? Later, when I know for sure that she is dead, I see, for the first time in years, in a gift shop, one of those enormous sand dollars, fragile and crisp shelled, and I buy one for her.

Twenty-four years ago I remember collecting them, delicate treasures, wrapping them carefully and packing them into my suitcase. Not a single one survived the plane trip home to Penang.

Drag, swim, push. Don't panic.

Drag, swim, push. Bring a rope!

I'm not sure of what I'm seeing at first, between the dip and swell of the waves; it's like an ant line of people appearing over the sand. But as they run closer I recognize some of them, the fat bartender and the manager from the hotel and the two waiters from the restaurant, including the pervy one who wanted to show us his porno collection, and, stranger still, my mother. Running.

Bringing a rope.

Later, she told us that in our cabana, far from the water, in the midst of unpacking she'd heard our voices, as clearly as if we'd been standing beside her. Immediately she'd run out and up to the main building, screaming that her family was drowning and they had to come quickly.

'You heard us?' I said. 'How is that possible, when Toni was standing on the sand and couldn't properly hear what Dad was saying.'

'I heard you,' she said. 'You were calling me and I heard you. Sometimes it doesn't matter how far away you are, you can tell when someone you love is in trouble.'

'Bring a rope,' we called.

And she did.

The third year

4 January

On our very first New Year's Eve together, Christopher and I stayed at a little cottage on the Central Coast.

It belonged to the hippie sister of a friend from work and we house-sat for a week while she chanted in an ashram somewhere and strained her own tofu.

The cottage was very sweet and rustic and full of homemade crafts and hand-woven rugs. The kitchen was full of recycled glass jars crammed with home-preserved vegetables and dried fruits. It reminded me of the first book in the Little House on the Prairie series, *Little House in the Big Woods,* with all its stored foodstuffs and preserves and Ma diligently making cheese out of the head of a pig and boiling maple syrup into sugar while Laura played with her cornhusk doll and plotted ways to kill or maim her perfect sister Mary.

That New Year's Eve was meant to be quiet and intimate, with just Christopher and I and some nice wine and candlelight and half a tab of acid each. The acid part was a new experience for me and naturally it ended in disaster. Instead of walking hand in hand through the moonlight and gazing in chemically induced wonder at the beauty of nature, I tipped a candle over one of the hand-woven rugs and spent the next eight hours obsessively picking wax out of every individual cotton fibre.

We spent this New Year's Eve alone together, too.

Just me. And Christopher. And the twins.

On 30 December, the seven-week scan showed two shadowy peanut shapes and two heartbeats. I felt my eyes become suspiciously moist.

The technician was excited. 'Look,' she cried, as she twirled the Dildo-Cam like she was whipping mayonnaise. 'There's bub!'

All suspicious eye moisture instantly evaporated. For some reason the word 'bub' coupled with her cheery upbeat tone and expectation that Everything Will Be Wonderful set my teeth on edge.

She twirled a little more. 'And here's ... other bub.'

'Other bub' was said minus the exclamation mark. Even with our geriatric eyesight, Christopher and I couldn't fail to note the discrepancy in size. Twin B was a week behind in development from Twin A.

As the technician measured the heartbeats, Christopher, the eternal optimist, said, 'I'm cheering for the underdog!'

The technician chuckled approvingly.

'Mmmm,' I said. 'And if Twin B fails, will I have a period?'

The chuckling stopped. She pursed her lips a little.

'Well,' she said. 'You may get some spotting. Or it may simply be reabsorbed into the body. But ... look, there's a sac and a heartbeat. I think we can give bub the benefit of the doubt! Let's go with Dad's attitude!'

So that's what we're doing. We're going with Christopher on this one. Go the underdog.

And in the meantime I've started eating for a family of six. It is unpleasant to feel constantly hungry. It is even more unpleasant to feel you would like to rip the head off your husband and devour it because he took you to a function where you didn't eat for four hours. That only happened twice. Now I never leave the flat without a handbag packed full of nuts and crackers.

I'm eight weeks pregnant now, which is amazing and incredible and gobsmackingly weird. My body is changing before my eyes (hey! I've got cleavage!), I fall asleep at the drop of a hat and I eat and eat and eat.

I'm terrified and I'm elated and cynical and trusting all at once.

I started well, reading baby books and making little notes but after having just seen the Narnia film I suddenly felt it was far more important to reread all the books in the C.S. Lewis series. I collect names of good doctors from my previously up-the-duff friends but then I keep putting off booking into a hospital. Apparently my subconscious thinks I can deliver on my own couch with my husband to bite the cord(s). There are times when everything seems too much and other times when I feel as if I've won the jackpot and this unsettled state is simply confusion because I'm finally getting what I want.

And meanwhile, the clock is ticking. I can pfaff about and read *Voyage of the Dawntreader* and Google potential doctors and freak out about scripts and shows, but inside me, I know that Stuff is Happening and will keep happening week by week.

On that first chemical New Year's Eve, all I could do was concentrate on picking the wax out of the rug, thread by thread, knowing vaguely that one day, one week, one year, the rug would finally be free of evil candle residue. I remember stopping for breath, lifting my head for a moment to stretch my neck and seeing the Milky Way through the lounge room window. The drugs were still coursing through my system and as I stared I saw that the stars were huge and pulsating, like enormous shining crystals. I could faintly hear their tinkling and I wondered for a moment if I was seeing my mother among the angels, hovering in the night sky, fuzzed over with their own brilliance.

Stuff is Happening. Something about that makes me happy.

8 January

Oh look I couldn't help it, all right?

We've told our families about it and the few very close friends who knew we were shooting up guinea pig gonad juice or whatever the hell that stuff is. We talk about it in hushed and sensible voices and the phrases 'still early days' and 'all being well' are scattered freely throughout the conversation. It's the sensible way of doing it, but frankly it's not very satisfying.

But then last night we were out chatting to some Not As Close Friends, one of whom has been through IVF and another who frequented the Chinese Fertility Goddess (and both of whom have two beautiful kids apiece) and we were talking about What We'd Been Up To Recently and *finally* I couldn't stand it anymore and I dragged the CFG recipient off to one side and said, 'Okay, I do have some other news.'

'You're having a baby,' she said.

'No,' I said. 'We're having *two*.'

'Oh my God,' she said. 'Oh my *fucking* God. I am *so fucking happy* for you!'

And then we did a little skipping hugging dance right in front of the theatre.

And it was deeply *deeply* satisfying.

17 January

Lucy lives in London, which is a ridiculously long way from me in Sydney, especially if I want to have a cup of peppermint tea with someone or discuss Things to Eat When Pregnant.

Over the years we have had some lovely bonding experiences, including having an enormous fight at university and then making up a year later and being staunch friends ever since; me being present at the birth of her first child, Conor, and becoming his godmother; and some years later both of us catching headlice from him and then having to spend several hours combing nits out of each other's hair.

This last experience was actually far jollier than it might sound. Christopher and I were visiting from Australia, Lucy was very busy directing rehearsals most of the time while we were there and the nits gave us a sort of enforced quiet time in the bathroom together. Also, the combing sensation was quite soothing.

Today I am ten weeks pregnant, which means I have a uterus the size of a grapefruit or an orange, depending on which baby book you refer to. My belly bloats at the drop of a hat and looks quite podgy, even this early, although that could just be me. My cleavage continues to delight.

I have been to my GP and I have booked myself into hospital. I decided not to have a second scan just to check the size of the twins and see if Twin B had managed to catch up to Twin A. Instead, I will wait till the twelve-week scan and, in the meantime, eat more.

I have also just finished working on the enormous show, which was for the Sydney Festival. I worked as a contributing writer but also as a sort of community liaison helpful backstage sort of person, such was the nature of this piece. It got fantastic reviews—the one in the *Sydney Morning Herald* made me cry because I couldn't believe the reviewer could have understood it so completely, but perhaps that was also the hormones.

The other big thing is that we're moving.

It's been wonderful living in our flat but the time has come to up stumps. We are actually going to be living in an enormous but unfinished house with … excited stamp of tiny feet … the Naughty Nephews! And their parents!

Yes, it's true. We are about to become our own sitcom.

On the weekend we went to yum cha with the Naughty Nephews and parents and grandparents and then had coffee/peppermint tea back at Keith and Neâ's house. Neâ had a swag of pregnancy books for me to read and I browsed through some as we ate cake and chatted about essential items for the New House. Like … a floor.

And then Neâ grabbed hold of the smallest Naughty Nephew, applied a slosh of anti-nit cream and started combing the offending bugs out.

It was a slightly surreal moment but it was also oddly soothing, possibly because for a moment I was taken back to those few hours in Lucy's sunny bathroom in Brixton, where all that mattered was the stroke and drag of the fine-toothed comb and the calm, unhurried talk and the here and now of slowly and methodically cleansing every hair.

In a few weeks, Christopher and I will be part of a bigger family. A family with an ongoing headlice problem, yes, but a family we love and cherish. And in a few months that family will be bigger again.

In my mind all these things swirl and bump about. The moving, the fixing up of floors and walls, the juggle of work and writing and nephews and shared living and of course the babies, floating calmly in their grapefruit- or orange-sized world.

There is plenty to be worried about, the potential problems both of the pregnancy and the Big Move. But mostly I am not worried. Mostly I'm calm. And maybe that's hormones too. I don't seem to fret the way I used to. And I know I can always make a pot of peppermint tea and dial London.

21 January

So last night while watching a concert at the Opera House I discovered that I had inadvertently taken up the loathsome habit of belly rubbing in public.

However, I did it not because I am a smug preggo who wants to show off her miraculous fecundity, but because I had shocking wind and needed to gently ease out a fart.

29 January

I was lying on the couch, drifting in and out of sleep as I listened to Christopher talking to some friends on the phone.

He was telling them that I was finally pregnant! With twins! Joyous shrieking emerged from the phone and Christopher and I smiled at each other and tangled our toes together happily. At the end of the call he looked at me and said, 'I don't think we should tell anyone else now. Not until after we really are twelve weeks.'

'It's okay,' I said. 'That's only six days away.'

Then we decided to watch an episode of *The Sopranos* and I got up to do a quick wee.

And then.

And then.

You know how this is going to go, don't you?

For a couple of seconds, as I stared at the blood on the toilet paper, I simply felt confused.

Like time had suddenly reversed itself and I was right back in that same place, in that same moment every month when I would hope against hope that this time, this month was our time, our month, and each time I was disappointed. It was as if I had been tricked. I was wrong. I had never been pregnant at all.

I looked down at the toilet bowl filled with bloody water and I moaned, just slightly, the tiniest of sounds, and Christopher who was in the lounge room setting up the DVD, heard that awful note in my voice and came running.

And when I saw his face, my eyes started to scrunch up and I folded into myself and I started to cry.

It was a public holiday and everyone was closed and I had no idea who I could call and what I should do, until in the end I rang the House of Groovy Love. And bless them, the Fertility Sisters were calm and soothing and understanding. They gave me advice and they wished me and Christopher luck and said they were crossing their fingers for us.

We got ready to go into Emergency, which means I packed a book to read during the inevitable long wait and Christopher ducked down to the shops to buy me some pads.

I was expecting some super strength, surfboard-sized monstrosities but instead he handed over a pack of ultraslim regulars. I started to say that maybe the thicker sort would be better but he stopped me.

'No,' he said, quietly. 'I decided not to get those. Because you're not going to need them. You're *not*.'

At that point there were more tears at his ever faithful optimism—and that's also how I know that babies have no kneecaps, because the sticky strips on the back of the ultraslim pads are decorated with whacky true facts.

Once we got to Emergency the triage nurse grilled me about blood colour (not bright red) and amount (consistent but not gushing) and pain (no) and clots (no), and finally she helpfully suggested that perhaps the blood could be coming from my anus rather than being related to the pregnancy.

'Ahhh no,' I said, firmly. 'It is not. It is related to my pregnancy.'

'Well,' she said, 'it could be constipation related.'

'No,' I said. 'I don't have constipation.'

'Well,' she said, 'I'm just warning you that the doctor may want to check that so don't be alarmed.'

Really, I wanted to say, I feel more alarmed at your enormously ugly headband, but thanks for the warning.

Two hours, half of *The Weirdstone of Brisingamen*, and one ultraslim pad later, we were in, sans anal probe, with the doctor who probed at my stomach, indicated that it would be several more hours wait for an ultrasound (due to the public holiday) and then sent me home.

His diagnosis was that the bleeding could be absolutely fine or it could be the start of a miscarriage, and either way there was nothing much that could be done. Did I want a blood test? There was still no pain, there were still no clots. I had my first appointment with the antenatal clinic the following morning. I decided to forgo the blood test and get some sleep.

Bright and early the next morning, we rocked up to the antenatal clinic. I was calm and collected. At the desk I managed to give my name in a steady voice. The midwife told me to wait for the clerical nurse.

'But here's the thing,' I said, and my steady voice suddenly went to shit, 'I'm bleeeeeedddiiing ...'

Three minutes later I was across the hall in Ultrasound.

As the wand glided over my lubed up belly, Christopher and I clutched hands and in my mind a little voice suddenly said: Please don't take them both.

I had already thought about the possibility that we might have lost the second twin, the one that was a week behind its sibling at the seven-week scan, but my greater fear was that we had lost them both and that now, my empty abdomen would be revealed in all its pathetic failure. That *once again* my crappy, infertile body had failed the test, only this time we got a little further in the ride, far enough to start discussing names and thinking about baby rooms.

Far enough for the universe to have a great hearty laugh at our clueless stupidity.

For a moment there was nothing to see but grey fog and amorphous sludge.

And then.

And then.

Suddenly, *suddenly*, it was as if the fog cleared and there was a baby there, a real live baby, a tiny little person with a head and arms and legs and it was dancing and Christopher was making bubbling, delighted sounds.

'Oh,' I said.

And then I started to cry, big racking sobs and the technician hastily handed me her tissue box.

'I can't see that second baby,' she said carefully.

And I nodded, 'I know, it's gone.'

One of my friends is at the same stage of pregnancy as me. We have started to chat about diet and delivery options, and for a while I almost felt like a normal pregnant woman. Except, I couldn't bring myself to buy my pregnancy vitamins in bulk. For a few weeks I was even beginning to feel that the ride was over. That I had finally arrived. But I see now that for people like me it never really ends until a healthy baby is delivered into your arms. And even that's just the beginning of a whole new ride.

Back at the antenatal clinic, the technician measured the heartbeat of Twin A and typed it onto the screen.

'It looks so cute,' said Christopher, 'so wriggly.'

The technician smiled. 'They're quite active at this stage,' she said. 'This little one looks very healthy.'

I was still crying and snotting into my tissue but I didn't do it in that way you do when you scrunch up your eyes and fold into yourself. Instead, this time, I kept my eyes wide open and I stared and cried and cried and stared, so I wouldn't miss one *nanosecond* of our beautiful dancing baby.

4 February

Here is a selection of some of the more classic lines served up to us over the past week:

'Oh well, it's all for the best.'

And:

'I think you'll cope much better with one anyway.'

And the utterly brilliant:

'Now you know how your sister felt.'

Because I am basically a kind person and I don't want people I care about to sound like complete fucknuckles, I have had to start taking evasive action when breaking our recent news.

First I tell them we lost a twin, then I allow them about ten seconds to begin their response.

If there is any sign of fucknucklery, as outlined above, I quickly start talking about how we need to acknowledge our loss as well as celebrate our joy and relief and usually, *then*, they stop talking shit.

And failing that, if I get any more comments about properly appreciating the pain of my sister Amanda's recent and tragic miscarriage, I shall have to rip out that person's catheter and shove it down his neck.

9 February

The Naughty Nephews have now been informed of Impending Cousin.

There is a variety of excited response to this.

Naughty Nephew the 1st (aged eight) gives me a hug and then says he hopes I have a boy as girls have 'no common sense'.

'That's ridiculous,' I say as I skateboard down the stairs with a carton of eggs balanced on my head.

Naughty Nephew the 3rd (aged three) goggles his enormous blue saucer eyes at me and then lifts my T-shirt so he can gaze reverently at my bulbous tummy.

And Naughty Nephew the 2nd (now aged six) grins happily and says a girl would be good because there are already a lot of boys in this family.

Although, he adds, he hopes I don't have to have the baby 'hoovered out'. This apparently happened when *he* was a baby. He had not wanted to come out because he was busy playing football inside his mother with the bones ...

He must sense my slight disbelief, because he adds that 'of course, it was a *special* Hoover'.

Of course.

19 February

The tiny dancing baby now has all its tooth buds in place. It is covered in fine fuzzy hair and for some time now has been able to urinate into its own amniotic fluid and then drink it, which could be a useful skill for impressing the other kids at end-of-school parties. Depending on the school, of course.

Last week at a christening, a friend asked me why I wasn't more excited. How could I be so calm? I smiled at her serenely.

'Oh well,' I said. 'You know. I'm pacing myself.'

I'm pacing myself.

It's true. It's as if I can only allow myself carefully measured spoonfuls of happiness.

I am now fifteen weeks pregnant. This means that we are past twelve weeks, which also means that we are past the point for the nuchal translucency (NT) scan. Which we didn't have.

Christopher and I talked long and hard about this, the possibilities and consequences that the NT might reveal, Down Syndrome being but one. I am after all, an older mother. A scan would probably affirm that the risk of abnormalities is higher and then the suggestion might be that we make sure by having the more accurate amniocentesis testing.

We lost our twin at eleven weeks. I didn't want to risk another miscarriage by having a needle inserted through my abdomen and into my uterus to draw up amniotic fluid for analysis.

In which case, we thought, what would be the point of having the NT scan in the first place?

A lot of women make exactly the same decision, but there is not a day goes by that I don't worry I've done the wrong thing, yet again, and that I'm just putting off the discovery of Something Bad.

I try to measure out the worrying in equal spoonfuls with the happiness but some days I can't help outpacing myself.

21 February

Labour ward or birthing centre?

Clinical white room with adjustable bed, readily accessible medical equipment and proximity to emergency caesarean and epidural? Or warm pastel-toned room with great big bed, readily accessible beanbags and mats for active labouring and almost as close proximity to emergency caesarean and epidural?

It's not much of a choice really, especially when we see the ensuite to the room at the birthing centre, with its bath built for about four people, or six if they're all immediate members of my family. Maybe more if we add the Naughty Nephews. Yes, there's a bath in the labour ward but it's *just* a bath. It's not a Great Big Party Bath!

We know what we want but we don't know if we'll get it. That choice will be made by the obstetrician who examines me at my next appointment. Our hoped for, briefly promised, *female* obstetrician disappears as suddenly as an IVF doctor on transfer day, and so instead we are appointed an alternative obstetrician: Doctor Fill In.

Male, large, rumpled, bleary eyed ('I did a caesarean at five-thirty this morning on a woman who weighed the same as me, it was like doing a caesarean on myself.') Doctor Fill In is cynical, opinionated and *almost* totally unlikeable.

He peers through my record, huffs over my yellow hospital card and congratulates me on reaching fifteen weeks. I tell him that we have chosen not to have the nuchal scan and he nods. Then he asks me if I have any questions.

'Well,' I say, 'now that I am no longer carrying twins and no longer considered high risk I want to use the birthing centre and be under midwife care. Is that all right?'

A pause.

Doctor Fill In glares at us from under his hooded lids and gives a snort of disgust. He could not be less impressed if I had told him I wanted to give birth at Taronga Park Zoo under the watchful eye of gorillas.

I had been warned about this attitude in obstetricians generally, so I am able to hide my surprise at the venom in his voice. Instead I sit calmly, nodding as he reels off the litany of crimes perpetuated by the evil Birthing Centre and its wicked handmaidens the Midwives.

When he sees I am unswayed he tries again.

'Not only that,' he waves my yellow card for emphasis, 'you've got MS!'

I am prepared for the Multiple Sclerosis argument; a midwife at the antenatal clinic has already warned me that another practitioner who had seen those two letters on my card (but not actually seen or examined *me*) has said I wouldn't be able to use the birthing centre because the MS made me high risk.

'Be ready to argue for yourself,' the midwife had advised.

As Doctor Fill In pauses for breath I point out that I would be seeing my MS specialist very soon, that the last time I saw him I had told him I was trying to fall pregnant and he said (and my research supported this) that pregnancy seemed to be of benefit to MS sufferers, that MS symptoms even seemed to be suppressed during the pregnancy.

Doctor Fill In predictably hits back with the story of a patient who was diagnosed with MS *after* she became pregnant and swiftly seemed to get worse.

'That's terrible,' I say calmly, 'but in addition, my symptoms are mild and I have never been placed on any medication.'

My mother's breast cancer, initially thought to have been beaten with a mastectomy and radiotherapy, came back after ten years. I was twenty-two years old and we were both students at the University of Newcastle when she became affected by a strange, unshakeable cough. She thought it was stress. Her friend Carrie urged her to give up her job. Then the lumps started coming back. This time the cancer was in her bones.

From that point until she died, my mother fought hard and her family fought beside her in any way we could. There were massages and diet changes and herbalists and naturopaths. My father, non-Catholic, non-religious, at best a mild sort of agnostic, not only allowed the Filipino lay preachers into our house at our mother's request, he burned all the wooden carvings and masks brought home from Asia that were hanging on the walls, as instructed, because the preachers believed they 'harboured evil spirits'. She wasn't cured but the house looked much better.

Towards the end we were waging small battles with the doctors at her hospital. We asked questions. We queried protocols. No, we wouldn't just leave her in their capable hands, thankyou very much. We refused to give her up. Instead, we camped out by her bedside, assisting with her bathing and toileting. We brought her other food, better food, wholesome tasty food and sometimes rubbishy junk food just because she wanted it. A nurse showed me how to give my mother subcutaneous shots in the stomach (I never imagined I would be doing the same to myself some day). We kept a book by her bed, an ongoing journal of doctor visits, medications, results of tests etc., so that when one of us went home or had a break, the next person would be able to read about the day's events.

In some ways I feel for them, we must have been an absolute pain in the arse. Because doing this, asking, talking, and above all writing *everything* down, we discovered when medication was forgotten, when treatment was ordered and didn't occur and ... when doctors lied.

She came home for a while and one terrible night she broke her leg in her sleep. In hospital, recovering from the subsequent operation, she was advised by a doctor that she could visit the hospital dentist to have her toothache seen to. When the same doctor saw her a couple of days later she happily told him that she had seen the dentist. The doctor was furious. Had she any idea of the risk she was exposing herself to? The germs that were being introduced to the bloodstream? Why on Earth had she done that?

My mother was a feisty and strong woman. She came alone to Australia as a seventeen-year-old Filipina migrant where she met and fell in love with my father, a seventeen-year-old English migrant. She had worked as a nurse for many years and then as a social worker. She was used to standing up for herself but the cancer and the hospital stay had weakened her resolve. She stammered an apology. She must have got it wrong ... she thought he'd said she could ...

But the thing is, he had.

I took up the argument. You said she could go. He flatly denied this and left the room.

I ran after him down the corridor. Yes you did. Look. It's written in the book.

Doctor Fill In taps his fingers against my yellow card and regards me for a moment.

Then he changes tack.

'Look,' he says, and his voice takes on a warm and caring tone.

'You're thirty-seven years old. You have MS, you've had infertility and you went through IVF. You've miscarried a twin. You didn't do the nuchal scan and that's fine, I completely support you in that decision. Now you're fifteen weeks and that's terrific—things seem to be going well. The next stage where a problem can occur is in labour. Wouldn't it be good to avoid all those additional risks by having an elective caesarean?'

For a moment his words ring seductively in my ears. He had acknowledged that Bad Things happened. He might have guessed that every day I worry that Bad Things will continue to happen. But he definitely knew how reassuring it was to say there would be *no more Bad Things if I just had a caesarean.*

'We're planning to do a twenty-week scan,' I say.

'Yes, you'd be mad if you didn't,' he chips in cheerfully.

'Mmmm. So we'll see how things are then. But, in the meantime, what I would really like to do is book into the birthing centre.'

Much beetling of brows. Much scowling without real menace, as he helps me onto the examination table and we listen to the baby's heartbeat.

Christopher and I smile like idiots, as is our wont. Doctor Fill In grunts his approval.

'Still alive,' he says gruffly. 'Okay, get up. I'm not going to sign anything but I can't see any reason why you can't go to the birthing centre, if that's what you really want.'

'Yeah,' I say. 'It is.'

As we leave the hospital Christopher gives me a hug. 'You were great in there,' he says.

I know this doesn't mean that everything will now happen smoothly. I know I shouldn't see it as a good sign for the future.

I'm still pacing myself.

But on this day, at this time, we got what we came for.

And even I have to admit, that is a Good Thing.

6 March

Half the belongings in our flat, the sturdy square-edged half, are packed into cardboard boxes; the other half taunts us with its gamut of weird knobbly unwrappable shapes and thin fragile edges.

I'm doing most of the packing because Christopher is working away building floors, knocking out ceilings and generally making the Big House habitable. My process is to pack a box, have a cup of tea, pack another box, eat five loaves and half an oxen, and on it goes.

The other movements in our life are much smaller, but so much more impressive.

We're at seventeen weeks now (!) and along with those tooth buds and the pissing-into-your-own-amniotic-fluid-and-then-drinking-it tendencies, if, apparently, the Tiny Dancing Baby is a girl she's growing *eggs*.

'Eggs!' I squeal at Christopher. 'Teeny tiny weeny little eggs in her teeny tiny ovaries! How bizarre is that? And one day, one of those teeny tiny eggs might be half of a new teeny tiny baby. Only teenier! And tinier!'

And then I stop because all that high-pitched squealing is hurting my throat and aggravating my overactive mucous membranes.

Surely one of the most attractive and endearing Facets of

Pregnancy must be the cascading waterfall of slime that forms within one's body. One moment I can throw out my arms and lustily inhale the warm Sydney morning through my nostrils, the next I am drowning in snot.

Snotty Nose rapidly becomes Evil Mucus Dripping Down the Back of the Throat. This leads to much hacking. Quite quickly, I manage to give myself a throat infection and a nasty chesty cough. This in turn leads to much lying down and feeling sorry for myself.

I speak to Lucy, in London, sans peppermint tea, and she regales me with tales of horrifically abundant saliva when she was pregnant with her second baby, Alexandra.

'I had to carry a little cup around with me everywhere,' she tells me. Lucy is a director who works on various big West End type musicals. All very glamorous but not, we agree, when you have to stop calling out directions to actors onstage every few minutes because you have to spit into a little paper cup.

About three days ago, while lying on the couch, I started feeling other sorts of movement.

Of the delicate flicking type.

As if a tiny dancing baby had decided it was time to give the uterus a bit of a clean with an equally tiny feather duster.

When I put Christopher's hand on my abdomen he could feel it too. For a moment we sat like that. Then he grinned at me and said, 'This is so exciting, I have to ring my mum.'

24 March

'Imagine ...' Naughty Nephew the 3rd said to me the other day, as he watched his big brother struggle to pull on his new rugby boots.

'Imagine what, darling?' I said encouragingly.

Naughty Nephew the 3rd sometimes gets overwhelmed by his two older brothers and has trouble completing his sentences.

'Imagine ... (long pause as he fingered the spiky underside of one of his brother's boots) if we could only eat these ... studs.'

I nodded thoughtfully.

Imagine.

With an almighty struggle of box-packing and a full day of scrubbing our flat clean (earning the following ambiguous and slightly retarded note from the real estate agent: THANKYOU FOR LEAVING THE FLAT EXCELLENT!) we are finally out and into the Big House that we will henceforth share with the three Naughty Nephews and their parents.

Except ... the Big House needed a lot of work done to it so for several days we have all been living in a building site. A building site full of cardboard boxes.

It is strange to go back to sharing a house again.

Especially a house with small children. The running stamping shouting kind. Each morning I wake somewhere between 6 and 6.30 am to the sound of children running up the hallway, demanding their breakfast. Maybe that's a boy thing. Nah, maybe not.

The other night as I was having a shower I heard a small voice calling my name and looked up to see Naughty Nephew the 2nd standing in the doorway of our bathroom. Not only was I stark naked with bulbous belly but I was also wearing the ridiculous polka dotted shower cap which somehow made the nakedness and the bulbousness seem far more extreme.

I put on a calm, this is entirely normal, face and said: 'Yes darling?'

'When you've finished your shower,' he said politely, 'would you like to come downstairs and read *The Lion, the Witch and the Wardrobe* to me?'

In the background I could hear the horrified calls of his mother as she realized where he had gone.

'Yes,' I said. 'That would be lovely. I'll come down as soon as I'm dressed.'

And off he went and when I had finished showering and laughing I went down to join him in Narnia.

This week Christopher and I saw our baby for the second time.

It was the nineteen-week ultrasound, the morphology scan, and it was a strange and slightly surreal experience. Christopher kept looking up at the screen and then down at my belly to make sure the probe was actually in contact with my body and that the technician wasn't fooling us and scanning some other hidden pregnant lady.

No longer a tiny dancer, this was a baby on the go, shimmying around its slightly cramped conditions, jabbing its hands and feet in front of its face like a guilty celebrity. *No pictures, No pictures* ...

The technician was bemused. 'Nothing like having an active one to start the day,' she said as we stared up at the screen. Soon she was reeling off the roll call of body parts: here are the kidneys, here's the heart, here's the spine. And the baby kept squirming and turning and I felt like saying, we're all tired now, can't we have some rest?

Before this day we had decided that we wanted to know our baby's sex. But when the technician paused delicately at one point and asked if we wanted to know, Christopher suddenly called out 'No!'

So ... no.

Today while visiting our friend Hadass with her six-week-old twins I had a strange epiphany. I held her daughter, a tiny wee pixie baby with soft downy hair, and smiled across at her son, who appeared to be blessed with the coiffure of a seventies casino entertainer.

The little girl scratched at me with her tiny fingernails and made funny burbling noises against the skin of my neck.

I realized that, as an infertile woman whose monthly state was despair and disappointment, I had become used to hardening my heart to other people's babies. I felt so much less inclined to cuddle a baby when it appeared I would never have one of my own. It simply hurt too much. But today, holding this little girl close, I felt an oddly warm sensation. It was anticipation. For the first time in so many years.

Soon, I thought, finally, I shall be holding my own baby. Imagine.

REIGN ON THE PARADE

Two days before the Glen Devon Primary School Easter Hat Parade, my mother makes me a costume out of wire and green and orange crepe paper.

My mother tells me I will be Titania, Queen of the Fairies, which I carefully repeat to myself. Secretly I would rather be Princess of the Fairies, as from my extensive research into the fairytale genre the princesses are usually prettier and exciting things are more likely to happen to them than to the queens.

On the day of the parade it turns very cold and so when my mother arrives at school to dress me in my crepe paper petal skirt, wings and flowery crown, she also brings with her a bottle-green, long-sleeved skivvy and a pair of flesh-coloured rib tights.

'No,' I say, 'fairies don't wear skivvies.'

'This one does,' says my mother, 'and I didn't bring the other top, do you want to go out there naked?'

'Anyway,' she says, 'it's green, see ... like a stalk.' I do see. She then gives me a special putting-on-tights lesson: first one foot, then the other, toes, heels, knees and right over my bottom in the cold concrete toilet cubicle.

'Here, I brought you this as well,' she says, and I know she feels a bit bad about the skivvy. It's a big crepe paper flower, slightly poppyish. 'I thought you could use it as your wand,' she says.

I love my Queen of the Fairies costume. I feel fantastic as I take my place beside the other predictable and dull Easter Parade entrants: Easter egg hats, bunny hats, flowery bonnets. I am in the character section with some baby chicks, a couple of pirates, a handful of Bo Peeps and about a million Easter bunnies. But I am Titania, Queen of the Fairies and I bestow fairy magic via the poppyish wand onto watching non-fairies. Round and round the asphalt we go and I wave at my mother, and my sister Amanda, who are among the onlookers, and even Mrs Redford on the judging table who looks away because she doesn't like me.

Mrs Redford likes Julia Pool best out of our whole reading and writing class, even though Julia cannot read as well as me. What Julia can do is write in small, neat handwriting. I try to copy Julia's neat handwriting in the hope that Mrs Redford will like me too, but it's no use. She shouts at me for writing too small. And one horrible day, she catches me trying to write my name in loopy grown-up running writing, like I have seen my mother write. She is so angry that she goes to the blackboard and writes my name properly in running writing over the whole blackboard. 'Can you do this?' She shouts at me as the chalk squeaks against the board. 'No you can't you silly little girl, this is writing, you can't do this, you can't do this, so stop wasting my time and print your letters properly.'

In the end it's Julia Pool, with a huge fluffy Easter bunny head made out of thousands of cotton wool balls, who wins best costume. I watch her receive her prize, a basket of chocolate eggs and a beaming smile from Mrs Redford. I shiver among the crowd in my skivvy and tights and crepe paper. I feel the sting of defeat, and I can't help feeling it's because I'm playing a Queen and not a Princess and I should have gone with my first instincts. I pout ungratefully and go over to my mother and sister. The parade is over.

'Never mind,' says my mother as she helps me out of the crepe paper skirt, 'at least now you know how to put on your tights by yourself.'

Legs up & laughing

The following year I decide to take an independent approach to the Easter Hat Parade. I will make my hat myself. No parental influence. No fairy costumes or bonnets.

I create my hat from an ice-cream container and lots of cut-out paper. I decorate the front of the hat with the clever pasting of a dinosaur card I find in a box of Weetbix.

The dinosaur moves its head up and down when you turn the card. This means if I move my head up and down while wearing the hat, the dinosaur moves his. I leave my hat at home during the morning, and my mother promises to bring it at lunchtime, before the parade. At lunchtime, my mother does not appear.

I prowl around the school gates becoming increasingly agitated. I become tearful. Hat. Hat hat hat. Where are you? Beautiful ice-cream hat with a moving, bobbing dinosaur.

Finally, I run to Mrs Redford's office. 'Please,' I say desperately, 'my mother hasn't brought my hat with her. I don't know where she is. I think she's forgotten. I have to go home and get it. Please Mrs Redford.' Mrs Redford stares hard at me. I am a troublesome child. She says I can go.

'But mind the cars. If you get run over don't come crying to me.'

I run the three or four blocks to my house. I do not mind the cars. Luckily I do not get run over. As I run panting up the front steps of our house, the door opens. My mother. She looks surprised to see me.

'Why aren't you at school?'

I start to cry.

'I thought you'd forgotten,' I sob. 'I thought you'd forgotten my hat.'

She takes it out of the bag she is carrying. It is now encircled with several meters of tinsel. It sparkles. The dinosaur bobs at me.

'I thought I'd just add a bit more stuff,' says my mother.

It looks beautiful.

In the parade I walk happily in the hat section. I nod and smile at the crowd and my dinosaur bobs and nods too. I look at the hats around me. Professionally rendered bonnets and boaters, shaped and tizzed and moulded into perfection. Hats by Mothers. Perfect hats untouched by any child's hand.

My ice-cream container feels tight on my head, like an ice-cream container. It looks like an ice-cream container. A very beautiful ice-cream container, yes, but an ice-cream container nevertheless. I am a small self-made boat in a sea of parentally constructed ocean liners. I feel the cold fingers of self-doubt against the back of my neck.

As we wait for the judging I sit next to my friend Lynnette, who has a to-scale model farm jauntily sitting on her head. Each animal is carefully constructed from matchboxes and pipe cleaners. I admire the beautifully painted barn.

She peers at me, confused. 'What is your hat?'

'Just a hat,' I say. She turns her head sideways to get a better view. A milkmaid falls to her death. 'I made it myself.'

Lynnette is fascinated. 'Really?' She stares hard at the front of my hat. 'Is that a dinosaur?'

'Yes,' I say. 'Watch closely.' I nod my head.

'Wow!' She nudges the girl beside her. 'Look at what happens when she wobbles her head!'

The girl pushes back her cardboard and crepe paper re-creation of the entire Beatrix Potter collection. 'Where'd you get that from?'

'She made it,' Lynnette says.

'I found the dinosaur in a Weetbix box,' I say. 'It's good isn't it?'

I bask in the glow.

In retrospect I think a People's Choice award might have seen me as a strong contender, but sadly it was not to be. Lynnette and I watch Julia Pool go up to accept first prize. Her Easter bunny family picnic bonnet sways precariously in the stiff breeze.

'What a lovely hat, Julia,' beams Mrs Redford. 'Did you help Mummy make it?'

'No' says Julia.

Lynnette says to me, 'You should get a prize, I reckon, for making your hat yourself. Everyone else's mum made theirs.' I nod guiltily. My mother's tinsel glitters around me.

'Nod your head again,' says a boy dressed as a baby chicken and I happily oblige.

But it's all right, I tell myself. I thought of the dinosaur all by myself.

6 April

We take the photo we were given from the ultrasound up to Newcastle to show it off to my family.

My dad guffaws cheerfully when he sees it and my stepmother squeals with delight and tells me the baby has my nose.

Grumpy Grandad says he can't see anything, but that might be because his spectacles are thickly coated with a yellowish layer of his own scalp tissue, which has taken to flaking off in chunks and floating about his shoulders. I offer to clean them (glasses, not scalp) and it takes me nearly half an hour with the Windex and the paper towels, and within a few minutes of him putting them back on and exclaiming with delight at how clearly he can see the TV screen, I notice the flakes start to fall and cling to his lenses again.

This week has been all about moving house and Lordy it's slow.

Well not the actual moving *out* part; that was reasonably fast because we threw everything into cardboard boxes. And not the actual moving *in* part because two strong burly Chinese fellows named Johnny and Bob hurled our boxes into their truck and then lugged them up the stairs of the Big House.

The slow part is the unpacking part.

We have a bedroom, a bathroom and a large room for everything else in our cosy upstairs section of the Big House.

At the moment this room features a couch, two desks, a dining-room table and an enormous mountain of boxes, all full and all needing to be unpacked and sorted and stored.

Most of these boxes are labelled 'books', or for a change 'large heavy books'. One of the boxes got broken somewhere between Johnny hurling it into the truck and Bob lugging it up the stairs and so a small collection of my childhood reading has been oozing out of the side of the box mountain. I can't collect all those books together because that would necessitate putting them on a bookshelf, which would in turn necessitate deciding where the bookshelves should go, because God forbid we double handle things.

This week was also the twelfth anniversary of my mother's death.

She was born in a village on the island of Luzon, in the Philippines. The country had been occupied by the Japanese army since 1941 and the local people hated and feared them. Within a few hours of my mother's birth the village received a warning that soldiers were heading their way.

The entire village immediately evacuated and headed into the mountains. They planned to hide in some caves until the soldiers had passed by and then return to the village. There was no time to pack anything more than a few essentials. The tiny brown newborn babe that would one day be my mother was wrapped in a rice sack.

It took over an hour of walking through forests and crossing a river to reach the caves.

The villagers hid themselves. One of the scouts told them that soldiers were close by and they must all stay very quiet.

And then.

My mother began to cry.

The cry of a baby is piercing. Like an alarm or a siren. Or a betrayal. My grandmother tried desperately to feed her, to comfort her, to rock her back to silence but still she screamed.

The other villagers were terrified, they pleaded with my grandparents. The sound would draw the soldiers, they cried, they would all be killed. They had to do something, they had to stop her.

So my grandfather drew his knife and put the blade to the baby's throat. He hesitated as my grandmother wept and prayed.

And then, just as suddenly, the baby stopped.

The soldiers passed, the villagers left the cave and made their way back down to their village. When they stopped to cross the river, my grandmother moved down to the water's edge and unwrapped my mother from the rice sack so that she could bathe her in the river water.

And there, she discovered the leech. It must have made its way into the sack when they had initially crossed the river. Now, hours later, it was firmly attached to the baby's heel: black, glossy, swollen with blood and so fat it was as big as her entire foot.

When I imagine this scene, I think about how, when he'd held back his knife, my grandfather had spared not only his firstborn child, but also me, his firstborn grandchild, and my sisters and our children too.

Today I should be unpacking boxes and writing things and Being Organized but instead I'm thinking about Mum and how much I miss her and love her. I look at the image of my unborn baby (week twenty-one—size of a banana), with its nose like mine and its aunties and the grandmother it will only ever know from photographs and stories and the la la la of the one Filipino song I remember her singing.

I feel the familiar squirming deep within as the baby turns and stretches in my abdomen.

And there's something more. Higher up, a soft pounding against my heart.

It's been twelve years but I haven't forgotten that grief kicks too.

14 April

So I'm lying on my back feeling the baby slide around inside me and as it kicks I realize I can see my stomach rippling.

This makes me laugh and so then there is more rippling.

And then my bellybutton bulges and heaves and other parts of my stomach contort as if a miniature earthquake is underway in my gut and I stop laughing, because to tell the truth it looks really quite disturbing and while it was funny before, now, frankly, it's just plain *creepy*.

28 April

I'm now willing to admit I'm pregnant, but it's a far larger leap of faith to say that at the end of my pregnancy there will be a baby. Other pregnant friends have started to fill their baby rooms with monitors and cots and dingly dangly things. Christopher and I have bought nothing (yet) but we *have* received a load of hand-me-down Naughty Nephew clothes from Neâ which have been hastily stuck in the cupboard where we can't see them.

Despite this, the time now seems right to shop for maternity bras.

I actually attempted this a couple of months back when my bra size changed dramatically, but I chickened out at the last minute and settled for a couple of non-maternity bras that were a bit bigger than my normal size. These are now right at the end of their row of little hooks and uncomfortably tight.

I am not a well-endowed woman; bras have generally only ever really been things to stop my nipples poking out of my T-shirt on cold days. Bra shopping in the past was a quick and haphazard event based on colour, pattern and Is This One on Sale?

It is clear I need the help of an expert. I had heard the rumour of the necessity for proper fittings and the dire warnings of back strain, wrenched shoulders and milk-pudding boobs that would ensue if Proper Fittings were not had.

Christopher and I wander into the 'intimates' section of a Large Department Store and linger awkwardly around the maternity section. Row after row of wireless, double-clipped, enormous-cupped, wide-strapped bras dangle from their racks, taunting us.

We look at them, we take them off the rack, we finger their odd little fastenings and marvel at their extra hooks and eyes. Then we put them back because those whopping big cups are scaring the bejesus out of us.

Diddly diddly dee goes the muzak.

A chill wind begins to blow and a lone tumbleweed scuttles across the floor.

Christopher and I clutch at each other's clammy hands. One of us whimpers.

'Someone will come,' we mutter to ourselves. 'Someone Who Knows About Pregnant Bosoms.'

At one stage a sales assistant *does* flit past, replacing frilly delicate non-pregnancy things as she goes.

'Why look! Here is Someone Who Can Help,' announces Christopher in his best Actorly Projected Voice.

'Yes,' I smile, relieved.

We take our eyes off her for only a second but when we turn back she is gone.

'Bugger,' we say.

Diddly diddly dee goes the muzak.

Finally we decide we can work it out together. Are we not grown-ups? Have I not received hours of valuable Bionicle Assemblage tuition from the Naughty Nephews? Did not Christopher once build a house (in a previous relationship *yes,* but the experience still counts) and has he not just spent days laying lovely wooden floors and doing fiddly carpentry bits in the Big House? Well then.

We select a few bras based on what appears to be my current size but also on colour, pattern and Is This One On Sale?

Then we locate the fitting rooms.

Then we enter the fitting room.

Then the shop assistant who had done the neat disappearing act early on suddenly appears in the doorway with a stern look on her face.

Then Christopher is barred from the fitting room on account of him being a loathsome bosom-less man.

Then I bravely re-enter the fitting room alone.

Then I bare my boobs and attempt to attach the first bra to them.

Then the bra twists itself round the wrong way and laughs at my ridiculous attempts to wind it round my body.

Then *all* the little clips in *all* the bras suddenly and maliciously spring apart. An image rears up before me, of me, struggling to survive in my scanty brightly coloured pre-pregnancy bra, now faded and torn with use and held together with pins and bits of sticky tape. I am destined to be bowed down with strained back and wrenched shoulders, shackled to the cold hard earth by the weight of my ginormous Milk-Pudding Boobs.

Then my face goes red and tears of frustration creep into my eyes.

Then I swiftly re-dress, do some deep breathing, and fling the bras down (but neatly) on disappearing shop assistant's plush padded seat thing as I storm out the door.

I look for my husband and weep bitterly because he has wandered off to the electronics section and also because, lo, the pregnancy hormones are surging through my body, and there is much wailing and gnashing of teeth, and odd looks from other customers.

Diddly diddly dee goes the muzak.

It is all too hideous.

Christopher blows my nose and swiftly administers skim hot chocolate and small evil sweety thing, and then we go into the Other Large Department Store.

Here, we go straight up to the counter and ask for Someone Who Knows About Pregnant Bosoms.

And finally, *finally* the Someone appears. And yes she knows pregnant bosoms and yes she knows how to wrangle the nasty little clips.

Christopher is once again banished from the fitting room but this time it is okay, I feel safe, I feel nurtured in the arms of wide experience, I am to be saved from back strain and wrenched shoulders (but alas probably not milk-pudding boobs). I try on bra after bra, am instructed on the mysteries of breast enlargement and shrinkage, advised on where my straps should sit, where my hooks should meet and where my nipples should point. The Someone is very nice and very good and I feel much much better.

However, after twenty minutes I realize that I don't actually properly fit into any of the maternity bras she has brought for me. If it fits at the back then the cups are too big. If the cups are just right then I'm straining at the end of the hooks. (My friend Michelle later tells me that I can buy a little extension thingy to increase the back of the bra for a few bucks and that will keep me going until I am ready for the next stage.)

Once upon a time, years ago, when Christopher and I were in those first few months (stretching to the first year) of trying to conceive, he *did* buy something for our unborn baby.

It was a handmade patchwork quilt, just big enough to cover a cot. Coloured frogs and rampant teddy bears were pieced together with boats sailing into clouds and wide-eyed geometric cats. It was expensive, indulgent, impractical and beautiful. And perfectly fitting for Christopher's enthusiastic optimism for our impending offspring. Who never made an appearance.

For years the quilt stayed folded up and hidden away. Once I unwrapped it, a year ago, when I was looking for blankets. It was a shocking reminder of our younger dreams. Instead of frogs and boats and teddies and cats I saw invasive tests and broken hearts and long, empty years stitched together with self-hatred and failure.

When we packed the flat and prepared to move to the Big House this year I found the quilt again. And the teddies were back and the quilt was beautiful once more.

Christopher and I have decided to meet up elsewhere in the department store and I saunter towards him swinging my black and white shopping bag. Christopher looks at it with interest.

'No bra,' I quickly tell him.

'No bra?'

'It's a long story,' I say, 'but basically they don't fit yet. So I bought a pair of trousers instead. They're not maternity trousers but they fit comfortably over my tummy. Also, I liked the colour. Also, they were on Sale.'

He nods. It all makes perfect sense. We hold hands as we wander out the door.

Behind us, racks of maternity bras jangle their fiddly hooks, waiting patiently for our inevitable return.

And *diddly diddly dee* goes the muzak.

3 May

Last night I dreamt that I was in the process of giving birth when I suddenly realized that Christopher and the midwives looked shocked and worried.

'What is it?' I shrieked at them. Somebody pointed a mirror at my nether regions and I saw that four woolly legs, complete with four tiny hooves, were protruding from my lala.

'Does this mean it's breech?'

The midwives shook their heads sadly. 'We think there's something wrong.'

At this point I grabbed Christopher and pulled him close.

'I bet this has something to do with the sheep sperm,' I muttered in his ear.

Even now, wide awake, I can't help wondering just what

exactly it was I had done with that sheep sperm. Had it been some sort of torrid arcadian affair? Or was it an IVF procedure gone terribly wrong? Part of me is disgusted at myself but another part is quite impressed with the way I didn't feel the need to dream the whole backstory, I just cut to the chase.

18 May

Letter to a twenty-eight-week-old mathematical genius

> Dear Tiny But Feisty Person Currently Occupying My Uterus,
>
> It's been a while but I'm finally putting fingers to keyboard. How's it all going in the Pink Palace? A little snug is what I'm guessing, what with all the feet I keep finding in my bellybutton.
>
> The other morning your father was feeling you kick about and he decided he'd do a little gentle prodding back, and then suddenly the two of you were engaged in some sort of bizarre poke-off where he would poke at you and you would poke back. I was banned from laughing because the movement was preventing him from feeling the full force of your amazing new power and anyway who am I, right, I'm just the large warm fleshy barrier lying between you both.
>
> When you both finally collapsed with exhaustion, Christopher said he was teaching you how to count.
>
> This week Christopher is away setting up a new project. I told him that you started doing that bellybutton poking thing again and he got sad because he was missing you. So then I said that I didn't poke you back because that was a special game you have, just between the two of you, and that made him feel better.

Of course, I was lying through my teeth and when he gets back on the weekend you can show off your long-division skills.

A couple of weeks ago your aunty Neâ did the Scientifically Proven Ring Test over my belly, which said that you must be a boy. And then, while I was at a playwrights' conference on the weekend a woman told me that, according to every Italian woman she had ever known, my bump was boy shaped. But one of my friends had a psychic episode and declared you were a girl and then last night I dreamt that I had already given birth to you and you were indeed a girl.

So who knows?

The dream actually went on to reveal you were also incredibly slippery and I dropped you a couple of times and then decided you really would be better off back inside me, and I'd only given birth so prematurely because I was impatient to meet you, and then I was working out the best way to swallow you whole and then, thankfully, I woke up.

Your cousins, the Naughty Nephews, have been very helpful with suggesting names and because we're not sure of your gender (although that woman with all the Italian women friends was very persuasive) they have given me both sorts.

Naughty Nephew the 1st has provided a selection of lovely names all based on girls in his class he fancies or boys who are among his best friends. Among the girls, he rates Chloe and Phoebe very highly and I was pleased to note that the other day he included Bronte as a suggestion. I am yet to meet Phoebe or Chloe but I have met Bronte several times and she is a lovely, thoughtful, polite little girl.

Naughty Nephew the 2nd, with his finger firmly on the literary pulse, has suggested Klaus, Violet or Sunny (being the names of the Baudelaire children in Lemony Snicket's delightful *A Series of Unfortunate Events*). Violet gets extra points because she is also the daughter in *The Incredibles*.

And finally, Naughty Nephew the 3rd, he of the blue saucer eyes, has suggested ... his own name. But with a '2' on the end. You know, like with *Shrek 2*.

Today, I went to visit Grumpy Grandad (that's Grumpy Great Grandad to you) and he suggested that I could use my deceased mother's name.

Just on the off chance that it hadn't occurred to me.

All suggestions are gratefully received, of course. But at the moment I treat names the same way I treat gifts of baby clothes and baby items: I just don't know what to do with them so I shove them in the cupboard to be dealt with later.

Even now, at just on twenty-eight weeks, it still seems a long time till you'll be safely in my arms.

Even with the dreams and the Ring Test and Poking Bellybutton games, it still seems surreal.

Yes, you might be a baby, but you also might be my liver, wearing boots and equipped with tiny fists.

Which would explain why you keep trying to beat up my bladder.

But despite the regular thrashings of various internal organs, despite the necessity to sleep sitting up, despite the sore back and shoulders ... things are good.

Sometimes I look at my belly in the mirror and am shocked at how quickly my body has changed. But shocked in a good way. I can be hypnotized watching the ripples in my skin caused by you turning over, or stretching, or sculling a little amniotic fluid (as I know you do). I feel you when I'm driving or watching Very Boring Plays or when I'm meant to be having important business-type conversations, and it makes me smile.

I don't mind too much when old ladies and friends of my parents touch my belly because I think it's amazing too. In fact I think it's a complete miracle and maybe it's my civic duty to provide a belly-touching service to anyone who needs it, because that's how incredible and wonderful it all is.

And above all, I'm happy.

That's *you* who's done that.

So thankyou.

But give the bladder a break sometimes, okay?

Vanessa

xxx

23 May

It was a name that seemed to have it all.

It was unusual.

It was applicable to a boy or a girl.

It had a literary background (Shakespeare's *The Tempest*).

We said it beside imagined second names and both of our surnames and it seemed to pass with flying colours.

We wrote it down on scraps of paper in a café, and in the car we shouted it out at the top of our voices, imagining we were standing at the back door calling our child home for dinner.

It had a familiar ring and yet an exotic tone.

It was, we felt, perfect.

And it all ended sadly, a few minutes after we arrived home and Christopher started working on his computer.

'I have some very bad news,' he said.

I walked over and peered at the screen. There, in black and white was Our Baby's Perfect Name.

Our exotic, literary, unusual, unisex, backyard shoutable name.

How could I have forgotten? I see it every day. And yes the spelling was slightly different but even so …

'I'm sorry to have to tell you,' said Christopher. 'But … ARIAL IS A FONT.'

30 May

When I was seven, my Filipino grandpapa made one of his rare visits and gave me an enormous stuffed Yogi Bear that was almost as tall as me.

I was delighted, not because I loved Yogi Bear but because it was just the right size and shape to protect me from Evil, Abducting Burglars. At bedtime I would spend ages building two me-shaped sentinels out of pillows, soft toys and discarded clothes. Then I would position myself carefully between them and settle in for the night. My thinking was that any Evil, Abducting Burglar who came into the room would see not one but three people sleeping in the bed and hence be spoiled for choice.

It saddens me to think of that paranoid seven-year-old painstakingly stuffing her teddy under the bedclothes, but then again, I'm still here.

Yogi's enormous size and girth saved me precious stuffing time and I could get down to the real business at hand, which was not sleep but praying diligently for all the souls in Purgatory. I might manage ten or so Our Fathers and a score of Hail Marys before dropping off to sleep.

This wasn't negotiable: if I tried to go to sleep before prayers, my guilt would create nasty punishing scenarios involving weeping souls and Evil, Abducting Burglars. I was a little confused about how many Our Fathers it actually took to release a tormented soul and obviously I wanted to spread it round, so after three or so prayers I would say firmly 'That's enough for you, these are for someone else'.

Thirty years later I find myself once again shoving pillows under the bedclothes.

Once there, I try to shape them carefully around my body in a variety of configurations in a desperate attempt to get comfortable. It's as if the onset of night adds several hundred kilos to my belly. Last night as I struggled, half asleep, to get up so I could go to the toilet, the word 'forklift' distinctly formed in my brain.

Two nights ago I think I managed to form what could be the perfect nest. I was actually able to lie on my left side in hitherto unknown comfort and ease. I nearly wept with joy. It didn't solve the forklift dilemma—if anything it made it slightly worse because now I had to heave myself over the additional humps—but in between loo stops I was in bliss.

I used about eight pillows of varying thicknesses, from the two latex super pillows my parents gave us a week ago to a flattened dustmite-ridden relic I think I was using at university. It was so comfortable I decided not to make the bed, in case I dislodged any of the pillows from their exact locations, and instead just draped the doona over the lot.

Of course the missing factor from all this is Christopher, who is away *again*. Not only does the nest take up *all* the pillows we possess (and every single one is *vital*), it takes up *all* the room in the bed. Luckily for him our couch is comfy.

Christopher is doing his own form of nesting, setting up another household for us several hours out of Sydney. It seems that we will be spending some time in the country while this new arts project gets underway. Having just spent months nesting in the Big House it's probably the last thing either of us wants to do.

In the meantime I'm getting ready to jet off to a youth theatre festival for a couple of weeks. I'm judging performances and giving feedback and hopefully writing a twenty-minute script for next year's theatre festival.

A few days after I come back I do a two-week workshop on my

new play with Edward (blimey!) Albee. (I put in the blimey! not because that's something he says but because I'm a bit stunned at this opportunity.)

There's one more scriptwriting workshop to teach in Newcastle in July and then that's IT. My work is DONE.

Sure there's shopping, there's breathing and stretching exercises, organization of cot and other baby paraphernalia, further eating (obviously), and many teeny wee clothes to wash and put away in preparation for the Arrival. There's the vexed question of classes for the Seriously Pregnant; we haven't managed to attend a single one yet, although I hear a rumour about an Antenatal Super Class where you get six weeks worth of lessons in a solid four hours, which sounds like it's got our names and the names of every other feckless disorganized over-committed parent-to-be written all over it.

Oh and then there's also that pesky little thing ... what do they call it? Oh yes, *birth* ... but very *best* of all, there's me spending quality comfort time snuggled in the nest.

Yogi Bear's long gone, but even so, it's pretty damn fine.

THE NEW ROMANTICS

On that day it was raining and we couldn't go to the car dump and smash windows like we usually did.

It was the eighties, and a Saturday, and the shops shut at midday. We had no money to catch a bus into the city to see a movie. There were no cafés to sit in and chat, we were too young for pubs and too old to play organized sports, and we weren't very sporty anyway.

So we simply walked.

Through the deserted park, down past the grey stone church, along the main street and right past all the closed shops.

We walked about two feet apart and sometimes, if he saw someone he knew, he let me walk on ahead while he pretended to gaze into shop windows.

We lingered at the fish and chip place on the corner and sniffed at the hot fat smell.

At the end of the main street we stopped to look at the river. We stood a moment, side by side, watching the swirling weed and litter, and then, after a quick look around, he pulled me close and kissed me.

It was lightly sprinkling and his face was cold and white beside mine, but his mouth was warm and soft. When I opened my eyes, just a fraction, I could see his long dark lashes scattered with tiny beads of water. The sky behind his head was grey and the clouds seemed to swirl through his hair. The river rushed beside us.

It occurred to me that this was romantic.

He stopped suddenly and took my hand and we walked along the path by the river. The grass was wet and my jeans were beginning to feel cold.

'Let's walk home,' I said and he nodded without saying anything.

We changed direction.

I hoped I hadn't said the wrong thing. Or the dumb thing. I didn't know anymore. We used to have fun and talk all the time and make jokes at school or on the bus going home. Now, everyone knew that we were going out together and it was suddenly shy and serious, and we were careful and solemn with each other.

I didn't know what he thought anymore. There were no more jokes between us. Instead, we laughed in groups with our other friends. I found it hard to understand how it had happened this way.

Sometimes I wished things had stayed just the same.

But I was happy, wasn't I?

Yes, I told myself. Because we were in love.

Were we?

I thought about it as we walked through the park towards the first group of streets near our houses.

That feeling, floppy, as if I couldn't take my eyes off him, sick in the stomach almost.

Was that love?

All those songs on the radio about love ...

... lost in

... all out of

... can't help

... it must be

... the power of

... tainted

... in action

... is a battlefield

I felt those songs. Sang along to them. Understood them.

Well then?

And he was so smart and funny and sensitive.

Or at least he was before we started, when we were just friends. Now we were too shy to look at each other. I would creep glances at him in English, keeping my eyes down, my cheeks red as I felt him creeping glances back at me. We didn't sit next to each other in English, although we did in other classes. Instead, we stayed in our old seats, our before-going-out-together seats: me with my back to the windows and him across the room in the centre row of tables.

He was shortsighted but I sat closer to the blackboard.

We sat together on the bus going home, but our friends would have remarked on it if we didn't. If you were going out together you had to sit together, too. I liked that, because then we might talk to each other, softly, or to our other friends, but while we talked he would press his leg up against mine.

His face might be turned away, he might be talking to someone else, might not talk directly for the whole journey except to say 'see you' when I got off the bus, but the warmth of his leg stayed with me all the way home.

We were walking now along the top of the hill. We had already walked past the tree he had spraypainted in silver with our initials. I wished it was gold or at least fluoro yellow so I could see it every day from the school bus. I could see the tree all right but not the writing.

'Let's go to the new school,' he said, 'maybe we can get out of the rain.'

It was not heavy rain, it was soft and grey and dull. It seeped into our clothing and skins.

We walked the long way around to the new high school, avoiding the streets closest to my house, my family's house. He was scared of my father, I knew, but that was all right because so was I.

The new high school was so new it only had one permanent brick building which was the office. All the classrooms were 'temporaries'. These were ugly, thin-walled fibro boxes with big aluminium windows and carpeted floors that wobbled when a class walked in.

Our English class was in a temporary as well, even though our high school was old and had been there for many years.

It was quiet at this new school, on a Saturday, in the soft rain, and we walked hand in hand and peered into windows and talked quietly. When he saw an open window he climbed in and opened the door from the inside so I could step through. He grinned, pleased, and I did too, it was funny and it was also familiar.

Not just because it was a classroom, but because it reminded me of being a child, playing house and making cubbies.

That was it, I felt as if we had just made a cubby.

It was an English classroom, we soon saw, and we laughed about that and about the homework still chalked on the blackboard from Friday afternoon.

'What will the world be like in twenty years?'

'We'll be thirty-five years old,' I said.

It was an eternity.

'I wonder what we'll be doing? Married with two kids?'

I blushed, it wasn't meant to sound as if ...

'Not to each other!,' I said quickly. 'I didn't mean to each other.'

But it had come out all wrong anyway, I realized, like I hated the idea of it or something.

He shifted beside me and we sat down on the green carpet. After an awkward pause we began to kiss again. The rain fell heavily onto the tin roof, the light was dim, filtered through the chairs and desks. We rolled over on the carpet, he put his hand down my jeans and I put my hand down his.

After a few minutes I stopped him. He looked at me steadily, his face flushed, his hair curly and tangled, his eyes huge and calm. I thought in that moment that he was beautiful and that I loved the look of him, and the feel and the smell of him and so maybe that was all the love I needed.

'Do you think—'

I stopped. Unsure of how to phrase it. I tried again.

'Why don't you get ... '

He knew.

Two weeks ago he had told me he'd bought a box of condoms. I had thought about that every day since. Imagined him, nervous, determined not to show it, asking the man in the chemist shop as casually as he could.

Now they were hidden in his bedroom, in his house. Just across the road.

'Are you sure? If you don't want to ...'

'Yeah I'm sure,' I said.

He stood up and fixed his fly and was gone. I waited for a few minutes, still lying on the floor, but the floor felt hard and the carpet itched my neck so I sat on the step outside and waited there instead, watching the rain and shivering until he came back. On his bike, I noted, so it was quicker.

He smiled as he walked up the steps.

'I just brought one,' he said. 'I didn't think you wanted the whole box.'

I laughed at the joke.

We both laughed.

'There's just one thing,' he said as we sat down again on the carpet. He held it up.

'It's blue. I had to buy the coloured ones. There were none of the other sort left.'

I stared at it, fascinated. There was only one pharmacy in the town.

'So ...' he said, not smiling now.

He lay down on the carpet and I lay down beside him.

So.

And then we started again, and it was serious and careful and solemn.

I thought later that it could have been a bit more fun, with the blue condom, and the fact that it was a classroom and all.

When we finished, we both looked at the condom, a little blue rubber sock filled with sperm. He tied a knot in the end and wanted to leave it on the carpet but I picked it up and wrapped it in a tissue. It was warm and soft. Like a secret in my hand.

We closed the door carefully and then he got on his bicycle.

'I better go home,' he said. 'Mum'll have cooked dinner. She gets the shits if we're late.'

He kissed me quickly on the lips. 'See you,' he said.

He rode off and I waited a moment and began the walk home. It was still drizzling and I pulled my jacket more tightly around me.

I kept an eye out for a rubbish bin as I walked.

I wondered where we'd be in twenty years.

15 June

I can tell I'm in the country now, because every time I walk into a shop or wait to cross at a traffic light or catch someone's eye from across a paddock stuffed with cows, someone will say to me: 'When is your baby due?'

Actually they don't usually say 'baby' they say bub, bubba or bubby.

I can also tell that pregnancy has mellowed me because my response is simply to smile and say, 'About ten weeks,' instead of something like 'I expect to be squeezing the little parasite out my clacker (clack, clacky or cla-cla) some time in August.'

My other response, and it depends on who asks and how they ask, is to say to people that it's been a very long road to get to this point which may or may not lead onto the topic of IVF.

I do this because I think if more people were open and sensible about infertility, the world would be a nicer place. Obviously the world would be an even nicer place if people could be open and sensible about, say, religion, but you do what you can.

I am here to be a judge for a youth theatre festival and also to start work on a short script for next year's festival. The theatre company running the festival are a jolly group. The festival director picks me up from the airport in a battered looking van that smells of fuel and old apples. It reminds me fondly of my days touring schools, writing and performing theatre-in-education. It is a lovely jobette to have. On the weekend Christopher visited me, which was excellent as I am staying in a little apartment near the main street and we could pretend we were in our courting days again.

Sadly, the nostalgia is limited. There was none of that initial attraction Hot Sex, for instance. Frankly, apart from being large and cumbersome, the belly is an enormous distraction for even Luke Warm Sex. Just as we get down to it, the belly will start to squirm and ripple and Christopher and I stop with the making out and instead begin to coo at how extraordinarily clever our unborn is ... look, it's rolling about in there ... look, there's an unidentifiable limb ... it's tapping, could it be Morse code?

In the good old days Christopher spent a lot of time under our doona while I spent a lot of time in heaven, but these days he gets as far south as my belly and then stops to hum a couple of verses of 'Teddy Bears' Picnic'. (This has been designated the 'daddy song', with the theory being that the baby will recognize his soothing baritone in utero and once out of utero will respond accordingly i.e. drop immediately off to sleep before Daddy can finish singing the first line.)

After this I usually drag him up to attend to my nipples, which these days means examining them under the bedside lamp and discussing whether they really are darker or not. Then there's a bit of pillow talk about who else will be in the birthing suite and then, exhausted, we have a little nap.

When we aren't reliving our glory days Christopher and I walk in the winter sun, picnic by the river and visit the farmers' market. Here there are stalls of cheese and lumpy bread and varying winter vegetables. It all seems very wholesome and rustic. We have several of these types of market in Sydney, but I feel certain that this is the genuine article, mainly because there is a predominance of men in Big Hats and women wearing boots with cow shit on them.

At one of the wine stalls, while Christopher discusses grape varieties with the woman behind the counter, I notice a large elderly man eyeing off my belly.

'WHEN'S BUB DUE?' he suddenly booms.

He is wearing a Big Hat so I know he's a farmer, but he also has crusty yellow sores on his nose. These, and his inappropriate volume level, remind me in a sort of endearing way of Grumpy Grandad.

I tell him when the baby's due and he humphs a little, which I take to be an indication of approval. I am about to move on to examine some potato varieties when he suddenly says, 'OUR JILLAROO'S PREGNANT'.

'Really?' I say. 'That's great.'

'YAIRS ...' he says. 'YOU KNOW WHAT A JILLAROO IS, DO YER?'

Actually I do know, I began to say, even though I may be an ignorant city dweller whose closest link to the country is a friend who script-edited *McLeod's Daughters*—but he cuts me off.

'A JILLAROO'S A GIRL WHO HELPS US OUT, ON THE PROPERTY.'

I nod. It's fascinating. This man is *exactly* like my grandad.

'IT'S A SORT OF ... HANDYGIRL. SHE AND HER HUSBAND WERE HAVING ...' he pauses delicately before bellowing '...DIFFICULTIES.'

I can't believe it. We are about to have the Conversation.

'YAIRS ... SHE HAD TO DO THAT ... IBF. YOU KNOW, IN MY DAY THERE WAS NO PROBLEM WITH MAKING BABIES.'

I look him in the eye.

'You mean *IVF*. My husband and I did that too. Sometimes you do need a bit of help.'

He seems genuinely surprised at the possibility that there could be two freakishly infertile couples on the Earth at the same time.

'DID IT TAKE A LONG TIME?'

'It took a little while,' I say, 'it didn't happen straightaway but we were lucky, we didn't have to wait too long. And your jillaroo? Did she ...'

'WORKED FIRST TIME.' There is a definite note of triumph in his voice.

'Isn't that terrific?' I say, a trifle coldly.

'BUT DID YOU GET ALL SWOLLEN IN THE BELLY? STRAIGHTAWAY?'

I glance across at Christopher, who has a big smile on his face and is well into the wine tasting. Bastard.

'Ahhh,' I nod sagely, 'there was some bloating yes, and a little discomfort. It's the injections you know, the hormones ...'

He waves the spectre of hormones aside like a pesky blowfly.

'YAIRS ... SHE'S TOLD US ALL ABOUT HOW IT WORKS. SHE SAYS SHE HAS TROUBLE GETTING AROUND OUR PROPERTY.'

By this stage Christopher is thankfully ringing up his purchase. It is time to move on; the gourds are calling us. I say goodbye to Farmer Grandad and he nods, thoughtfully fingering his scabs.

I hesitate a little. The thought of their jillaroo having to lug grapes or whatever it is they grow at the PROPERTY is worrying me a little.

'You know ... they do recommend you take it easy,' I say as we start to move away. 'Especially early on.'

'OH YAIRS,' he nods, 'SHE *IS* TAKING IT EASY. IT'S JUST RIDING THE MOTORBIKE SHE FINDS A BIT PAINFUL'.

11 June

Not surprisingly, with my low bladder tolerance, I missed the final post-credits scene of *X-Men 3* because I had to rush to the loo. Not only that, someone had obviously rushed in before me and had been in too much of a hurry to aim, flush or wipe the seat. No matter, I was just pleased to have beaten the queue. There are few things that can really disgust me these days.

For instance, the other night while I and my fellow judges were lolling around at the back of the theatre, a fellow judge who is also a parent confessed that he was late because of a bath mishap with his one-year-old.

'What's the worse thing that can happen?' he asked.

One of the child-free judges looked at him aghast, with obvious images of near drownings and horrid scaldings flashing into his head.

'Poo in the bath?' I suggested.

And indeed it was.

The other judges winced at the thought. The Parent Judge rolled his eyes and groaned loudly at the memory.

'Well,' I said 'that's not that bad is it really? A bit of baby poo?' After all, it's not like he found it in the tea towel drawer.

'But it's what you have to do when you *find* the poo,' he said. 'You have to put the one-year-old on the bathmat while you empty the bath and hope the poo goes down the plughole, and then you have to get out the disinfectant and sterilize all the bath toys ...'

'Still,' I said. 'It's just poo.'

Later that night I was given a graphic illustration of how much my body has mutated in the past few months as I played a hilarious game of Where's My Intestines?

Several hours earlier I had consumed a small can of baked beans, which are of course high in fibre and protein and low in fat. All very good things. And I had ample time to meditate on the general goodness of baked beans as they gurgled through my bowels, which now seem to be located just under my ribs.

Not only could I hear those beans gurgling I could *feel* them, lumping their way along, and at times, oh joy, even hear the ominous bubbling and popping of bean gas. It was as if my breasts had miraculously developed the ability to fart. As one of Doctor Xavier's erstwhile mutant students, I could fight villains by causing small but lethal earthquakes with my nipples as the epicentres. Whenever trouble seemed to loom I would receive a text message from Wolverine saying 'Time to Bean Up, Windy Woman'.

That night as I built and rebuilt my pillow nest in a vain effort to halt the mammary winds, I reflected on how disgusting I found *this* particular pregnancy oddity.

Poo in the bath? Ha! Bring it on.

15 June

Michelle wants to organize a baby shower for me. Apparently this is a *normal* celebration for people expecting babies. Through her various sources (i.e. old school friends from Toronto High School) Michelle has even learned a variety of special little games that people can play at these things. I had no idea that baby showers have their own party game genre.

For instance, one choice example involves putting mini chocolate bars into disposable nappies, microwaving them and then passing them round, licking the chocolate and determining exactly what chocolate bar left the poo-like smear within. Another involves small plastic baby dolls frozen into ice-cubes and dropped into people's drinks, the winner being the first person to declare their 'water's broken' and plastic baby floating freely in no-longer-chilled beverage. I can only presume that these events start early with something appropriately de-inhibiting. Like a bucket bong.

Is this sort of event an Australian thing? I have no idea. But then, I've never been to a proper hen's night either. (Except Michelle's, but that was a civilized lunch at a nice restaurant in Melbourne.) Somehow, even though I spent many formative years in Newcastle, I missed getting an invitation to one of those hen's night pub crawl things where the bride-to-be is decked out in an apron and veil decorated with toy plastic cooking utensils. Or coloured condoms. Or a sign inscribed 'chook'. For my first wedding, Lucy organized a 'kitsch tea' which was hilarious because people gave me heaps of ugly things like garden gnomes, Australiana tea towels and badly written poetry. But this later proved to be a pain in the arse because I had heaps of ugly things like garden gnomes, Australiana tea towels and badly written poetry to now dispose of.

Michelle agrees that the baby shower will be low key and there will be no chocolate poo or ice-cube babies—even though the latter is kind of appropriate, what with it being a frozen embryo transfer and all. I laugh and say yes and hum and ha as I think about who should be emailed and invited. But the truth is, even now, the whole thing seems like tempting fate. I am torn between wanting to neatly sidestep the whole thing and wanting, desperately, to be normal.

21 June

'Has anyone here ever been arrested? Apart from me?'

Just another question to the writing class from play-writing legend Edward Albee.

This past fortnight I have been head down and ever-increasing-in-size bum up in a writing workshop with the Arrestable Mr A. One of my plays won an award this year (well, co-won with two other writers) and the fortnight with Albee, workshopping my script, is part of the prize.

It's been a great experience, but a fairly gruelling one as well. Physically I seem to get heavier and more tired every day, but also mentally it's as if my brain is starting to shrink and I can focus on only one thing at a time.

In the first week Mr A looked at the seven plays (there are seven playwrights involved, seven directors and about twenty-eight actors) and gave feedback. This week has been more about working with the director and actors to present an extract at the end of the week. And in between are, of course, the rewrites.

I feel like I'm running some kind of hormonal race with my play—it was written at a time when I felt really really angry with my country, my industry, my crap fertility, my stupid immune system, with a lot of things really, and that's all apparent in the script. It's a black comedy and I've written a couple of those quite successfully, but this one is *very* black.

This is probably why one of the notes for me was: 'You have

to be careful this doesn't slide into parody.'

I'm okay with that because a few of the comments he made about other writers' plays included: 'These characters are a bunch of turds', 'This is actually a fifteen-minute play' and 'Now don't get offended, but what you have here is a perfect opera libretto'.

Perhaps the biggest problem with my play is that I'm just not that angry anymore. Sitting in a room, hearing the words read aloud, I can feel my baby squirming inside me and all I want to do is smile like an idiot.

One of the other things Mr A said to me was, 'Are you eight months pregnant?' I was horrified at the suggestion. At eight months pregnant the last thing I planned to be doing was a week-long play-writing workshop, even if it *was* with the writer of *Who's Afraid of Virginia Woolf?*.

I'm becoming increasingly aware of how little I'm going to get done on *all* my writing as time ticks on. A kind of creative desperation is setting in. Our friend Peter, whose wife Leonie is due around the same time as me, tells me about a woman in their antenatal class who had her baby *three weeks early*. I tell him to shut his mouth. (We have that kind of tough love friendship, Peter being a fellow Novocastrian and theatre-in-education survivor.)

'Three weeks early!' I shriek. 'There's too much to do! There's scripts and teaching and Christopher is working in the country, seven hours away launching a new project and there's setting up baby stuff and there's cleaning stuff (when is that damned nesting urge going to take over and inspire me to clean?) and there's me and Christopher going away for a week on our own to relax and Be A Couple for the last time in our lives. In fact, what I really want is for the baby to come *late*.'

Peter smiles. Like my uni friend Michelle, he too was in the infamous production of *A Midsummer Night's Dream*.

He knows that Christopher and I are notoriously late for most things (me—an hour late for our wedding, for instance). Surely, I plead, our own offspring isn't going to let the team down?

4 July

I left home at the age of nineteen. My parents were not impressed. For starters, my timing was seen as rather poor. A couple of weeks earlier my paternal grandmother had died of thyroid cancer.

My mother, being a trained nurse, had taken on the role of carer in that last stage of the cancer, my grandfather being hopelessly out of his depth both emotionally and physically.

It wasn't just my mother who waited out those final weeks. Our entire family—Mum, Dad, Amanda, Toni, Kerry and I—had decamped from Newcastle and were now living in the fold-up bunk beds and strange faux-holiday ambience of my grandparents' caravan. Once the getaway vehicle for countless family adventures on the Central Coast, it was now permanently parked on the pebblemix drive, a few feet away from my grandparents' bedroom window.

Grandma eventually died after a few weeks of this strange, sad caravan limbo and then Mum and Dad took us kids away to spend some time at a friend's beach house. The idea was to have some family time, some grieving time, some quiet reflective time.

The problem for me was that I had left behind a boyfriend and an active social life, both of which I was missing. I understood the need to support my grandfather and look after my grandmother, I respected my parents' wish to spend precious post-funeral days in a sparsely furnished two-bedroom fibro minus television and telephone, but afterwards, when we got back to Newcastle, I packed a bag and announced my intention to stay with my boyfriend in Sydney over the weekend so we could go sailing.

And my parents hit the roof.

Looking back, I imagine they felt it was disrespectful to be enjoying myself so soon after such a sad event. My father, who had said little to me about his grief at losing his mother, was probably disgusted at my blatant desire to hang off the edge of a speeding catamaran, not to mention my unspoken desire to hang off my boyfriend.

I argued that I needed a break, that I wanted a holiday ...

'You just had a holiday,' my father snapped back. 'We just spent a week in a beach house.'

But the thing is, I wanted to say, the holiday I want is from my family. From you.

I didn't say those things, some vestigial sensitivity must have held me back. Instead I began to whine to get my way, always a useful tactic when dealing with disapproving parents. In this instance, my piercing tones finally burst the emotional dam in my father; he was able to shout that I was an ungrateful bitch, which obviously went down very well with me, and finally he offered this ultimatum: *if you walk out that door you're never coming back.*

It was a no-brainer.

'Fine,' I shouted back. 'I'll move out when I get back from Sydney.'

My face was grim, my eyes hard and stony but as I walked down the stairs I suddenly heard my mother break down and cry. It was this, more than any of my father's threats, that nearly propelled me back up the stairs, but instead I kept going, knowing a line had been crossed.

I would go to Sydney, I would come back and move into a friend's place, close to the university. After a few months my parents would visit the new house, bringing presents and hugging me close. I would return for visits to the family home, we would move beyond the incident and never speak of it again, but on that day, standing on the stairs that led to the front door, hovering between anger and regret, I realized that for the first time I had knowingly broken my mother's heart. I could have taken a knife out of the kitchen drawer and stabbed her and I knew it could not have hurt her more than the sound of my feet marching out the front door.

I had caused this pain. I had done it willingly. And I cried bitterly at the thought.

A few years earlier I had kept a diary, and one particularly ugly day I had written about how much I hated my *fucking parents*, both of them, *my fucking mother* and *my fucking father* and how I wished they would both *just fuck off*.

I have no idea why I had written this, I can only remember the words scrawled in pencil, jagged, furious scribblings inarticulate with a fifteen-year-old's rage.

And I remember coming home from school to find my diary open to that page on my desk, a pointed message that my parents had found the page and read it.

For several years whenever I thought about this discovery I became furious all over again at the invasion of my privacy. But then, not long ago, I thought about this incident and instead of feeling the familiar white-hot incandescence of my teenage indignation I wondered how *I* would feel, reading *those* words, about me, in *my* child's handwriting.

It was a strange sensation and oddly painful.

These and other memories came back to me this week following a phone call from a friend I hadn't seen in a long time.

'I hear you're pregnant,' he said. 'Congratulations, I think you'll be a great mother.'

He asked where we were having the baby and we discussed the hospital, the same place his wife had her baby recently. '... Except,' I said, 'we're hoping to use the birthing centre and be under midwife care.'

My friend made a small derisive sound. His wife had had an elective caesarean.

'Oh,' he said, 'you're having one of those "natural" births.'

'Well,' I said, 'we're going to try. It's very possible I'll be wheeled screaming straight into the labour ward and the warm comforting arms of Mr Epidural, but I'm going to try my best to have a "natural" birth, yes.'

I didn't mention the squatting practice and the birth plans and the support team, it seemed pointless.

'I just don't understand why you'd put yourself through all that ...' and then with a Herculean effort at civility he changed his tone. 'Oh well,' he said cheerfully, 'to each their own.'

The word he had omitted was *pain*.

I understood that he saw pain as a needless exercise, as an unnecessary element of the child-bearing procedure. Nobody likes pain. God knows I don't.

Pain is unpleasant. Pain makes you cry. Pain makes *other* people cry for you because there's not much they can do to help, and also because in an effort to alleviate one's pain one might reach for one's husband's gonads and scream *Breathe Through This, Cunt*.

Oh yes, it's all ahead of me.

I didn't say to my friend that I'm afraid of pain too, but I *am* looking forward to the birth of my child. That I struggled long and hard to bring this soul into the world and one of those struggles has been giving up things like coffee and wine and painkillers and anything else I thought might possibly harm or hurt my baby. That to avoid pain in the way he preferred I would need to agree to the use of drugs that might possibly harm or hurt my baby. That I would need to undergo invasive major surgery.

I'm not inflexible about this. I know I might become exhausted, the baby may become distressed, there are a myriad of crisis situations that may necessitate intervention, and I'm prepared to do what it takes. Including the drugs and the surgery and whatever else I have to do to ensure the birth of a healthy baby.

But just here, just now, with six weeks left to go, yes, I do want to have a 'natural' birth.

And the thing is, I should have said to my friend, that pain you can't even bring yourself to mention? That's just the start buddy. You've got a daughter whom you adore more than life itself. I saw

Legs up & laughing

the photographs you sent via email, the radiance in you and your wife's faces as you held up your precious bundle.

But among the many golden moments of joy, there will still be pain, blackly stitched-in fear, in illness, in injury or accident, in anger, in rage, in death.

How does a father feel when his daughter writes that she *fucking* hates him or leaves home under a dark cloud with her mother crying beside him?

And for some parents, the pain is overwhelming. Last week an eight-year-old girl was found murdered in a shopping centre toilet. The week before that a father accidentally ran over his toddler as he reversed down the driveway.

There is no anaesthetic for parenthood.

In the last days of my mother's life, we, her daughters and husband, were gathered around her bed, day and night, like moths drawn to the intoxicating glow of her dying. Now it was *my* turn to have my heart broken, and not fast or cleanly, but slowly, in splintering fragments of grief. I was losing the person I loved most in the world and there was nothing I could do to stop it.

In one of my last precious moments with my mother, curled up beside her on the bed, while my sisters and father were getting dinner, or sleep, or simply walking their own patterns of distress around the hospice corridors, she asked me to forgive her. I was resentful at the thought that, now, with death twiddling his thumbs nearby, she felt the need for forgiveness.

'Why?' I asked, my blind, stupid tears welling up immediately. 'Why do *you* need to be forgiven by *me*?'

'For all the times I made you cry.'

Our faces were very close together, our voices little more than whispers.

'Oh yes,' I said, 'oh yes.'

'And,' she continued, 'I forgive you for all the times you made *me* cry.'

We lay like this for moments, or perhaps it was hours, this

woman and her firstborn child, mentally snipping together at the black stitches of our past. We had twenty-six years together, my mother and I.

When you forgive the pain caused by each other, that seems so very much more.

11 July

I rang Christopher in a state of great excitement.

For a long time I have been fearful of Mush Brain, that evil pregnancy-induced state of vagueness and general 'Sorry what was that?' syndrome.

But *now* I had proof positive that I could beat it!

Being school holidays Neâ had arranged a chess tournament. Just us and the Naughty Nephews. Slightly reluctantly, I agreed to take part.

Chess, you see, is not my game. As a kid I played draughts and Chinese Checkers and a sort of dropping-beans-in-a-little-wooden-pot game. But not chess.

But then, the tournament started and an amazing thing happened for lo ... I won ALL my games! Every single one! Even the grand final!

At chess! *Chess*, I say! Which I only learned to play as a grown-up. And is much harder than that game where you drop the little beans in a wooden pot.

'Did you hear me, Christopher?' I shouted down the phone. 'Every single game! I was the champion! And that means I AM NOT IN THE GRIP OF MUSH BRAIN!!!. How can I be, when my focus, concentration and strategy skills are obviously razor sharp?'

There was a delicate pause.

'But ...' Christopher said, 'you were playing against a six-year-old.'

'AND a nine-year-old, AND their mother,' I retaliated.

'... who was playing in tandem with the four-year-old,' Christopher pointed out.

'But it was *chess*,' I whined. 'Chess is *hard*. Some pieces go one way, some pieces go another. And the six-year-old kept making up rules which sounded like they might be true, so I had to keep checking with his mother.'

'Mmmm,' said Christopher.

'It's *not* like dropping beans in a little wooden pot,' I said crossly. 'In fact I don't even know if that was a real game, it might just have been me liking the *plunkety plunk* sounds.'

'*What* are you talking about?' asked Christopher.

I'd really like to end this neatly with some sort of witty observation about chess and playing against one's nephews and so forth but ... it all seems suddenly too much for me, and my, it's a nice day today and where did I leave my cup of tea?

14 July

It's no secret that I was lagging at the back of the line when they dealt out 'organization'. I pack at the last minute. I arrive at the last minute. I understand not *the list* or the *timetable*. These are strange and foreign beasts.

In a pivotal moment in my early schooling career, when my family lived in Victoria, my third-grade teacher, Miss Featherstone (from Minnesota, USA but enjoying an exotic year overseas in beautiful Werribee, Australia), discovered that I had somehow failed to get my looseleaf binder into any form of useful filing system.

Instead of neat cardboard dividers separating my subjects, each nicely decorated with a hand drawn picture depicting SOCIETY or MATHS, I had a haphazard sheaf of paper and cardboard all flung in together. I distinctly remember that on the GEOGRAPHY divider I had drawn a duck.

'But *why*?' she asked me, uncharacteristic crossness in her voice. '*Why* would you throw all your papers into your folder like this when I asked you all to organize your work *and* I even showed you how to do it?'

Had she? I was speechless. I felt my face grow red even as I racked my brains to remember when we had studied FOLDER ORGANIZATION.

Luckily, Wendy, my desk neighbour, was able to recall that I had not been at school that day, that I had been off sick and so had missed all the crucial tips for keeping my folder nice.

I burst into tears with sheer relief.

Miss Featherstone was instantly all smiles. 'There's no need to be upset,' she said. 'I wasn't angry. Did you think I was a bear?'

I laughed, as required, but inside I thought: a bear, no, an evil bullying cow, yes.

Having been in Sydney for the last week, Christopher has gone back to the country town where he is setting up the new arts project. The launch is on Wednesday and the *Plan* is for him to come back on the Thursday or Friday. During that time I will finish a couple of writing deadlines. Then, the week after next I will be free to pack hospital bag, place rubber sheet over mattress, wash barrels of baby clothes I have been given *and* find the time for Christopher and I to get away, on our own, just the two of us. And, tomorrow, I'm meant to be having the baby shower.

Cue outrageous laughter at so-called Plan.

Last night I was woken with *nasty* period-like pains. Every fifteen minutes. They were so unpleasant I had to get out of bed. Each time they hit I would do a little belly dancing which seemed to help.

This morning I rang the birthing centre. 'I'm having these pains,' I told the midwife. 'Every ten to fifteen minutes. And ... I'm just on thirty-six weeks.'

'That's fantastic,' she said cheerfully. 'Although, if you *are* in labour you'd have to go to the labour ward, you can't come to the birthing centre until you're thirty-seven weeks.'

I have rung Christopher to let him know that we might have to go to Plan B. Not that there was ever a proper Plan A.

'It's all right,' he said. 'It might not be It. Some people keep having contractions for weeks before they go into labour.'

'Oh *goody*,' I said.

'The thing is,' he continued, 'we can't control this. It doesn't matter about the washing, or the packing or the deadlines. If this is going to happen there's nothing we can do about it.'

Thanks to Wendy I finally managed to organize my folder. I delighted in seeing my subjects set out neatly, my precisely placed dividers with appropriate pictures (the duck was deemed more suitable for NATURE). I was delighted, but not enough to retain the desire or the knack over the next thirty-odd years. Organization was a short-lived pleasure.

'Keep me posted,' the midwife had said when I spoke to her this morning.

I've put that on my list. Right next to 'Hold on for another week'.

15 July

Here is an Important Community Message:

When you start to do the whole labour/contraction thing, DRINK LOTS OF FLUIDS. Then, when you have drunk lots of fluids, DO LOTS OF WEEING.

If you don't, you will end up with a bladder the size of a bowling ball. Amusingly, you will assume this large swelling is baby's head and you will tell your husband to feel it and maybe even give it a little kiss.

Won't you feel a dill later on!

The contractions will intensify. They will come at two to three minutes apart and you will be feeling very ordinary indeed. You will go back to the hospital that night, absolutely certain that *this is it*. There you will find, to your great displeasure, that you are *still only 1 centimetre dilated*. There are *nine* of the little buggers left to go!

Plus, your enormous bladder will need to be catheterized to remove the 1 litre of fluid so diligently drunk by you during the day.

After a night in the hospital you will be again discharged and sent home, except this time you will be tested for a urinary tract infection.

On the good side, if this goes on for, say, five more days, your unborn baby will no longer be considered premature. The birthing centre midwives will welcome you back.

On the bad side, you will be completely knackered.

A LITTLE BIT EACH NIGHT

1994 Raymond Terrace.

There is a tank in her room—this is how these things start—and the glass is grimy and filmed over with a membrane that darkens at the perimeter into a deep bile green.

Inside is a fish. A goldfish named Bit. Originally there were two, named after Bit and Bot, the Play School fish, but Bit nibbled at the flimsy, soft tail of his partner, who then developed fin rot and was later found belly up in a gelatinous island of his own death secretions. Bit bit Bot's bot off.

So now here is the tank, uncleaned, and Bit is listlessly creeping through the tainted water and I say: 'You should get another fish, what about a gourami, they're nice.'

As I speak, I am setting out the massage oil, digging out the ambient music cassette, dimming the bedside lamp. She doesn't answer; instead, she stares up out of the window at the black. The crack of the Milky Way flecks the sky.

My mother is looking for God.

She can't just get up and stand at the window, because she broke her leg recently when she rolled over in her sleep, so she just looks. Her eyes are deep brown, black like mine, like all her children, and I don't go too close to them in case I fall in.

She scans the sky for a glimpse of God. When exhausted by the effort her eyes close shut, and I catch God furtively peering down at my mother. Through the crack in the night sky he sees her lying thin and brown on her bed, and then he sees me looking at him and he quickly turns away.

In the Chinese restaurant near where I live there is also a tank. And there is one fish, a large mirror dory, tarnished silver disc, listlessly creeping through the tainted water.

'A big fat silver Bit,' I say out loud and my husband says 'What?' And I say nothing.

When the young Chinese waitress takes our order my husband has to pick because I'm in a mood now. I'm watching the big silver fish spinning slowly in the tank. I'm thinking about Bit, sullen and lonely, and I'm wishing I'd taken Bot out of the tank earlier—kept him separate in a jar—until they'd both settled down and then put them back together again. Instead, I'd watched, fascinated by the cannibal nibble nibble nibble of Bot's tail down to a stump of flesh and tiny, thin bone.

In front of me, rice steams softly on a plate. I fan out my hands on the red linen tablecloth. My mother's hands. Small and brown, slim fingers, pink nails.

Even the mole on the back of the left hand is the same, and the biro tattoo dot on the right.

Fucking Slopeheads. I hear these words very clearly from the table behind me. I look round. A table of five men, eating hungrily and speaking aloud on Where to Get a Fuck in Thailand. One voice of dissent among them protests that All Slopes Have Disease and I wouldn't touch them with a 10-foot Pole Let Alone My Dick. Roars of laughter from the other four.

I get up to leave. 'Are you all right?' my husband asks. He pays the bill.

I stop in the doorway to thank the waitress. She smiles and her eyes slide past me to the Loud Table.

'I'm sorry they are rude,' I say, and she shrugs.

As I walk on she says suddenly: 'You are Chinese,' and quick as a flash I say, 'No no, my mother is Filipina, you see I am half and half.'

She looks confused, so I say, 'I like your fish.' She smiles.

'We can cook him for you,' she says.

My mother asks, painfully, 'How was your dinner?' It hurts her to speak.

I say I had to leave the restaurant early but I don't say: And I am leaving my husband for good. It hurts me to speak also. I don't know why I can't tell my dying mother that I am leaving him. If I can keep them separate, one in a jar and one in a tank, then maybe one day I can face them together, but not yet.

Except, I know she loves him and maybe this is one pain I can spare her. I love him too but I know it's not enough. Even if she was strong and healthy it would not be enough. And with her like this, it's as if the spluttering spark of our relationship is being deluged by a great black wave of despair.

Instead I say, 'How 'bout that massage now?'

I look at her. Her face is worn with the effort of dying. I wish, harder than anything I've ever wished before, that there is a God and that he reaches down with even his littlest finger and touches my mother's chest so that the ulcer closes over and her right breast reappears and her poor broken leg is fixed. I wish until it hurts but it doesn't happen.

She reaches up with one hand, smooth and brown, my hand, and touches my face.

She says don't cry but this makes me cry harder.

She says: 'I'm not afraid, I'll be with God,' and her eyes start to search the sky again.

God remains hidden.

I start at her feet, massage them good and proper with lavender oil and she grunts with pleasure and giggles at the tickle spot. I massage her all over. In the Philippines there is a type of healer, you take chickens or a pig to his hut. You lie on a thin bed and he feels for the source of your disease and then he plunges his fingers into your flesh. Thick, bloody gobbets of tissue and tumour are drawn to his fingers and plucked away from your body, and when his fingers withdraw the edges of the wound pull together and heal. A miracle. My mother said it was faith.

But when we saw it on the telly, the reporter said it was fake.

As I rub at my mother's skin, cancerous nodules slide beneath my hand. They feel like marbles embedded in her flesh. I wonder if it would hurt to split her skin with my fingernail and flick the marbles into the corner of her room. Her breathing slows and deepens beneath me. She's asleep.

My mother told me once about the time she weaned me. I had screamed and pulled at her blouse with furious indignation. And I said, righteously, 'Well it's barbaric, why would you wean a child at that age, anyway?' and she said: 'No it wasn't like that. You were biting me.'

With my thin sharp milk teeth I bit until she bled.

My mother opens her eyes. 'That was a wonderful massage,' she says.

I say 'Yes, well, you were supposed to be visualizing your healing while I massaged you, did you visualize or did you just go to sleep?'

And she says mmmm and looks guilty and then we both laugh. She is a naughty one sometimes, my mother. I love her so hard, so much, that it hurts, but even that is not enough. Not enough to stop her gums from ulcerating, her chest from rotting and pulling apart, her bones from crumbling and breaking in her sleep. Her pain.

It even hurts her to speak.

'Before you go home tonight,' she says quietly, 'will you feed Bit?'

I nod, yes of course. I get the can of food and stand over Bit's tank, sprinkle flakes on the slippery skin of the water's surface. Bit nibbles. I wonder what he thinks, if he sees my mother through the distorting glass, if he forgets every three seconds like they say about goldfish, and gets resurprised, over and over, at how thin she's become.

My mother will be forty-eight next birthday. Perhaps I will buy her another fish.

I sprinkle on and look up at the sky for a glimpse of my mother's shy God. If she was to be healed, perhaps there would be a sign, some sort of lesser miracle first. The words IT WILL ALL BE OKAY might spell themselves out in the stars.

I begin to make out an A and a T when my mother sings out: 'That's enough!'

The surface of the water is thickly coated with fish food.

It is time to say goodbye again.

I lie next to my mother, with my arms carefully wrapped around her. She kisses my face and whispers to me. We lie like that with our eyes closed. When I hear a sound beside us I don't open my eyes. I don't want to scare God. Sometimes he's shy.

In my mind I see the tank boiling and churning, swirled by God's littlest finger. Full now to the brim with seething, writhing fish all pushing at the glass of the tank and ready to burst forth upon my mother's carpet in a golden cascade. I can sense the fine web of cracks racing across the glass with the weight of a million shining gold Bits bearing down upon it. And the brittle sound that fills the air is the sound of the tank being pushed to the limit.

Like a thin white bone that snaps in the night, or a family of hearts being broken.

And in the End

Two days earlier it had been a full moon.

As we drive home along the ocean I watch it hanging, still hugely round and golden, above the waves.

'Maybe the moon will bring the baby,' I say to Christopher, and we laugh because we have been told that the full moon *does* bring the baby and so, lacking any better idea, we have planned around it—our pre-baby holiday away, the baby book reading, the writing down of the birth plan, my sister Amanda booking her ticket from New Zealand two days before the due date, the last-minute intensive antenatal class ... all scheduled before the full moon.

The *next* full moon.

'You're one lunar month away,' says my sister-in-law Neâ later that night, and I think about the time we have left and the time that has passed and how much has moved and changed within the ocean of our lives, and the moon rises, and the waves crash and suddenly, shockingly, there is no more time.

On Thursday, Christopher goes back to work, several hours away, and I potter at home. I wake late at night, back cramps, waves of period-like pain, bearable but uncomfortable.

It's the gnocchi, I think. Earlier in the evening I babysat the Naughty Nephews and we had dinner together. The pasta had been a month past its use-by date.

I, on the other hand, am a month early.

The pain continues, regular, unsettling, and the next morning I ring the birthing centre to see what I should do.

'Come in,' the midwife says, 'but if you are in labour we can't take you because you need to be at least thirty-seven weeks. You'll have to go to Delivery.'

I am horribly disappointed and indeed, when later Neâ and I

arrive at the birthing centre, a midwife steers me back down the hall to the other doors.

No, I want to say, *I can wait, please! I can do better. I can hang on. Give me another chance.* But she's gone.

All through Friday in the delivery suite the pain continues to wash over me, stops while I am in the bath where I sway and sing through my contractions and the warm water slops over my belly, rising like an island from the deep.

And we wait and wait and wait ... *should I stay, should I go, should Christopher fly home now, or next flight, or last flight, or drive, or wait?* Neâ is waiting with me, calmly updating Christopher, giving me arnica but *no, stay don't rush, don't panic, not happening, don't go ...*

Fifteen minutes after Christopher's last possible flight leaves, the midwife examines me again. My cervix is 1 centimetre dilated and fully effaced. I'm staying in hospital.

Christopher swears loudly and exclaims delightedly within the same breath. He will pack up, drive back, be here in several hours—around one in the morning.

Kerry arrives from Newcastle, her fiancé Troy has driven her the two hours and will drive back again immediately. 'You look after your big sister,' he tells her. 'Don't leave her alone.' Kerry is nervous, excited, didn't read *Active Birth*—she did order it from the bookshop but it didn't come in time ...

No time, no time ...

That night, after Christopher arrives, I am given sleeping tablets and have three blessed hours of pain-free sleep. But I'm still only 1 centimetre on Saturday morning so we go home again.

Saturday is the day of the cancelled baby shower and a couple of girlfriends turn up. We have tea and cake and lavender oil back massages and the day passes in a beautiful blur of love and sugar.

By Saturday night the contractions are much harsher and I hang off the walls and breathe. Neâ is telling me to 'float above the waves' and indeed at the height of the pain I do see myself floating above ... something dark and far away, a canyon, impenetrable, mysterious ... and then the wave recedes and I find my feet on the other side.

Minute after minute, breath after breath, hour after hour.

Walking down the hallway at home to return to the hospital, I have to stop and breathe and float on the walls directly outside the Naughty Nephews' bedroom. I am vaguely aware of their bright eyes, their curious voices.

Earlier, Naughty Nephew the 2nd had asked his father why it was hurting so much, and he begins to explain ... 'Well, the baby has to come out through her vagina ...' Naughty Nephew the 2nd's eyes goggle. His mouth drops open. Struck temporarily speechless, he covers his cheeks with his hands.

After the birth he will draw a card for me showing a picture of me 'dilating' and 'being dilated by Kerry'.

After a gruesome but mercifully short drive, which I spend on my hands and knees in the back of the car, we reach the hospital, where the midwife discovers my bladder is hugely distended. She uses an in–out catheter to draw off a *litre* of urine. Kerry, Neâ and Christopher carry dish after dish to the sink and drain it away.

Sometime during the night will come the first of many discussions concerning my multiple sclerosis. 'Could the MS have caused the bladder retention?'

'No,' I say, in between breathing and floating, 'nothing to do with it.' But it will come up again and again, and underlying the question is the Potential for Problem and the need for intervention.

I breathe and float and argue.

They examine me again and disappointingly I am only 3 s dilated. The contractions on top of an overfull bladder have made me seem far further progressed than I actually am. This time I get a shot of pethidine to help me sleep.

On Sunday morning nothing has changed and I am sent home again. This time Christopher decides we will have no visitors, nothing but quiet and nourishment and breathing and rest.

By Monday afternoon I am back at the hospital. This time they tell me my bladder is retaining again, although not as badly as two nights before. ('Are you sure this isn't the MS?') A decision is made for me to have a catheter throughout the labour and I mentally doff my hat to Grumpy Grandad.

A midwife suspects I could have a bladder infection ('Could it be the MS?') so another decision is made. I will be on IV antibiotics until after the baby is born. A canula is inserted into the back of my hand and throughout the labour I will snap at people who touch it. *Stop it! My hand, you're pressing my hand!*

I am aware of voices and murmurings around me but by now, time, which seemed to be so short before, has become slippery and elastic and I slip and slide in and out of now and another state, a more liquid state of consciousness, full of strange imagery and half dreams.

A midwife breaks my waters and they gush hotly down my legs.

Sometime during all this an obstetrics registrar has appeared, more MS discussion, more concern that this labour is taking so long, I am now, after all this time, only 5 centimetres and he is concerned *because ... because ... because ...*

... the voice weaves around me, he is talking Syntocin to hurry the labour along and I think of how this will throw me straight into the deep end of these crashing wave contractions, and I know I am not ready.

I ask for pethidine to let me sleep, let my body try to finish the job.

My support team is around me, rock solid: Neâ has come home early from work and I have asked her to stay for the birth, Kerry is holding my hand, Christopher is with me and around me whispering *you are so beautiful, you are doing so well, you are so strong ...*

They work tirelessly, massaging me, applying the heat pack and whisking it away when I screech *too hot too hot* on the eve of each contraction. I am silently congratulating myself for not swearing, for staying calm even though it is patently obvious that the massage is *all* wrong, that the hot packs are *too* hot and then in the *wrong* place, that Kerry's hands are *too small* and *in the wrong place* ...

Christopher tells me later that I would snap out instructions and the three would roll eyes and smile at each other and patiently work on around me. *You said that Kerry's hands were too small and like monkey paws,* he tells me and I gasp at the meanness and cry with laughter at my cranky shitty labouring self, forgiven over and over again.

And eventually I am given an ultimatum.

Pethidine, yes, but then in two hours, I'll be reassessed, to see if Intervention is Required to Speed Things Up.

Two hours only ...

Time, time, so little of it, so much of it, not yet, not yet, not yet ...

Christopher and Neâ withdraw to restrategize.

They are aware that I am rapidly being seen as a Problem, there are tight little knots of staff discussing me, they hush up when any of my team walk past. Christopher and Neâ create their own tight little knot while Kerry stays with me.

The pethidine only lets me sleep between contractions, and these are getting stronger, the waves are rushing down my body from head to toe, my back arching up in between. In these moments I moan and sigh and think *yes*, I understand why women choose epidurals, I understand fearing and hating this pain, I understand elective caesareans and my little sister despairs as I whisper all my fears to her.

I'm scared, I'm scared, I can't, I don't want, it's not fair ... I'm scared

But in between these moments I am drifting at the entrance of that dark world, that strange half life, illuminated by pain. Flickers of face and image and strains of music and words. *I have never seen that image before* I say to myself, *I have never heard those words before* ...

And later we say this may well have been transition, the doorway into stage two of the birth, because when I am finally examined, exactly two hours later, I am fully dilated.

Fuck your Syntocin, I think.

In stage two, fully dilated, the door to our world as fully open as it can ever be to the baby squeezed deep within my body, a light in the darkness, a path to follow through the incessant squeeze and writhe and push ...

Push, I hear people saying, *it's time to push* ...

... and I do, for nearly two hours, with nothing to show for it. I hang from my husband's arms, my sister rubs at my legs and squeezes my toes, my sister-in-law rubs at my back and stops and starts and talks me through, her voice is a clear bell in the storm brewing about my body.

Here now is the dark place, the black place, the canyon I floated over during earlier contractions. The world has split wide open, full of stars and the bright lights of faces I can't place or properly glimpse.

All love and all hell rests here and I see suddenly how thin the veil is that lies between us. Only women glimpse this place, I think. Only women see this power.

The shock of this.

The sprawl of this.

The intense terror and beauty that winds me through this landscape, winds this place to me, marked by the contractions breaking against me.

Push, I hear the voices calling, and I push and I push but I know it's not enough.

We're running out of time, I hear someone say ... that word again ...

With each wave I push with my first breath, push hard at something but when I break to gulp air and push again it's as if whatever I'm pushing against has slipped further from my reach.

... *the time* ... the registrar is saying. His eyes are like green orbs, they seem sorrowful and fanatical all at once and I hear him saying *ventouse* but then also *forceps* and *maybe even emergency caesarean* and I think *no, that's not fair, after all this, that's fucked* ...

So, push again, he says ... *your baby's head is flexed, I'll try to turn it now, but if this doesn't work we need to look at the options, it's been two-and-a-half hours now ... do you understand?*

Do I understand?

I do, but I don't. I understand the logic but I don't understand the enormity, the power of what I'm experiencing.

He reaches into me and twists and I scream and hang and clutch and berate and groan from the arms and hands of people who love and support me, until my body, my vessel, slides further into the heaving waters of this new ocean, this new storm ...

We're running out of time ...

Time

Time

Time

And the time it takes is one breath, perhaps, or the combined heartbeat of me and the child trapped within me, or one hour, or one year, but when the next wave hits me, deep inside my mind, I silently scream.

Mum.

Get the baby out. Mum!

Breathe.

Breathe.

Push!

Muuuuuuum! Get the baby Mum. Please.

Breathe.

Breathe.

But there's nothing. And then, time's up.

The voice is asking me: *the ventouse?*

And I open my eyes and see Neâ's face. I know she had the ventouse with her second child: Naughty Nephew the 2nd has told me about how he was 'hoovered' out of his mother because he wanted to stay inside and play football 'with the bones' ...

She nods. *Yes*. The bell in the storm.

And I say *yes*.

And *bang*! the room fills with staff who seem to have been hovering in the hallway, waiting for the word.

I am told to get up on the bed, the doctors are waiting, and I mutter *the doctors can fucking well wait* as I heave myself up onto the bed. I am tired beyond tired and sore beyond sore.

And now, a new kind of scream, a new kind of sensation.

But it's all part of the same ocean, the same journey, the same road that led me past that huge golden moon so many years ago.

The ventouse is slipping and the baby's heart rate is dropping but here now perhaps is where my mother is able to do her own intervention, or perhaps it's luck, or love, or skill or all these things, or none of them, but suddenly I hear people say:

Here comes your baby's head!

And I feel that burn, that stretch, that I have read about, heard about ... and now the head is out ... and now, impossibly quick after all that has gone before, the rest of my baby comes slithering out and suddenly there is a new person in the room, a new soul ... and people are laughing and gasping and my sister is sobbing.

It's a he.

And he's on my belly, large and wet. And his bright eyes look at me in amazement.

Mother.

And I stare back, in amazement, *this is you*.

Oh.

We saw you being put into my body, in the end of a pipette.

We saw you sparkle in the night sky of my uterus, beside your sibling's smaller, weaker beat.

We saw you alone, a tiny dancing baby, shimmying beneath the ultrasound.

We saw you pushing and batting at my flesh ...

We saw you coming from far far away. And we thought we loved you then.

But we were wrong.

Because now you're here, and so the world has changed.

And the stars have wheeled and turned.
And the moon has come and gone.
And time has stood still for you.
And oceans have run dry and refilled for you.
And my love. And your father's love. Immeasurable.
This is you.
This is you.
And things will never be the same again.

acknowledgments

Ooh! It's a book!
Thankyou!

To Hazel Flynn, Rhiain Hull, my editor, Karen Gee, and to my agent, Elizabeth Troyeur, for your patience and encouragement. And to all at Murdoch Books for your commitment and enthusiasm.

To Annie, who read beyond the call of duty, and to Peter, Marky, Lucy, Michelle, Helen, Hadass and George who cheered me onward.

To my beautiful family, Peter and Dawn, Amanda, Toni, Kerry, Ros and Paul and Grandis for your continued support and caring and for your love.

To my wonderful extended family and housemates, Keith and Neâ, and my Nephews Max, Louis and Oliver (who are hardly ever Naughty) for stories and laughter and painless injections and so much more.

To all those who read and commented and supported me on my blog, 'L'Eggs Up And Laughing', throughout the events of this book. You shared my grief as well as my joy. You made me feel part of a community who knew exactly how I felt. You kept me writing.

And finally, to Christopher, for your unwavering faith in my ability both as a mother, and as a writer. You believed enough for both of us. You still do. And for that I will always be thankful.